Business

Karen Hough • Jackie Tye • Nick Colburn

OCR
National Level 2

www.heinemann.co.uk
✓ Free online support
✓ Useful weblinks
✓ 24 hour online ordering

01865 888058

Heinemann
Inspiring generations

Heinemann is an imprint of Pearson Education Limited,
a company incorporated in England and Wales, having its
registered office at Edinburgh Gate, Harlow, Essex, CM20 2JE.
Registered company number: 872828

Heinemann is a registered trademark of Pearson Education Limited

Text © Nick Colburn, Karen Hough, Jackie Tye 2005

First published 2005

10 09 08
10 9 8 7

British Library Cataloguing in Publication Data is available from the British Library on
request.

ISBN: 978 0 435401 22 1

Typeset by Tech-Set Ltd
Original illustrations © Harcourt Education Limited, 2005
Printed in China (SWTC/07)
Cover photo: © Zeta

Acknowledgements
Every effort has been made to contact copyright holders of material reproduced in this book.
Any omissions will be rectified in subsequent printings if notice is given to the publishers.

Contents

Acknowledgements

The authors and publishers wish to thank the following for permission to reproduce material:

ACAS

ASA

Barclays Bank plc

Buckingham Palace

Devon Ceramics

GMB

Office of National Statistics

Tesco

The Duke of Edinburgh Award Scheme

Virgin Enterprises Ltd

Alamy pages 6, 38, 39, 79, 144 (bottom), 159, 161, 172, 190, 228, 247, 303; **Corbis** pages 21, 34, 83, 166, 187, 242, 246, 248, 263, 299; **Digital Vision/Rob Van Petten** page 68; **Getty** pages 279, 286, 297; **Harcourt Education Ltd** page 144 (top); **Harcourt Education Ltd/Gareth Boden** page 309; **Harcourt Education Ltd/Corbis** pages 65, 73; **Harcourt Education Ltd/Haddon Davies** page 28; **Harcourt Education Ltd/Getty Images** pages 47, 158, 176; **Harcourt Education Ltd/Jules Selmes** page 267; **Nokia** page 167; **Press Association/Empics** page 163; **Rex Features** pages 4, 23, 25; **Bea Ray** pages 151, 152; **Rolls Royce** page 232; **S&R Greenhill** pages 24, 33, 82, 276; **Sainsbury's** page 284; **Topham** pages 1, 12, 19, 84, 124, 188, 201, 203, 215, 218, 225, 233, 268, 302, 324; **Which?/Bea Ray** page 277.

Crown copyright material is reproduced under Class Licence No. C02W0005419 with the permission of the Controller of HMSO and the Queen's Printer for Scotland.

Every effort has been made to contact copyright holders of material reproduced in this book. Any omissions will be rectified in subsequent printings if notice is given to the publishers.

Introduction

This book has been written to help you achieve your OCR Level 2 National Certificate in Business.

In order to achieve the qualification you are required to pass six units. Units are achieved by the preparation of assignments. Four of these assignments are mandatory – this means they are compulsory. The other two assignments are chosen from option units. All units are weighted equally and each contributes one-sixth to the overall qualification.

In order to pass an assignment you will need to produce evidence, that is proof that you have met the requirements of the unit.

Evidence could be:

- completed assignments or projects
- products of real work that you have completed during work experience
- statements from witnesses
- records made by your assessor when observing you carrying out your work.

Evidence can be anything that proves:

- what you can do
- how well you can do it
- the level of knowledge you have in relation to what you do
- the level of understanding you have about what you do, how you do it, and why you do it.

The mandatory units are:

- Unit 1   Investigating business
- Unit 2   Enterprise and operations
- Unit 3   Finance in business
- Unit 4   Communication in business

The four optional units included in the book are:

- Unit 5   Working with people in business
- Unit 7   Promotion in business
- Unit 11   Keeping customers happy
- Unit 12   Career planning for business

All units are broken down in exactly the same way. Every unit is introduced with a learning outcome. The learning outcome section describes what you will achieve while completing the unit.

Assessment objectives describe what you are required to do in order to achieve the learning outcome. You must achieve every assessment objective in the unit.

Assessment objectives are further broken down into knowledge, understanding and skills. This section provides further clarification of the type of evidence required in order to achieve the assessment objective.

Your assignments will be marked against clearly laid-out grading descriptions.

You are able to achieve a pass (1 point) merit (2 points) or distinction (3 points) for each unit. You must achieve all units in order to pass the qualification. In order to calculate your overall grade you will need the following points:

- Pass – 6 points
- Merit – 10 points
- Distinction – 14 points

The layout of the book has been designed to enable you to work through each unit easily. Each unit is laid out in assessment objective order. All the knowledge, skills and understanding have also been clearly explained. Each section contains exercises to help you understand the theory being covered. You will also find portfolio tips to help you build up your assignment.

Remember that if you find some of the information confusing or overwhelming at the beginning of the course seek help from your course tutor.

We hope that you find the book interesting, enjoyable and that it fully supports you through your studies.

Nick Colburn
Karen Hough
Jackie Tye

April 2005

Investigating business

Getting Started

In your daily life you come into contact with many different types of organisation. You are probably studying in a school or college and some of you will have a part-time job in a business. We all go shopping and at times we may need to make use of doctors, hospitals or other medical services. This unit investigates the different types of business organisations that exist.

To complete this unit successfully, you will need to produce portfolio evidence which includes an investigation into such a business organisation. You will need to address the eight assessment objectives in the specification. In this unit you will look at various types of business organisation, the aims of organisations, how they structure themselves and the different industrial sectors that they operate in. You will look at how and why organisations may change, the various groups which have an interest in the activities of business (known as stakeholders) and how businesses are affected by changes and by competition. You will also consider factors which influence where the business is located.

This unit will cover

- AO1 Describe, using examples, different business aims.
- AO2 Describe, using examples, different types of business ownership and show why business ownership may change over time.
- AO3 Illustrate the organisational structure of the selected businesses, and show other ways in which the business could be organised.
- AO4 Describe the different stakeholders the selected business has, what their interests in the business are and why some stakeholders' interests might differ.
- AO5 Describe the trends of growth and decline for the sector in which the selected business operates, and compare with other sectors.
- AO6 Identify the main competitors of the selected business, describing how they compete and how the selected business remains competitive.
- AO7 Describe the current location of the selected business and explain why this location is used.
- AO8 Suggest and justify changes that could be made to the location of the selected business in the future.

AO1 Describe, using examples, different business aims

Business organisations will have a number of aims, that is broad goals, which will influence the way in which they behave. Some of the most common business aims are shown below:

- to make a profit
- to increase market share
- to provide services to customers
- to improve the quality of the product or service.

Making a profit

Total revenue is the total amount of money coming into the business from selling the product or service. It can be found by:

number of items sold $\times$ selling price = total revenue

All private sector businesses have the key aim of making a **profit.** If the total revenue coming in from selling a product or service is greater than the total costs involved in making or supplying it, the business has made a profit.

The owners of a business, sometimes called **entrepreneurs**, risk their capital in a business and profit is their reward for risk-taking. If a business is to grow it will need to earn profit. Some of the profit can be put back or reinvested into the business to buy new equipment or vehicles, expand the premises or take on additional staff. Individuals may gain great satisfaction from running their own business but in the long run the business must generate a profit if it is to survive and grow.

ACTIVITY

Arpacko Ltd had sales last year of £650,000. It had the following costs: wages £210,000, materials £90,000 and overheads of £100,000. Calculate the annual profit.

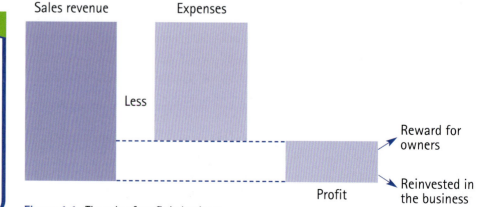

Figure 1.1 *The role of profit in business*

Increasing market share

Market share is the proportion of the total market sales that are made by one company or brand or product. The market sales figure is the total value of all the sales made by all firms in the market during one year. Market share can be calculated by the formula:

<u>Sales of Brand X</u>

Total market sales $\times$ 100 = Percentage market share

Example

Last year *Woof!* brand of dog food had sales of £30 million in a total market worth £100 million. *Woof!*'s market share was:

$$\frac{£30m}{£100\,m \times 100\%} = 30\%$$

The firm or brand that has the biggest market share is known as the **market leader**. If a firm is able to increase its market share, it shows that it is winning customers from its competitors; so many businesses have increasing market share as one of their key aims. If a market is growing then all of the businesses in that market may see their sales rise. However, not all will be able to increase market share. For example, Walkers is the market leader in the UK crisp market. Golden Wonder is one of their smaller competitors. Golden Wonder may have increasing their market share as one of their aims. They will need to win customers from Walkers and other crisp manufacturers if they are to survive in this very competitive market and increasing market share shows that a brand is succeeding against the competition.

> ## Real business
>
> *Tesco is the market leader in the UK supermarket business. In the 6 months to August 2004, Tesco enjoyed sales worth £16.5 billion, well ahead of rivals Asda and Sainsbury's.*

> ### QUESTIONS
>
> The UK burger market is dominated by McDonald's and Burger King.
>
> 1 How can you find out which is the market leader?
>
> 2 Why might Burger King have increasing market share as an aim?

Providing services

The majority of UK businesses do not manufacture a product but instead they provide a service to their customers. Businesses such as banks, transport firms, advertising agencies and retailers are all examples of service industries. Some important services are provided by central or local government and are free for their users, for example NHS hospitals and local-authority schools. Most business services, however, charge their customers for providing the service and aim to make a profit. A business such as the Post Office has mixed objectives. It is owned by the State but it is run as a business and charges for its services. However, it is expected to fulfil certain social obligations e.g. providing daily postal deliveries in rural areas which may not be profitable.

QUESTIONS

Outline the type of service(s) provided by:

1 Your local NHS hospital

2 Lloyds TSB plc

3 British Airways plc.

Improving the quality of the product or service

In most markets, customers have a choice about the product or service that they use. If the quality of a product or service is not as good as that of its competitors it is likely to lose market share. Customers expect high standards from products and services so businesses must work to continually improve their products if they are to stay competitive. This may mean improving the design of products, making them more reliable or giving quicker service. A restaurant will need to provide good-quality food at reasonable prices in a pleasant environment while a taxi firm will need to offer a reliable service. In the longer term, businesses which cannot produce good-quality products or services may not survive.

A Virgin train

QUESTIONS

How might the following businesses improve the quality of the product or service that they offer?

1 A train operator such as Virgin Trains
2 A manufacturer of crisps and similar snacks
3 A leisure centre
4 A water company such as Thames Water plc.

Other business aims

As we have seen, all businesses need to make a profit if they are to be successful in the longer term. However, for a new business its first aim may be to survive, as many new businesses fail in the first year. In the early days, the owners may be satisfied to simply **break even** until the business is established in its market. A larger organisation may aim to develop and launch new products or break into new markets overseas. Some businesses aim to take over their rivals or drive them out of the market. The aims that a business organisation has will affect its behaviour and the way in which it organises itself.

Break even point occurs when the revenue coming into the business just covers the costs of the business. There is neither a profit nor a loss.

GLOSSARY

Break even point: The business has covered its costs and makes neither a profit nor a loss.

Mission statements

We have looked at a number of possible aims that businesses might have. Many businesses now produce a **mission statement** or vision statement. A mission statement gives the key aims of the organisation and how the business intends to operate to achieve its aims. The mission is a vision of where it wants to be and how it wishes to be viewed by others. For example, Ford Motor Company's vision is 'to become the world's leading company for automotive products and services'. Vodafone's mission states 'our shared vision is to be the world's mobile communications leader'. In contrast, the mission statement of the charity Oxfam states that 'Oxfam works with others to overcome poverty and suffering'.

ACTIVITY

Identify the companies/ brands which are the market leaders in the following markets:
1 chocolate snacks
2 cars
3 mobile phone networks
4 car insurance.

ACTIVITY

In pairs or small groups, decide what you think are the aims of the following organisations:
1 Your school or college
2 Asda
3 A new nail bar set up in your area by two friends who have just completed a beauty therapy course at a local college
4 Kellogg's
5 Arsenal Football Club
6 The RSPCA.

Portfolio tip

It may be useful to start your assignment by giving a clear statement of the main objectives of your chosen business. You could include a mission statement if the business has one.

AO2 Different types of business ownership and why it may change

Some businesses may be operated by one person

Businesses in the UK range from small, one-person businesses, such as a mobile hairdresser, to large organisations, such as banks and oil companies. When setting up in business for the first time the owners will have to decide upon the legal structure of their business, based upon their aims, the amount of money they have to invest and how much risk they wish to take. Over time, the business may grow and its aims may change. The owners may then decide to change the legal structure of the business to adapt to the new circumstances. The main forms of business ownership are shown below:

- sole proprietors
- public limited companies
- partnerships
- franchises
- private limited companies
- co-operatives.

Sole proprietors

Sole proprietors or sole traders are the simplest form of business organisation in the UK. Typical sole traders might be small newsagents, hairdressers, decorators and window cleaners.

In most cases there are very few legal formalities to set up as a sole trader, although a licence may be required to run certain types of business such as a pub or a taxi firm. The owner may employ workers to work in the business but there is only one legal owner. This means that the owner has a great deal of freedom in how they run the business and they are able to make all their own decisions and keep all of the profits. However, they are likely to have a heavy workload as they will have to deal with customers and suppliers, market their products, do their own accounts and all of the many other things involved in running their own business. Taking holidays can be difficult and a prolonged period of illness may mean that no income is earned.

Sole proprietors have **unlimited liability** meaning that if the business fails the owner may have to sell off their own assets, such as their car or house, to pay off debts of the business. This can make being a sole proprietor a stressful occupation if the business is not going well.

Dan the carpet fitter

Dan Wilton set up his own carpet fitting business four years ago. He now employs one young assistant who is learning the job. He enjoys being able to arrange his own work and likes being out and about meeting customers. He is not highly paid but he earns more than in his previous job working as a sales assistant in a carpet superstore.

1 Outline three advantages of Dan running his own business.
2 Outline three drawbacks of Dan being self-employed rather than working for someone else.

Partnerships

A **partnership** is a business usually owned by between two and twenty partners. Partnerships are quite common in professions such as solicitors, accountants, vets, doctors and dentists. They are quite easy to set up although it is usually sensible to draw up a partnership agreement which sets out how profits will be shared, how much salary each person will earn and what will happen if a partner wishes to leave. Silent or sleeping partners are partners who invest money in the business but take no part in the running of it.

Advantages of partnerships

- Taking on new partners is a way of bringing new capital and ideas into the business.
- The workload can be shared among the partners.
- Partners may be able to specialise in the area in which they have skills and experience.

A **deed of partnership** is just another name for a partnership agreement. It outlines things such as how much money each partner has contributed and how profits will be shared.

Drawbacks of partnerships

- In an ordinary partnership all of the partners have **unlimited liability** and they are all liable for the debts of the business so it is important that they trust each other and know what is going on in the business.
- There may be disagreements between the partners which can make decision-making a slow and difficult process.
- The retirement or death of one of the partners can cause serious problems for the partnership. The retiring partner or the family of the deceased partner will probably want their share of the assets and the remaining partners will have to find the money to buy them out.

CASE STUDY

The healthy burger bar

On leaving college Tej, Sal, Billy and Leah decide to set up a burger and salad bar. Tej, Sarah and Leah each provide £5,000 capital while Billy contributes £10,000. Sarah and Tej will be working in the business full-time but Billy and Leah will be working part-time.

Working in pairs or small groups, draw up a partnership agreement outlining how profits/losses will be shared, how major decisions will be reached and what will happen if one of the partners wishes to leave the partnership.

Private limited companies

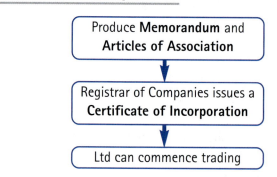

Figure 1.2 *Setting up a private limited company (Ltd)*

Private limited companies range from small-scale businesses with only a handful of shareholders to firms as large as the Virgin Group or Littlewoods organisation. The majority, however, tend to be small or medium-sized businesses such as local building firms, printers etc. Most football clubs outside the Premiership are Ltds.

Private limited companies (Ltds) are businesses owned by **shareholders** who have bought shares in the company. They enjoy the advantage of **limited liability**. This legal term means that if the business fails, the shareholders only lose the money invested in the business. Their own personal assets, such as their home or car, are not at risk. This might make people more willing to invest their money in the business as the risk is reduced.

There are more legal formalities involved in setting up this type of business compared to sole proprietorships and partnerships. Two important documents that are required are outlined below.

- **Memorandum of association.** This gives the outline of the company with information such as its name, registered address, its aims and the amount of authorised capital. In some ways it is like the birth certificate of a company giving the business its legal identity.
- **Articles of association.** This document gives details of the number of directors, how meetings are conducted, voting rights and other information about the company's ownership and structure.

Limited liability means that shareholders only risk the money that they have invested in the business. Their own assets are not at risk if the business fails.

The business must comply with various Companies Acts and the company's accounts must be independently audited. Profits are subject to Corporation Tax rather than income tax. The company has its own legal identity meaning that it can sue and be sued and it will still exist even if one or more of the shareholders dies.

The shareholders elect a **board of directors** to run the company and if the business is profitable the shareholders may receive a **dividend**. Ordinary shares carry voting rights at the Annual General Meeting (AGM) and the more shares a shareholder owns, the more votes they have. If one shareholder has over 50 per cent of the shares they effectively control the business. Selling new shares is a way of raising more capital to expand the business and shareholders know that they have limited liability. However, in a Ltd, shares cannot be sold to the general public and so the shares are not traded on the Stock Exchange. If shareholders wish to sell shares they can only do so with the consent of the other shareholders. In a small private limited company there may be only a small number of shareholders and quite often the directors and the shareholders are the same people.

> **GLOSSARY**
>
> **Board of directors:**
>   The group of senior managers who make all the key decisions in a limited liability.
> **Dividend:**
>   the share of profits paid out to shareholders.

> **QUESTIONS**
>
> 1 Give two advantages and two drawbacks of setting up a business as a partnership rather than as a sole trader.
>
> 2 Give two advantages and two drawbacks of setting up a business as a private limited company (Ltd) rather than as a partnership.

Public limited companies

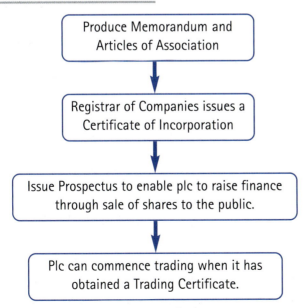

Figure 1.3 *Setting up a public limited company (plc)*

Public limited companies (plcs) account for only a very small fraction of the total number of limited liability companies but they are the giants of the business world, such as Barclays plc, Vodafone plc and Tesco plc. Their shares can be bought and sold on the Stock Market and, because shares can be sold to the general public, the business is able to raise millions of pounds of capital. When the plc sells shares on the Stock Market for the first time, this is known as a **flotation.** They must sell at least £50,000 of shares.

However, plcs are expensive to set up as there are far more legal formalities than for any of the other types of organisation dealt with so far and it is not realistic to float on the Stock Market unless the business wishes to raise several million pounds. Plcs have to abide by the Companies Acts, Stock Exchange rules and publish their accounts.

Likely investors in a plc, such as Marks & Spencer, can look up the share price in the financial pages of newspapers or on the Internet. They can then contact a stockbroker if they wish to trade shares. It is not possible to keep the affairs of a plc secret as accounts are published.

There is also a risk that plcs may be taken over. If an organisation or individual buys more than 50 per cent of the voting shares, they will gain control of the company. This is known as a takeover. If the share price of a plc falls they will become vulnerable to such a takeover because a potential buyer is able to buy the shares cheaply.

The divorce between ownership and control

The phrase 'divorce between ownership and control' means that in larger businesses, the owners do not necessarily run and control the business. A limited liability company is owned by shareholders but the decisions about how it is run are made by the directors. In a small family-run private limited company, it is likely that there will be only a handful of shareholders and they may well be the directors. However, in a large plc there will be millions of shares issued and possibly thousands of shareholders owning only a small number of shares and so they have little influence over how the business is run. The result is that most do not attend the AGM and they do not exercise their voting rights, either in person or by post. In these circumstances, the owners (shareholders) are separated from the day-to-day control of the business.

CASE STUDY

Gregory Electricals Ltd

Gregory Electricals Ltd is a well-established family business selling a wide range of household electrical equipment through eleven stores in the south of England. The Gregory family currently owns 70 per cent of the shares. The Board of Directors wishes to expand the business by opening more stores in the Midlands and is considering converting the business to a plc and floating on the Stock Market.

Produce a short report for the Board of Directors of Gregory Electricals Ltd outlining the advantages and drawbacks of converting to plc status.

ACTIVITY

Key in the table below and fill in the details showing some of the key features of different business organisations.

Type of organisation	No. of owners	Liability	Control/ management	Sources of finance	Distribution of profit	Other points	Examples
Sole Trader							
Partnership							
Private Limited Company (Ltd)							
Public Limited Company (plc)							

Figure 1.4 *Table comparing various types of business organisation*

Franchise operations

The best known type of **franchise** is the business format franchise. The potential entrepreneur (**franchisee**) buys a licence to trade under an existing business name from the parent company (the **franchisor**). Some familiar high-street names such as Body Shop, Benetton and Pizza Hut operate in this format.

Advantages

- The franchisee benefits from buying into an already established business and they usually receive training, support and national advertising from the franchisor. The result is that a franchisee is far more likely to be successful than if they started up their own business from scratch.

- The franchisor benefits because it can be a way of expanding the business rapidly without the need for large sums of capital and they usually receive a percentage of the profits earned by the franchisee known as **royalties** as well as the licence fee.

- The franchisee is likely to be far more motivated than a manager as they have invested their own money in the business and will be keen to succeed.

ACTIVITY

Select a number of companies from the share pages of a newspaper such as the *Financial Times* or the *Daily Telegraph* and track their share prices over the course of a number of weeks. You may like to plot their prices on a graph and comment upon the movements in the share prices.

Drawbacks

- A large amount of capital is usually required to buy into a successful franchise such as McDonald's although less well-known brand names will be cheaper.
- The franchisee also has to purchase all their stock from the franchisor, generating more revenue for the franchisor.
- The franchisee is usually required to follow quite strict guidelines so they will not enjoy the same amount of independence as if they had set up their own business.

QUESTIONS

1 What might be the attractions of buying into a well-established franchise business such as Pizza Express?

2 What are the drawbacks of this compared to setting up a new pizza business?

3 Why might Pizza Express wish to encourage franchisees to buy into the business?

Co-operatives

The familiar face of the Co-op

Co-operatives are a fairly uncommon type of business in the UK. They are a special type of limited liability company owned by the members. Each member has one vote, regardless of how much money they have invested in the business. There are two main types of co-operative in the UK: worker (or producer) co-operatives and retail co-operatives.

Retail co-operatives

The best known type of co-operative in the UK is the co-operative retail movement set up in Rochdale in 1844 and which now includes the retail stores, the Co-operative Bank, insurance and funeral services. The original aim of retail co-operatives was to provide good quality products at reasonable prices for their members. Members are able to join a

Co-operative Society with a minimum investment of £1 and for this they are able to vote on Society policy. Voting is democratic in that everyone has the same voting rights regardless of how many shares they own. The Co-op retail stores face strong competition from other stores such as Tesco and Sainsbury's and critics argue that Co-operative Societies are outdated.

However, the Co-op is proud of its unique approach as the following quote outlines:

'Our members are what help set us apart from other businesses. Our members give us our co-operative vision – our different outlook. Making money is not their sole goal. Profit that's reinvested in their communities making a real difference to the lives of their neighbours, friends, people they see in the street – that's what matters to them.'

Worker co-operatives

Worker co-operatives often arise when a business is threatened with closure. The workforce raises money to buy the company to protect their jobs. The workers then become the owners of the business and so make all the decisions regarding how the business is run. These organisations are quite rare in the UK. The workers are likely to be very well-motivated but may sometimes lack the necessary business skills.

Portfolio tip

You should comment upon the legal structure of your chosen business and consider the liability of the owners. You may also want to examine why the owners opted for this particular type of legal structure.

AO3 The organisational structure of businesses

We will now look at how businesses organise and manage themselves internally on a day-to-day basis. It is possible to use diagrams called **organisational charts** to show the relationships between different employees in the organisation. In a small business, it is quite possible for the owner to deal directly with all of his or her employees face to face. The owner is personally able to explain his or her ideas and workers are able to report any problems to the owner. Important information can be quickly exchanged. This is sometimes called the entrepreneurial model.

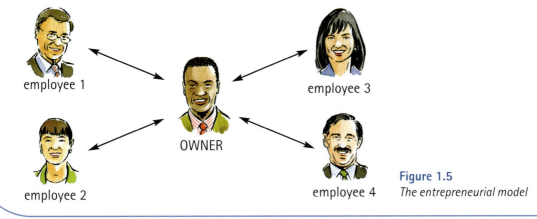

Figure 1.5
The entrepreneurial model

Large organisations tend to be **functionally** organised with workers belonging to a department or section in the company according to the function or job that they perform in the business e.g. marketing, finance, personnel etc. **Line managers** are responsible for getting work done in their department, area or section.

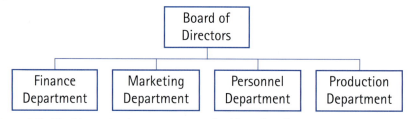

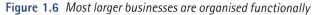

Figure 1.6 *Most larger businesses are organised functionally*

QUESTIONS

In which department would the following employees probably work?

(a) a cost accountant (b) a sales manager (c) a recruitment officer (d) a production line worker (e) a market researcher (f) a fork lift truck driver (g) a credit controller.

Hierarchical structures

Large organisations such as banks are usually organised as **hierarchies**, that is, they have layers of management. When an organisational chart is drawn it resembles a pyramid with a small number of senior managers at the top and a larger number of workers lower down. This gives rise to a promotion ladder as staff can see how they can work their way up the hierarchy, gaining more authority and responsibility as they go up the organisation. Staff know their position in the hierarchy.

The **chain of command** shows how orders and instructions work their way down the hierarchy from the senior managers to the shop floor workers. Superiors (managers) have authority over their subordinates, that is, they are able to ask them to carry out tasks but the manager remains responsible for seeing that work is carried out. The **span of control** refers to the number of subordinates that a superior has direct authority over. It will be difficult to closely supervise a large number of employees if they are carrying out complex tasks. Figure 1.7 shows a hierarchical structure with four different levels and small spans of control.

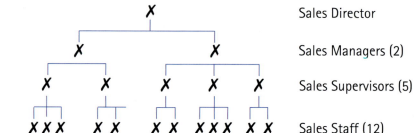

Figure 1.7 *An example of a hierarchical structure*

Flat structures

In a flat structure there are fewer levels of management. This can encourage a team approach but fewer promotion opportunities exist as many of the staff are on the same level or grade and there are a limited number of managerial or supervisory grades. Spans of control will be larger, making close supervision more difficult. Figure 1.8 shows a flat structure with only two levels of authority and larger spans of control.

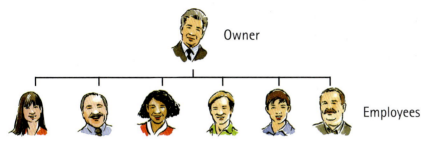

Figure 1.8 *An example of a flat structure*

CASE STUDY

Locks Heath Manufacturing Ltd

Locks Heath Manufacturing Ltd is led by a managing director and has four main departments: marketing, production, finance and distribution. Each department is headed up by the relevant director. Within the finance department is the finance manager who manages five finance clerks. The production department has a works manager and twelve production line staff. The marketing department has a sales manager who manages a market research supervisor and a team of five sales staff. The market research supervisor manages a team of three market researchers. The distribution manager has two supervisors, one supervises the six staff who work in the warehouse and loading bay and the other supervises the five van drivers.

1 Draw the organisational chart for Locks Heath Manufacturing.
2 What is the span of control of the marketing manager?
3 How might a decision to change marketing strategy move down the chain of command?

Matrix management

As we have seen, workers tend to be organised along functional lines so they usually work alongside colleagues doing similar work. For example, an accounts clerk will usually be working in the finance department alongside other finance assistants, accountants etc. However, a business may decide to put together a team drawn from different areas of the business to work on a specific new project. This is known as **matrix management**. The advantage is that this team will have a range of skills and experience. The team members will not have their usual line manager as their boss while they are working on the project.

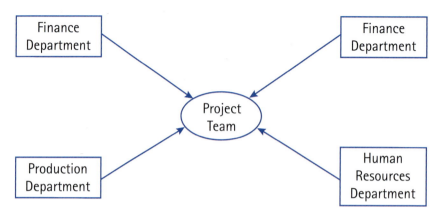

Figure 1.9 *An example of a matrix management structure*

CASE STUDY

Simpsons Luxury Chocolates

Simpsons Luxury Chocolates wish to develop a new chocolate product. The board of directors believes in matrix management and a team has been set up to develop and launch the new product. The team is led by a senior marketing manager and is made up of a production manager, a cost accountant, the distribution manager, two marketing assistants and a human resources assistant.

What is the advantage of setting up a team such as this to manage the product development?

Portfolio tip

You will need to either produce or obtain an organisational chart for your chosen business to illustrate its structure and discuss other ways in which the business could be organised.

Delayering

Many organisations in recent years have implemented a **delayering** process. This means removing layers of hierarchy to create a flatter structure. The firm is able to reduce its costs by having fewer layers of management and junior staff may find that they have more interesting and responsible jobs as they take on some of the supervisory and managerial work. However, delayering may damage morale as jobs are lost and it may just increase the workload of the remaining staff. Over the last ten years, thousands of jobs have been lost in banking, insurance and many other industries as a result of this type of restructuring.

A04 Different stakeholders and their interests

When business owners set up their businesses we have seen that they do so primarily to make a profit. However, other groups and individuals in the business may have different interests. There are also outside groups which may be affected by the behaviour of a business organisation. The term **stakeholder** refers to any individual or group who has an interest in how the business is run or who is affected by its activities. Some of these individuals and groups are shown in the diagram below.

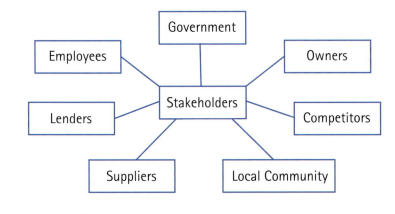

Figure 1.10 *Typical stakeholders in a business*

Internal stakeholders

Stakeholders can be divided into internal stakeholders and external stakeholders. Internal stakeholders are those individuals or groups within the organisation. Typical internal stakeholders are:

- **Owners.** The owner, partners or shareholders of the business have invested their money and want the business to be profitable. They will expect the business to be run efficiently and that managers will be committed to increasing revenues and controlling the firm's costs. Wages and salaries are often important costs for businesses so there is the potential for conflict between the interests of the owners and the employees.

- **Employees**. The employees are another important group who have an interest in the business. They will rely upon the business to provide them with a regular wage or salary. They will hope for job security, safe working conditions and perhaps training and the chance of promotion. They need the business to be successful and profitable but, equally, they will hope to see their wage or salary rising. Managers on the other hand may be expected to hold down staff wage costs to improve the profitability of the business so there is the potential for conflict.

QUESTIONS

List the internal stakeholders in your school or college.

External stakeholders

External stakeholders are those individuals or groups outside the business who are affected by its activities. Typical external stakeholders are:

- **Customers**. Customers will expect products and services to be safe and reliable. They will also expect that the price charged appears fair given the quality of the product and that any complaints will be dealt with quickly and fairly.
- **Suppliers**. Firms that supply the business with raw materials, components, packaging or services will expect to be paid promptly. They may also rely upon regular orders to ensure the success of their own business. Marks & Spencer plc were heavily criticised when they decided to end links with some of their British suppliers and use cheaper foreign clothing manufacturers in North Africa and Eastern Europe.
- **Local communities**. Some businesses have a considerable impact on their local communities. Sometimes the impact is positive, for example, a business may be one of the few sources of employment in an area of high unemployment and generate positive publicity for the area. However, a business may also be a source of pollution, noise and traffic congestion in the area.

Sustainable businesses

Owners set up businesses to generate profit. However, there is now a widespread view that businesses should take the interests of others into account. Customers are becoming more demanding, environmental controls are becoming tighter and bad publicity can seriously damage a business. There is a view that to survive, businesses must become **sustainable**. A sustainable business is one that does not simply pursue profit, but one which takes into account the interests of various stakeholder groups.

Real business

Travis Perkins is a leading UK builders' merchant. The company sells a wide range of building materials from a national branch network. The company fully intends to be a sustainable business and to be this it needs to:

- *generate profits for its shareholders*
- *provide good employment conditions for its employees*
- *trade fairly with suppliers*
- *look after the communities in which it operates*
- *act as a guardian and improver of the environment.*

QUESTIONS

Below is a list of some possible stakeholders in your school or college. For each group, explain what their interest is in the school or college or how they may be affected by its activities.

- pupils/students
- teachers/lecturers
- parents
- governors
- the local education authority
- the government
- local residents.

CASE STUDY

Waterford Wedgwood

Wedgwood china

In June 2003, the pottery firm Waterford Wedgwood announced that more than 1,000 jobs would go with the closure of two of its factories at Hanley and Tunstall in Staffordshire. The company had decided to move production of its lower priced earthenware to factories in the Far East where costs are much lower.

Tony O'Reilly Jnr, the Chief Executive of Wedgwood, said that the business was not generating sufficient return for shareholders.

Mark Fisher, the Labour MP for Stoke-on-Trent, commented:

'Wedgwood have not made a single effort to try to save these jobs.' He added: 'That lack of concern for the community is breathtaking.'

The company announced pre-tax profits of £5.2m for the year to 31 March compared to a loss of £38.3m the previous year.

Source: Adapted from BBC news article 4 June 2003.

How might the following feel about Waterford Wedgwood's decision?

1 a worker at Waterford Wedgwood in Hanley or Tunstall
2 a shareholder in Waterford Wedgwood
3 a local shopkeeper in Stoke on Trent

Conflicts between stakeholders

Some stakeholder groups share similar aims. For example, the owners of the business want it to be successful and profitable. Workers want the business to be successful because then their jobs are likely to be more secure. However, conflicts will also arise. Workers will be looking to increase their wages and other benefits while managers will be trying to control wage costs. This may lead to tension or even industrial action such as a strike. The owners of a local airport may be planning to lengthen the runway and increase the number of passengers to boost profitability while local residents may well object to more noise and traffic in the area.

CASE STUDY

EnviroClean Ltd

An industrial plant

EnviroClean Ltd is a business which employs over 200 staff processing hazardous industrial waste. Waste is brought to the business where it is rendered safe and some can then be reused in various industrial processes. The business is located on a river estuary rich in wildlife and popular with weekend sailors. The business has a good safety record and growing demand for its services has meant rising profits. The company has applied to the local council for planning permission to extend the factory to cope with larger quantities of waste. The expansion plans would create at least 50 new jobs in the area. However, local residents have opposed the plans.

1 List some of the possible stakeholders of EnviroClean Ltd.

2 What interest do each of the stakeholders listed above have in the business ?

3 Give reasons why the local residents may object to the plan.

4 Imagine that you work for the council that is considering this application. Produce a report outlining reasons for and against allowing the expansion to go ahead and make a recommendation.

Portfolio tip

Think about who the key stakeholders in your chosen business are and whether there are any conflicts or tensions between the different stakeholders.

AO5 Trends of growth and decline in different sectors

Over the last 30 years the structure of business activity in the UK has changed significantly. For example, up until the 1980s, the majority of retailers were not allowed to open on Sundays. Now Sunday is the busiest day for many retailers such as DIY stores and garden centres. Similarly, 30 years ago there was no mobile telephone industry as such in the UK. The industry only developed during the 1980s and 1990s and now Vodafone is now one of the UK's largest companies and the mobile phone industry employs more workers than mining, steel and car manufacturing put together. New technology is constantly being developed and the shape of the UK economy continues to change at a very fast rate.

Businesses in the UK operate in a wide range of sectors from farming to telecommunications and from coal mining to leisure centres. This assessment objective examines the three different types of business activity – primary, secondary and tertiary sectors in the UK and some of the important trends and changes taking place in the different business sectors.

Primary industry

Farming is a primary industry

Primary industries are involved in obtaining resources from the natural world. They include businesses such as arable, dairy and fish farming. Some of these primary industries are called **extractive industries** as they extract or obtain resources from the natural environment and they include industries such as coal mining, quarrying, drilling for oil and water supply industries. The number of people who work in these industries in the UK is relatively small but the production of foodstuffs to feed the UK's 60 million population, and obtaining natural resources for business, is clearly vital for our success as an economy. In 2004, less than 2 per cent of the workforce worked in the primary sector.

Secondary industry

Secondary industries are involved in the second stage of the productive process which involves taking raw materials and resources and transforming them into finished or semi-finished products. For example, a brewery such as Scottish and Newcastle takes hops and barley which have been grown by farmers and combines them with water to produce a finished product – beer, which can be sold to consumers, pubs, hotels and restaurants. Brewing is, therefore, a secondary process. A steel manufacturer which takes iron ore and processes it to make steel sheets is also in the secondary sector. The steel sheets are, however, a semi-finished product as they will need further work by other manufacturers. These steel sheets may be used for, example, to make body shells in the car industry or cases for DVD players. As well as manufacturing, the construction industry is also usually included in the secondary sector of the economy as the building industry uses raw materials such as sand, cement, steel and timber to produce homes, roads, hospitals, bridges etc.

Tertiary industry

Tertiary industry covers all of the thousands of services provided in the UK economy. The tertiary sector does not make products as such but it provides valuable services that consumers and other businesses are prepared to pay for. There has been huge growth in this sector of the economy over the last 50 years and over three-quarters of all workers work in the tertiary sector. Some of the largest tertiary industries are retailing, banking, transport, hotels and communications.

Figure 1.11 shows the three sectors of industry working together. The flow diagram shows hops grown on a hop farm in Herefordshire (primary) being used to brew beer (secondary) and being sold in a pub (tertiary).

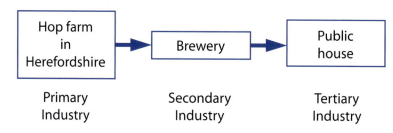

Figure 1.11 *The three sectors of industry*

ACTIVITY

Working in pairs or small groups, identify which sector of the economy the following belong in:

(a) a beauty salon

(b) a salmon farm in Scotland

(c) a taxi firm

(d) a bakery

(e) a slate quarry

(f) a housebuilding company such as Barratt

(g) a vegetable canning business

(h) a television company such as Sky TV

(i) Tesco plc

(j) an oil refinery

(k) Southern Water plc

(l) *Heat* magazine

Patterns of growth and decline over the last 30 years

As was mentioned earlier, there have been enormous changes in UK industry over the last 30 years and the number of people employed in the different sectors of business. There are three main changes that can be identified in recent decades:

- the continuing decline of the primary sector
- the decline of manufacturing in the UK
- the growth of the tertiary sector.

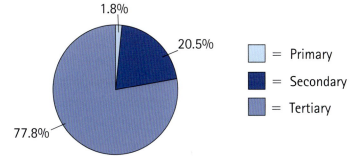

1.8%

20.5%

77.8%

■ = Primary
■ = Secondary
■ = Tertiary

Figure 1.12 *UK Workforce by industrial sector spring 2004*

Real business

P & O operate a large fleet of ships from their headquarters in Portsmouth. They run cross-channel ferry routes to France for passengers and vehicles and they also have a number of luxury liners such as the Aurora *and* Oriana *which provide cruises for their customers.*

ACTIVITY

	Number employed in thousands	
	1980	**2002**
Agriculture, forestry & fishing	361	255
Energy and water supply	726	177
Manufacture	6,940	3,668
Construction	1,252	1,186
Services	13,693	20,375
Total	22,972	25,661

1 Calculate the total number of workers working in each of the primary, secondary and tertiary industries for 1980 and 2002.
2 Plot this data on a graph.

Source: Office for National Statistics

The continuing decline of the primary sector

Agriculture

Over the last 30 years the number of people working in agriculture has fallen significantly. Small farms have closed or been swallowed up by larger farms that make use of more machinery and are able to produce food more cheaply for the big supermarket chains. Changes in the European Union's (EU) Common Agricultural Policy (CAP) have also affected farmers' incomes, causing some to leave the industry.

Fishing

The fishing industry

The UK's fishing fleet has reduced significantly over the last 30 years. In 1975 there were 22,134 sea fisherman employed in the UK. By 2003, the number employed had fallen to 11,774 (DEFRA figures). These job losses have hit areas such as Hull, Cornwall and Peterhead in Scotland. Stocks of many fish species have reduced as a result of over-fishing and the EU has responded by introducing quotas and other measures aimed at reducing the number of fish caught. Many fishermen have found it hard to earn a reasonable income and have left the industry.

Mining

The mining industry

In 1947 there were approximately 750,000 people working in mining in the UK. By 1993 the number had fallen to around 31,000 and by 2002 there were less than 11,000 coal miners in the UK. The main demand for coal comes from the generation of electricity and now only 30 per cent of electricity comes from coal-fired power stations. Gas is the main competition although some electricity is generated by nuclear and hydro-electric power stations. The UK coal mining industry has also suffered as a result of cheaper imported coal.

Manufacturing industry

Manufacturing is another sector that has seen a huge fall in the number of workers employed in it and during the 1980s the term **deindustrialisation** was coined for this process. The trend has continued and between 1997 and 2002 over half a million manufacturing jobs disappeared. One reason to explain this is that manufacturing has become more capital intensive, meaning that it has become more automated and computerised. Far more technology is used in manufacturing, resulting in fewer workers being needed. At Ford Motor Company, for example, robots rather than people carry out all welding in the manufacture of cars and vans.

A second factor is that cheaper foreign-produced products have replaced many UK-manufactured goods and some UK companies have decided to switch production overseas to lower wage economies to cut costs. For example, Dyson the vacuum cleaner business has switched some of its production from Wiltshire to Malaysia to take advantage of lower wage costs.

The service sector

The service sector

ACTIVITY

Carry out a survey, either of the part-time jobs done by students in your class or the jobs done by your parents.

1 How many work in each of the three sectors discussed?
2 Do your findings reflect the main pattern of employment outlined?

There has been a massive expansion of this sector over the last 30 years and the vast majority of workers in the UK are employed in the tertiary sector. In 2002 there were over 20 million people working in the service sector of the economy. As citizens have become wealthier the demand for services has increased significantly. Consumers are now far more likely to eat out, have bank accounts and credit cards, own a mobile phone, take foreign holidays and belong to a fitness club than ever before. The service sector of the economy has grown to meet consumers' needs.

The interdependence of industry

The primary, secondary and tertiary sectors are not completely separate from one another but instead they are often inter-connected and dependent on one another. Dairy farmers need to send their product to a dairy where it may be pasteurised and perhaps turned into cream, butter, yoghurt or cheese. The big retailers, such as Sainsbury's, rely on farmers to produce foodstuffs and on manufacturers such as Heinz and Birds Eye to process them if they are to meet their customers' needs. The demand for mobile phone services has increased so companies such as Nokia and Motorola will need to manufacture more phones.

A change in one sector may have a knock-on effect in other sectors. For example, when foot and mouth disease broke out in England and Wales a few years ago, the initial impact was on livestock farmers. However, very quickly hotels, pubs and leisure facilities in rural districts saw their incomes fall as fewer people visited the countryside. The disease thus had an impact far beyond the farming industry.

QUESTIONS

How might a boom in the housing market with more people moving house influence the following businesses?

(a) A removal company such as Pickfords

(b) Nationwide Building Society

(c) A new car dealership

(d) A DIY superstore such as B & Q

(e) A travel agent specialising in luxury holidays

AO6 Competitors in business

Almost every business has some form of competition. This means that every business will need to consider not just its own products and prices but will need to take into account the actions of its main rivals. The business must carefully analyse who it considers its main competitors and this inevitably makes the firm think carefully about the market it is operating in and how it will stay competitive.

Competitor audit

The competitor audit is the process of carefully analysing who the competitors are in the market. There are usually some obvious competitors who are providing an identical or very similar product or service. However, competition may also be less obvious and can be from firms which are providing a product or service which is an alternative for customers. For example, a ferry company such as P&O is obviously in competition with other ferry operators such as Sea France and Britanny Ferries. However, passengers who wish to travel to France could also use Eurostar or fly. The competitor audit forces managers of a business to take all forms of competition into account. They are then in a better position to decide exactly how they will compete with them.

Means of competition

There are a variety of ways in which businesses may choose to compete. Some of the main forms of competition that will be examined here are:

- price
- product
- marketing and promotion
- customer service.

Price

Price is often seen as the main form of competition. If there are several firms offering a product or service in a market then offering a lower price than competitors is one possible way of trying to increase market share. However, when firms in a market all try to undercut each other's prices this is known as a **price war.** The result is that each firm's market share is usually unaltered but they are all earning lower profits because of the lower price. Firms will usually try to avoid a damaging price war by competing in ways other than price. However, a large, powerful firm may deliberately start a price war with the aim of driving weaker businesses out of the market and thus gain market share. Some businesses are fiercely competitive on price e.g. low-cost airlines.

Product

It is important to realise that price is not the only form of competition. The majority of businesses do not set out to be the lowest-cost supplier in the market and the vast majority of television advertisements make no reference to the price. Most businesses prefer to compete in other ways. One method is to differentiate a product or service from rival products either through design or through advertising. Some products have a **unique selling point (USP).** The aim here is to persuade the customer that the product or service is worth buying because it is different or special or special in some way. The USP for the Dyson vacuum cleaner was that it was the first bagless cleaner designed so that the suction would not weaken as the bag filled up.

In the market for lager, Stella Artois does not claim to be the cheapest on the market but rather its advertising slogan is 'Reassuringly expensive'. A high-status product such as a Rolex watch or a designer dress sells on its exclusive image, not on having a lower price than its rivals.

QUESTIONS

What do you think is the main selling point for the following:
(a) McCain micro chips
(b) Bold 2-in-1 washing powder
(c) a Ferrari
(d) Flora pro-active margarine
(e) Head and Shoulders shampoo?

Marketing and promotion

Most products and services operate in markets where there is a significant amount of competition from similar rival products. It is not always possible for a product or service to have a unique selling point. Businesses will often develop a **brand name** and spend large amounts of money on developing this brand name and an accompanying brand image. The aim is to persuade customers that a particular brand is better in some way. The majority of washing powders are similar in their chemical structures so manufacturers spend large sums of money on advertising, with the aim of

GLOSSARY

Brand name: an identity for a particular product

convincing customers that their brand washes whiter or is gentler on colours than rivals. A successful brand name will provide consumers with reassurance about the quality of the product and make it easier to develop new products or services under the brand name.

Television advertisements for many products, for example, beers such as Fosters, Carling and John Smiths, give little or no information about the product but use humour to create a brand image for their product. Some businesses will use celebrities or sport stars to endorse their products e.g. Thierry Henry and Renault.

Branded products are important marketing tools

Smaller businesses will not be able to afford high-profile celebrity endorsements and television advertising campaigns but they will still usually promote their products and services. Advertisements in the local press, on local radio stations and endorsements by local sport stars and minor celebrities may all be used by businesses to promote themselves to potential customers.

Above the line promotion

Above the line promotion involves using independent media to promote the firm's products or services. Popular examples of this type of activity include television, national and local press and radio advertisements.

Below the line promotion

Figure 1.13 *Buy one, get one free is a popular promotional offer*

Below the line promotion involves promotional activities that the business has more direct control over such as trade promotions, sponsorships, money-off coupons etc. Offers such as 'Buy one, get one free' (BOGOF) and '50p off your next purchase' are typical examples of this form of promotional activity. Events such as the Southampton Boat Show and the Ideal Homes Exhibition provide important promotional opportunities for businesses operating in these industries.

Customer service

Both domestic and industrial customers are becoming much more demanding. Customers have higher expectations of the quality of the product or service that they are paying for and they are far more likely to complain if products do not meet their expectations. There are a few markets such as domestic water supply where there is only one supplier. However, in the majority of markets customers have a choice of supplier and if a product offered does not seem to offer good value they will take their custom elsewhere. In the longer term, it is difficult to see a business surviving if it does not offer an acceptable level of service to the customer.

During the 1980s, a number of businesses such as British Telecom introduced the concept of **Total Quality Management (TQM)**. This is a management approach which puts the customer first and BT's aim was to give the customer what he or she wants first time, every time. The business may not always achieve this aim but it demonstrates that the company takes customer satisfaction seriously. If a customer buys a tin of beans there is less need for an after-sales service than for a car dealership. Many businesses have a customer service department which deals with complaints and queries but it is obviously better if the firm produces a high-quality product or service and does not receive complaints.

Portfolio tip

You should comment upon the level of competition in the market. Who are the main competitors and how fierce is competition? In what ways does your chosen business compete?

QUESTIONS

What customer service/quality issues may arise from the following?

(a) a meal in a restaurant

(b) a car insurance claim

(c) a package holiday to Ibiza.

AO7 The location of business and why this location is used

There are thousands of businesses located across the UK. Some of the smaller businesses such as newsagents and pubs may be found throughout the country, even in small villages, whereas oil refineries tend to be located at particular coastal sites such as Fawley and Milford Haven. Some industries have a long association with a particular region of the country while others have grown up quite recently. This section of the unit looks at some of the factors that may be relevant when a business is deciding where to locate.

Some of the factors which may be relevant in the decision about location are:

- economies of scale
- the local labour force
- local employment levels
- wage levels
- customers' suppliers
- historical reasons
- demographic change.

Economies of scale

Economies of scale can be divided into two types: internal and external. **Internal economies** are the advantages that a firm enjoys as it grows. For example, a large firm is able to employ more specialist staff, afford more expensive equipment and gain bulk-buying discounts which may not be possible for a smaller firm.

External economies arise when an industry becomes concentrated in one particular part of the country. Local colleges may well develop specialist training courses to meet the needs of the industry and businesses will be set up supplying specialist services to meet the needs of the dominant industry. For example, for over 100 years Sheffield was known for its steel industry and in response, the local universities and colleges developed metallurgy and other specialist courses. Businesses grew up offering repairs, maintenance and support services for the steel manufacturing industry and associated trades. Sheffield thus became attractive as a location for a steel-related business.

The local labour force

The size and quality of the local labour force may also be relevant in deciding where to locate a business. If a manufacturing business needs to recruit 400 workers for a proposed new factory then this will be difficult in a rural district with a small population. In these circumstances a location near to a large population centre is preferable. If the business needs to recruit skilled workers, for example, those with computer skills, it will need to locate in an area where there is a skilled workforce with appropriate skills. University towns can be a useful source of well-educated and trained workers. Significant numbers of hi-tech and research businesses are located on business parks on the outskirts of Cambridge and Oxford. A pool of skilled labour grows up in an area where particular industries are concentrated, encouraging more new businesses to locate there.

ACTIVITY

Explain the difference between internal and external economies of scale.

QUESTIONS

Was the workforce in your local area known for having a particular type of skill in the past? Is this still the case?

Local employment levels

The local unemployment rate may play a part in the decision where to locate. The UK currently has one of the lowest unemployment rates in Europe. However, unemployment is not evenly spread and some parts of the country have high levels of unemployment e.g. Northern Ireland, parts of west Cornwall and the north-east of England. If a business needs a large supply of semi-skilled or unskilled workers it may well consider locating to an area of high unemployment. It will be easier to recruit workers in this sort of area where there are significant numbers of unemployed workers looking for work, whereas it will be much more difficult in a prosperous area with high levels of employment.

Government assistance

Because certain parts of the country suffer from high unemployment, the government uses regional policy to encourage businesses to locate in areas of high unemployment. The areas are classified by the government as Assisted Areas and businesses may be able to obtain government grants if they create jobs in these areas.

A number of foreign companies, including Nissan and Samsung, have over the last 20 years received millions of pounds from the UK government to locate in areas of high unemployment. The government also designates some small areas of particularly high unemployment as Enterprise Zones and gives them extra help. They tend to be run-down inner-city areas or towns that have suffered from the closure of one large employer. Firms wishing to locate in these areas and create jobs may be eligible for a significant amount of government assistance. A business which has no need to locate in any particular area, sometimes referred to as **footloose**, may decide to take advantage of government financial incentives when making its decision.

Wage and salary levels

The average wage offered by businesses varies significantly in different parts of the country as is shown in the table below. Wages in the south-east of England tend to be higher than in, for example, south Wales. For some firms, wages account for a significant proportion of their total costs so a business may decide to locate in an area of relatively low wages. These areas tend also to be areas of above average unemployment as workers are keen to find work and are prepared to accept lower wages. However, if a firm needs workers with a skill that is in short supply they may have to accept that they will have to offer relatively high wages. A shortage of computer analysts or bricklayers in London or the South East will force up wages and businesses will have no choice but to offer higher wages if they are to recruit and retain workers.

ACTIVITY

Wage differences by region, winter 2003/04

Region	Average gross weekly earnings (£)
North East	356
North West	393
Yorks & Humberside	390
East Midlands	403
West Midlands	404
East	485
London	548
South East	491
South West	410
Wales	381
Scotland	417
Northern Ireland	369

Using the table, answer the following questions:
1 Rank the 12 UK economic regions based on average earnings.
2 Which two regions have the highest average wages?
3 Which two regions have the lowest wages?

Based on data from the Labour Force Survey – National Statistics

Nearness to customers

Department stores are usually located in towns or cities

For many businesses nearness to the customer is of great importance. There is a limit to how far customers will travel to buy fish and chips even if they are of excellent quality. Usually a fish and chip shop will need to be situated in an area where there are plenty of local customers. For the same reason a department store will usually be situated in a reasonable-sized town or city. Marks & Spencer will only consider locating a new store in an area of relatively high population density.

Similarly, some finished products are heavy or bulky to transport so it makes sense to locate the business near to the customers to reduce transport costs. For a business that sells its product nationally or internationally nearness to the customer may be less of a consideration when deciding where to locate.

Nearness to suppliers

For some businesses, a site near to suppliers of key raw materials and components may be the main factor in deciding where to locate. There are a number of vehicle manufacturers in the West Midlands such as Rover, Land Rover and Jaguar. Over the years, a wide range of suppliers have grown up in the area such as companies supplying electrical fittings, tyres and other important components. A new business or a relocating business will want to be confident that it will have easy access to all the materials that it needs in production.

Up until 1979 the UK imported all of its crude oil. It made sense to locate oil refineries at sites on the coast such as Fawley and Milford Haven so that the crude oil could be refined where it was brought ashore. Vegetables and fruit can be heavy and costly to transport so it may be sensible to locate a vegetable canning or freezing factory close to the growing areas. For example, sugar beet is a bulky root vegetable. There are sugar refining businesses located in East Anglia, close to the growing areas to reduce transport costs.

ACTIVITY

Consider how important is nearness to customers when deciding upon the location of:
(a) a 10-pin bowling alley
(b) an Internet bookseller
(c) a cycle repair shop?

ACTIVITY

How important is nearness to suppliers when deciding upon the location of:
(a) a wine bar (b) a fish processing plant (c) an advertising agency?

Some businesses locate near to their raw materials

Historical reasons for location

A business will sometimes stay in a location long after the original reasons for locating there have gone. This is known as **industrial inertia**. Once established in an area a business may be reluctant to relocate, with all the expense and upheaval that this involves. The area around Stoke on Trent is known as the Potteries. This is because during the 18th and 19th centuries a large number of pottery and earthenware businesses set up in the area because of the availability of suitable fireclay. However, despite the fact that production methods have changed, earthenware and chinaware businesses such as Waterford Wedgwood and Royal Doulton still operate in the area.

Demographic change

Demographic change refers to changes in the population over a period of time. Over the last thirty years, some parts of the country have experienced increases in population as people move into the area in search of work. Other areas have experienced falls in population as people move away from the area because of high unemployment e.g. parts of west Cornwall. These demographic changes will have a significant impact on local businesses. If population declines in a locality then businesses, particularly small shops and cafes, will find that they have fewer customers, revenue falls and they may decide to close down.

However, in other parts of the country a rapidly increasing population may mean more customers for businesses. This may encourage entrepreneurs to open new businesses or expand existing ones. However, it may mean traffic congestion, shortages of housing and pressure on local schools and hospitals. This is very much the case in parts of London and the south-east of England.

ACTIVITY

Which industries were traditionally associated with the following places in Britain?
(a) South Wales
(b) the Clyde Valley in Scotland
(c) Sheffield
(d) Cornwall
(e) Northampton.

Portfolio tip

You should describe where the business is located and explain why this particular location was chosen by the owners. In some cases the location is of great importance while for other businesses the particular location is relatively unimportant.

QUESTIONS

1 List five factors a business may take into account when deciding where to locate.
2 Which factors are likely to be most important when deciding to locate the following businesses?
  (i) a sandwich bar
  (ii) an airport
  (iii) a boat repair business
  (iv) a horse riding centre

AO8　Possible changes that could be made to the business location

Businesses are constantly having to respond to changing circumstances. The fact that a business is thriving and profitable today does not guarantee that it will even be in existance in five years' time. New competition may arrive in the market place or customer tastes and preferences may change. A business will need to be aware of these trends and a business may need to assess from time to time whether it is appropriate to stay in its current location or relocate.

Relocation due to business growth or decline

Most new businesses start off on a relatively small scale usually in rented premises or perhaps even based at the owner's home address. A successful and growing business may quite quickly outgrow its existing premises, prompting the owners to undertake a search for new, larger premises. In some cases this may simply mean moving to a larger site on the same industrial estate but in other cases it may mean moving to a different part of town or even out of the locality altogether.

In other cases a business may decide that it needs to move to smaller, cheaper premises or out of the area altogether. If sales are declining the business may aim to lower its fixed costs by moving to cheaper premises. In the worst cases, the business may decide that there is no point in continuing to trade in the locality because of its falling sales.

QUESTIONS

1 Have any businesses closed down or moved away from your area recently?

2 Have any new businesses opened up in your area recently?

Portfolio tip

Discuss the location of the business and consider whether changes in the market may mean that a change of location will be necessary in the future.

Redevelopment of current location

A business may be quite happy with its current geographical location but feel that the actual premises are inadequate for its needs. The current premises may be old and in need of refurbishment to improve facilities for staff and customers or the premises may simply be too small due to the growth of the business. An expanding manufacturing business may decide to build on adjacent land that it owns to increase its capacity or a department store may feel that it needs to undertake a complete refurbishment and decoration programme to maintain its competitiveness with other retailers in the area.

CASE STUDY

Splatter!

Julie and Shaun operate a paintballing centre on the outskirts of Swindon called 'Splatter!'. The business has grown rapidly over the last 6 years but two issues are causing some concern. Firstly, a go-carting centre is to open nearby and, secondly, the landlord has indicated that the rent on the site may rise next year. Shaun feels that they should consider relocating the business but Julie is not so sure.

Outline the arguments for and against remaining at their current location.

PORTFOLIO GUIDANCE

To meet assessment objectives 3 to 8, you must produce evidence based on a business that you have chosen. To achieve a pass grade you need to examine the structure of the business, its stakeholders and the main trends in the market. You should identify the main competitors and how the business competes. You will also need to consider the location of the business and any possible changes in the future.

To achieve higher grades you will need to analyse issues in much greater depth, use examples to support your points and show a thorough understanding of the trends that affect the business based upon research.

SKILLS CHECK

1 What is meant by the term 'mission statement'?

2 Explain using examples why different types of business organisations have different aims.

3 What is meant by the legal term 'unlimited liability'?

4 Four college friends are thinking of setting up in business either as a partnership or as a private limited company (Ltd). Outline some of the issues that they might take into account before deciding upon the legal structure of the business.

5 Why might a successful private limited company (ltd) decide to convert to plc status?

6 What is meant by the following terms?

    (a) hierarchy
    (b) functional management
    (c) chain of command
    (d) span of control.

7 (a) What is meant by the term stakeholder?
    (b) Explain, using examples, why the aims of some stakeholders in a typical business organisation may conflict.

8 (a) Distinguish between primary, secondary and **tertiary industry**.
    (b) Outline some of the main trends in primary, secondary and tertiary industry over the last 30 years.

9 Apart from price, examine some of the ways in which businesses may compete with each other.

10 Explain 4 factors that a new business may take into account when deciding where to locate.

11 Outline some of the factors that might cause a business to consider relocating to new premises.

Enterprise and operations

Getting Started

A surprising number of people have a dream of one day running their own business. Unfortunately a lot of these businesses fail, because the owner(s) have insufficient business skills.

Throughout this section you will learn how to start up your own business. This will entail considering everything you will need to do to ensure that your business does not fail at the first hurdle. You will develop an understanding of the processes necessary to ensure your business venture remains successful in a highly competitive market.

To complete this unit successfully you will need to produce evidence to show that you understand how businesses identify opportunities, how they obtain support for new ventures, and how they operate to give the venture the best chance to succeed. Your work will focus on a single business venture devised independently or as part of a group. If you choose to work within a group you must write up your evidence independently. You will need to produce evidence to achieve the five assessment objectives that are contained in the specification and which are shown below. This unit is split up into five sections which match the assessment objectives and contain information to help you achieve them.

In order to understand the unit, all of the illustrations and examples will be based on Richard and Megan starting up a mobile car valeting business called 'Squeaky Clean Cars'.

This unit will cover

- AO1 Research and describe the current business environment relating to the proposed business venture.
- AO2 Describe the different forms of business ownership suitable for the proposed new venture and recommend the most appropriate.
- AO3 Research and present the information required to construct an outline business plan.
- AO4 Describe the operational systems needed to make the intended business successful.
- AO5 Carry out a presentation to pitch a proposal for the new business venture to a key stakeholder.

AO1 The business environment relating to the proposed business venture

In this section you will learn how to undertake different kinds of **market research** and identify the business environment in which your new proposed business venture will compete.

Market research

It is vital that before starting any new business venture, sufficient market research is undertaken to assess the potential demand for the service/product being offered. Market research is classified into two sections – primary and secondary.

Primary market research

Primary market research is where the business undertakes its own research. There are different ways that a business can gather information. It could question people, hold focus groups, ask the general public to try out its products or services and feedback their comments, or it could observe customer behaviour.

Primary research is very time consuming and can often be expensive. Another major problem can be the accuracy of the results. In order to achieve results that represent the whole of the country a large number of people need to be included in the **population**.

> **GLOSSARY**
>
> **Population:**
> The total number of people included in a survey.

Market research can take many forms

The population is the total number of people that are involved in the research.

Before undertaking market research the business must first decide who its potential customers are. Will the product/service just be suitable for young people, families, males or females?

Once the business has decided who its customers are, it needs to consider how many of them they need to question in order to get reliable results. This process is known as sampling.

Sampling

Sampling is the term used to describe how a business chooses who to question about its product or service. There are two sampling methods:

- random sampling and
- non-probability sampling.

Random sampling can be further broken down into simple, systematic or stratified.

Type	Description	Example
Simple random sampling	Every member of the population has the same chance of being chosen for the survey.	This method is used when the business considers that the product could be used by any member of the population, for example, toothpaste.
Systematic sampling	The business will question every 'nth' person.	This method is used when the product is targeted at a particular section of society. If your school/college wanted to find out students' opinions of the canteen they could get an alphabetical list of all the students in the school/college and question every 20th person in the school/college.
Stratified random sampling	The business will break down the population into groups, for example sex, age and occupation. Each one of these groups is then randomly sampled.	This method is used when the product is aimed at the whole population and the business wants to ensure they manage to talk to everyone within each selected group. For example, a business wants to find out people's opinions on a new flavour crisp. They have decided to divide the population according to age. They will then randomly sample each selected age group.

Table 2.1 *Random sampling*

Non-probability sampling involves picking the sample randomly and there is no way of knowing who will be included. Anybody could be questioned simply because they were available at the time. This method of research is often cheaper. Non-probability sampling can also be broken down further.

Type	Description	Example
Quota sampling	The interviewer will select who they want to interview by age, gender or occupation.	This method is used when the business has already decided who their product/service will be aimed at.
		If a business were launching a new luxury chocolate bar they may have decided to aim it at women. Interviewers would therefore only speak to females.
Purpose sampling	This involves the business deliberately biasing a sample depending on the market being investigated.	The business only wants to find out the opinions of those people who already use the product/service or a similar product/service.
		For example, a lot of running magazines get their readers to test clothes or running shoes. The results are biased because the product has only been used by the people who already use a similar product.
Cluster sampling	This involves selecting a random sample from a selected area.	A business may decide that it can only afford to trial its new product or service in a certain area of the country in order to reduce costs.
		For example, a business is trying to launch a new type of soap. They have decided to trial it in Manchester due to high costs of market research. The business hopes that the results gained will be representative of the whole country.
Convenience sampling	This is probably the cheapest form of sampling. It involves talking to those people who were available at the time of the survey. To improve the results of convenience sampling, judgement sampling can be used. This involves the interviewer selecting respondents who are judged to be the potential purchasers of the product/service.	This method of sampling is likely to be less reliable than other sampling methods as it may only question a biased sample.
		For example, if you questioned people outside the local leisure centre at 2 pm on a Monday afternoon in June you are likely to only speak to mothers or fathers with young children, shift workers or people who are retired or unemployed.

Table 2.2 *Non-probability sampling*

Questionnaires

Once a business has decided what type of sampling method it is going to use, the next problem is how to compile the questionnaire.

Before a business starts designing a questionnaire it must first consider what it hopes to find out. Does it want to know:

- who its customers are going to be?
- how much will they pay for the product/service?
- how often will they purchase the product/service?

First choose your research sample

In order to collect the correct information the questions need to be carefully planned and worded. Many a poor response has been received by interviewers because the quality of the questions was insufficient to gain the information required by the company conducting the research.

Questions can either be 'closed' or 'open'. Closed questions will generally produce quantifiable responses. A business is then able to turn their responses into statistical data. For example, if a business wanted to know how many people swim at the local leisure centre, they could simply ask 'Have you been swimming within the last two weeks?' The business would then be able to calculate what percentage of their survey had actually swum within the last month.

Open questions give a business much more information and would include opinions. For example, within the leisure centre questionnaire the next question could be 'What do you think of the swimming pool?' This would encourage the respondents to pass on their own ideas and these would be more difficult to turn into statistical data. For example, 6 people thought the pool was often too cold. The rest of the sample did not make a comment.

QUESTIONS

You have been asked to find out what the students think of the food being served in the school canteen. Working in small groups, design a questionnaire that could be used for this purpose. Include open and closed questions.

Secondary market research

This is research that has been collected either by another organisation or within the business for other reasons. This could include using past sales figures in order to predict the potential sales of a new product.

Alternatively, the business could use statistics collected by the government as an indication of how many people take two holidays a year. This information may be free and available to anyone or there may be a charge for its use. Government statistics are freely available from the reference section of public libraries or the Internet.

Other forms of secondary research include:

- trade journals
- periodicals
- professional associations
- national organisations
- organisations which specialise in collecting data, for example Mintel and Key Note.

CASE STUDY

Mobile car valet

Megan and Richard are thinking of starting up in business offering a mobile car valet service. This would involve them travelling to people's homes and washing, waxing and internally cleaning customers' cars. Customers would have the option of which service they required.

There are three services on offer as outlined below:

Gold valet	Silver valet	Bronze internal valet
• shampoo bodywork • rinse, leather and dry • polish bodywork • clean wheels, arches and door frames • dress tyres, trim and bumper • vacuum interior • shampoo seats and carpets • clean headlining • clean and dress interior plastic • clean windows	• shampoo bodywork • rinse, leather and dry • polish bodywork • clean wheels, arches and door frames • dress tyres trim and bumper • vacuum interior • clean headlining • clean and dress interior plastic • clean windows	• vacuum seats • shampoo seats and carpets • clean headlining • clean and dress interior plastics • clean windows
Price: £50.00	Price: £30.00	Price: £30.00

Table 2.3 *Mobile car valet services*

They are aware that they need to conduct some market research prior to starting this new business. They have decided to undertake some market research of their own. They are hoping to attract private customers and local garages who sell second-hand cars. Eventually they will try and target businesses that have a fleet of cars, for example a local taxi firm or car hire business.

They have asked you to make the following recommendations.

(a) **What type of sampling method would you suggest? They think they will only get customers from their local area. Justify your reasons.**

(b) **Outline the information that Megan and Richard need from conducting this research.**

(c) **From your list in (b) design a suitable questionnaire they could use within the locality.**

(d) **What secondary market research could the couple undertake?**

Business environment

The business environment looks at where the new product/service is going to be placed and how external influences might affect its performance. The business environment will examine where the business is going to be located, how the economy will affect the sales of its products/services, what is the competition, how will the venture be financed and who are its potential customers.

Market environment (economic)

The current state of the economy affects all businesses. It includes the rate of inflation, how high or low interest rates are and levels of employment. At the time of writing the economy has seen a recent **boom**. People are confidently spending money and the demand for goods and services is high. This in turn keeps people in business as goods have to be manufactured and services provided. In December 2003 there were 28 million people in employment.

Inflation

Inflation is the rise in general prices and the reduction in value of money. Inflation is the sustained increase in prices measured monthly, quarterly or annually. It is usually measured by the retail price index (RPI). The RPI is a set basket of shopping the government compares over a period of time. The increase in the price of the basket of shopping is the rate of inflation. Housing prices are not included in this measurement. At the time of writing, the government's inflation target is 2.0 per cent. This means that the price of goods and services is only rising slowly. As a result, people's wages will continue to maintain their **standard of living** and wage rises remain relatively small. Standard of living reflects the goods and services that people can buy with their income. This could be a new car every two years and a holiday abroad.

When inflation is very high, people will be able to buy less and less with their money. They will need large wage increases in order to maintain their standard of living. Businesses are then pressured to meet these higher wage costs and therefore their costs rise. This may be passed on to the customer, fuelling inflation.

QUESTIONS

How do you think rapidly rising inflation would affect Megan and Richard's dream of setting up Squeaky Clean Cars?

Interest Rate

This is the amount charged by external organisations in order to borrow money. The Bank of England sets the base rate for the country. At the time of writing, interest rates have been slowly increasing. The reason for this is to reduce consumer spending and encourage more people to save their money. The recent fear of the government has been that consumer spending and borrowing have been too high and therefore there is a risk of inflation increasing. If interest rates are high, people's **disposable income** reduces as they meet higher mortgage payments or increased payments on loans. If interest rates are low, people will have more money available to spend on consumer goods or services as they will be spending less on their mortgages and loans.

Disposable income is the amount people have available to spend as they choose.

Employment/unemployment

At the time of writing, employment levels are considered to be high, standing at 28 million in December 2003. People are actively employed and have a higher disposable income which enables them to purchase more goods and services which increases the demand for non-essential goods and services. For example, more people are now able to afford to take short breaks as well as a summer holiday.

When people are unemployed, their ability to purchase goods and services decreases as they have less disposable income. They will only be able to purchase essential items and will avoid making unnecessary purchases.

> ### QUESTIONS
> Discuss as a group
> how you think
> increasing interest
> rates would affect
> Megan and Richard's
> dream of setting up
> their own business.
> How would
> decreasing interest
> rates affect their
> dream?

> ### QUESTIONS
> Discuss as a group: how do you think increasing unemployment would affect Megan and Richard's new business of washing and valeting cars?

Potential competition

Competition will always affect a business as customers will often spend their money where they feel they are going to be getting the best deal. Potential customers will often have different ideas of what a 'good deal' is and therefore any business must decide how it can compete within its selected market.

A business can choose to compete on price. High prices may represent to some people extreme quality, and people are often heard saying 'you get what you pay for'. A low price can also encourage people as everybody likes to feel they are getting a bargain.

Another way a business can compete against its rivals is to offer better customer service. This could include longer opening hours, home delivery, extended warranty on goods etc.

> ### QUESTIONS
> Organise yourselves into groups of four. Two of the groups should consider how your local supermarkets compete with one another.
>
> The remaining two should consider how Megan and Richard could compete with other businesses offering car washing and valeting services.
>
> Discuss your ideas together as a group. Decide how you think Megan and Richard should compete to attract customers.

Sources of potential finance

New businesses need money in order to start up. This can either be supplied by the owners or borrowed from an external source. If the money is supplied by the owners of the business this is known as capital.

There are various methods a business can use to borrow money and these are covered in detail in Unit 3: Finance in business. A business could borrow from friends or family, bank overdraft, bank loan, or selling shares in a private limited company to friends and family.

Let us look at the possible ways that Megan and Richard could raise the finance necessary to start up their new business. The first decision they have to make is how much money is required to get the business up and running.

Business mortgage

A business mortgage enables a business to purchase land and buildings. This is a long-term loan, often 25 years, from a financial institution which is secured on the **assets** of the business.

Assets are items that have a life expectancy of more than one year and will be used in order to help the business run. They include buildings, cars, machinery.

Securing a loan against fixed assets means that if the business is unable to meet its loan repayments the fixed assets can be sold and the loan paid off. Mortgages carry an interest charge which must be considered when a business decides how much it can justifiably borrow.

Loan

A loan from an external financial institution, usually a bank, will be secured on the assets of the business. Loans are often for smaller amounts of money and are paid back over a shorter timescale than a mortgage.

Bank overdraft

This is an arrangement with the bank whereby a business can spend more money than they have in their bank account. It allows the business to borrow small amounts of money over a much shorter time scale. The total amount that the business can overspend is agreed with the bank and this is known as the business's overdraft limit. If the business goes over this limit it will be charged a penalty and the interest rate will be higher. Illustrations of how this works can be found in Unit 3: Finance in business page 76.

Share issue

Private limited companies start up by issuing shares. These will only be issued to the owners of the business and this is often the people who are running and working within the business. However, they can be sold to other people who will not be directly involved with the day-to-day running of the business. Shares can only be issued to other people with the full approval of all the other shareholders. When someone buys shares in a business it increases the capital available within the business.

CASE STUDY

Getting the business up and running

Megan and Richard have sat down and discussed what they need to buy in order to start up this new business venture. They will conduct the administration side of the business from their home. They have come up with the following list:

- a van
- high-power wet and dry commercial vacuum cleaner
- steam cleaner
- industrial cold water washer
- car washing equipment, such as buckets, sponges, leathers, wax
- computer
- office equipment – filing cabinet, desk, telephones, fax machine
- initial advertising of the business.

Megan and Richard have asked you to suggest how they should raise the finance necessary to start up the business. They have £4,000 of their own money available. They have seen a suitable van for £5,200 and estimate that the remaining equipment will cost them a further £2,600. They are also worried about how much money they will have in their bank account to keep the business afloat in the early days before they have become established.

How do you consider Megan and Richard can raise the required finance?

Potential customers

All business must identify the people they consider make up their potential target market. These are the people you expect to purchase your product or service. If a business gets this wrong they are likely to fail. Once a target market has been identified the business can then aim its advertising at that particular market.

QUESTIONS

Who do you think Megan and Richard's potential customers will be?

Businesses must identify their potential customers

Location

Unit 1 assessment objective 7 looked in detail at the various reasons businesses locate in different parts of the country. Let us consider some of the factors that will affect Megan and Richard's choice of locations:

- they will need to be located near to areas of high population in order to attract customers
- they do not want to be too close to their competitors
- they will need good road access to be able to travel to their customers easily and quickly.

Portfolio tip

The key to this assignment is undertaking detailed and accurate market research. You will need to use both secondary and primary research. Don't try and make your business idea too complicated and think very carefully how each of the above stages will affect your chosen venture.

QUESTIONS

In groups, using your notes from Unit 1 and based on local knowledge, choose a suitable area where Megan and Richard could target their business. Justify your choice of location.

AO2 Different forms of business ownership suitable for the proposed new venture

Before any business can start up, its owner(s) must decide what form of business ownership would be most suitable. The decision is usually based on the number of people who will be involved within the business and how big the enterprise is expected to be. For example, if a business venture is likely to be a large financial risk the owner(s) might wish to have limited liability in order to secure their own personal possessions.

In Unit 1 you looked at the different types of ownership. In this section you will look at how different types of ownerships suit different kinds of business ventures.

This section will cover the following type of businesses:

- sole proprietor
- partnership
- private limited company
- public limited company
- franchise
- co-operative.

Sole proprietor

Many sole proprietor businesses are started up because someone has always wanted to work for themselves and run their own business. They are often not aware of the long hours and dedication needed to make it successful. This type of business is run by one person who takes all the risks. On the positive side the owner is able to reap all the rewards. A sole proprietor is often a small business, but may be large enough to have employees in order to share the workload. If the business gets into financial difficulties and cannot meet debt repayments then the owner can be sued. This means that the owner could lose all their own possessions including his/her home, car etc.

One of the benefits of being a small business is that the owner is able to offer a personal service and adapt to customer's wishes and demands quickly and easily. On the downside, it is very difficult for the owner to take holidays as there is often no one to run the business in their absence. The owner also has to make all the decisions and be multi-skilled. In order to be successful they will have to have financial, marketing and organisational skills alongside the service that they are offering.

Partnership

This type of business is owned by two to twenty people. The instant benefit is that the business will have more capital available to start. There will also be shared decision-making and staff can begin to specialise. For example, one partner could take responsibility for the financial side of the business and the other marketing and customer service. It becomes easier to take holidays and time away from the business as there are other people with equal responsibility.

The business still has unlimited liability which means that partners may be sued rather than the business, should the business run into financial difficulties. All partners are responsible for each other's debts. If your partners run up a debt for £5,000 which you did not know about you would still be responsible for that debt.

The profits and losses of the business are shared amongst the partners according to the agreed ratios. One of the major problems with a partnership is possible disagreements. This can be largely overcome by the drawing up of a **Deed of Partnership**. This is a document which clearly outlines how the business is going to be run and how the profits and losses will be shared amongst the partners.

Private limited company

The major benefit of being a private limited company is having limited liability. The business is seen as a separate legal entity from its owners. Should the business have financial difficulties the only money the owners/shareholders will lose is the money they have invested in the business through the purchase of shares.

ACTIVITY

As a group identify a sole proprietor business in your local area and discuss why you think they chose this kind of business ownership. Discuss whether you think this type of ownership would suit Megan and Richard. Justify your decision.

Did you know?

If the partners agree to share the profits in the ratio of 2:2:1 and their profit is £90,000, partner one and two would each receive £36,000 and partner 3 £18,000.

ACTIVITY

As a group discuss the advantages and disadvantages of Megan and Richard starting up in partnership.

ACTIVITY

As a group identify a private limited company in your local area and explain why you think this kind of ownership suits them.

Individually list the advantages and disadvantages of Megan and Richard adopting this type of ownership. Discuss your list with the rest of the group. Does the group think this is a good type of ownership for the car washing and valeting business?

A private limited company can be started up by just one person. There is a legal process which can be time consuming and costly. The company has to register a memorandum and articles of association with Company House.

The accounts of a private limited company are also available for the general public to see.

Often private limited companies are owned and run by the same people. Several companies in the Virgin group are private limited companies and as such do have the ability to become as large as the available capital allows. A private limited company can only sell shares to other people with the agreement of all the other owners. This can limit the cash available for expansion and is one reason they often remain small. Another reason for not wishing to expand is the desire to remain in control of the business.

The rights in the Virgin signature logo are the property of Virgin Enterprises Ltd

Figure 2.1 *Several private limited companies come under the Virgin group umbrella*

Public limited company

These are the largest businesses and are often owned by thousands of different shareholders. Divorce of ownership from control is clearly visible within a public limited company. Due to the high number of shareholders the only power they have is to vote collectively on a board of directors at the annual general meeting to run the business on their behalf. The shareholders do not have a say in the day-to-day running of the business. They put their confidence in the board of directors to make the right decisions on their behalf and make as much profit as possible. The shareholders will then receive good **dividends**.

Dividends are the shareholders' reward for investing their money in the business. They are paid out annually but some companies do pay an interim dividend after only six months' trading.

It is very expensive to become a public limited company and the business must have a minimum share capital of £50,000. This type of ownership is therefore only suitable for large established businesses.

By becoming a public limited company the business is able to sell its shares to the general public and these are freely available to anyone. This means that the business is able to raise large amounts of money in order to expand and become highly competitive.

ACTIVITY

Think of a public limited company that trades within your local area and explain why you think this type of business ownership is suitable for them. Why would this type of ownership not be suitable for Megan and Richard? Justify your answer.

Figure 2.2 *An example of a public limited company*

Franchise

A franchise is connected to one person's good business idea. The original owner comes up with a product or service and starts their own business. The business becomes very successful but the original owner does not have sufficient capital to expand the business. The original owner decides to let another person use their idea and trade under the same name for a fee. The person who shares the idea is known as the franchisor and the person who buys into the business is known as the franchisee.

The franchisee will have to run the business as instructed by the franchisor but will have the benefit of help with the overall running and marketing of the business. Marketing is usually conducted centrally and relates to all branches of the business.

Franchises allow someone who has always wanted to run their own business an opportunity to do so with the added support of the franchisor. In exchange for this the franchisee has to give a certain percentage of their profit to the franchisor.

Franchising is an excellent way of expanding a business without having to take on the financial risk of expansion.

ACTIVITY

If Megan and Richard's business became very successful, explain the advantages and disadvantages of franchising as a possible method of expansion.

Co-operatives

The idea behind co-operatives is that everyone has an equal vote and say within the company. In a worker co-operative the owners are also the workforce. The ethos behind the idea is that if you have a vested interest in the business and are going to receive some of the profits you will be more interested and dedicated to the business. One of the problems with this type of ownership is that the workers who take over the business do not always have the managerial skills to run it efficiently.

Retail co-operatives started because an organised group of people could negotiate cheaper prices for food if they bought in bulk. These savings were passed on to the members of the co-operative society.

Portfolio tip

You will need to choose at least two types of business ownership that would be suitable for your new business venture. You will then need to recommend which one would be most suitable for your business.

ACTIVITY

Can you identify a co-operative in your local area? What are its aims and objectives? Does it still follow the same values as when it first started?

QUESTIONS

Megan and Richard have asked you to choose one type of business ownership that would be suitable for their new venture. From all your class and group discussions identify which type of ownership you would recommend, fully justifying your choice.

AO3 The information required to construct an outline business plan

A business plan is a document which outlines how a business is going to develop over a set period of time. It will cover how the business will market itself, how it will raise/control its finances, how many people it will need to run efficiently and the materials and equipment required in order to meet customers' demands.

It will be produced in order to help formulate the business's **strategic plans**.

One of the most common reasons a business produces a business plan is due to the fact they do not have sufficient funds to start up or continue running without the use of external funding. The plan will not only help sell the business to the people being approached for the external funding but will also give the business a plan to work towards and monitor their progress against.

Throughout this section you will learn the skills necessary to put together a business plan that can be presented to a key stakeholder. The key stakeholder could include:

- banks or other financiers
- potential customers
- potential employees or colleagues
- potential shareholders or co-owners.

Figure 2.3 *Examples of documents available to help businesses set up*

Marketing

Marketing is about a business identifying and satisfying customer needs. It is about the business being able to sell their goods to the right people, ensuring that they are totally satisfied with the product so that they become repeat customers. In order to do this a business needs to ensure that its products or services meet the needs of their customers and they are easily available to them at the right price.

In order to do this we are going to look at two marketing tools: a SWOT analysis and the marketing mix.

SWOT analysis

This involves the business looking at its internal strengths and weaknesses and the external opportunities and threats. This will help the business identify if their idea has any chance of survival in what will probably be a very competitive market.

Let us look at the example of two friends, Pete and Tejal, who decided to go into partnership and start up a new kind of burger bar. Tejal had the idea that if they made their burgers healthy by only using fresh ingredients they could charge a higher price than their major rivals, McDonald's and Burger King. They were to be known as the 'Alternative Burger'. Pete and Tejal had no experience of the fast food market and were therefore relying very much on learning as they went along. They could not afford a location in the middle of town but were able to place their burger bar just off the main street. A lot of people walked up and down this side street as it led to the major car parks in the area.

Let us look at the SWOT analysis for the two friends.

Strengths	Weaknesses
They had a new idea. 'Healthy burgers' had received excellent reviews from their initial product testing. Their chosen location, although not on the high street, did get a lot of passing trade.	They had no previous experience of the fast food industry. They did not have a prime location. Their market research was limited to just a small group of people – mainly their friends and relatives. They were having to borrow a lot of money from the bank and did not have limited liability.
Opportunities	**Threats**
The government is currently campaigning for people to follow a healthy lifestyle and with the correct advertising this could be a major selling point. Convenience food fits into modern-day life and this new concept could bring in a different kind of customer.	Every other fast food chain in the town and surrounding area. Competition could also be seen as all other restaurants due to the higher price of the burgers on offer in the new establishment.

Table 2.4 *SWOT analysis*

QUESTIONS

Using the SWOT analysis above do you think the Alternative Burger could survive? Justify your answer.

Devise your own SWOT analysis for Megan and Richard. You will need to make some assumptions about their skills and experience.

The marketing mix

The marketing mix consists of the four Ps. These are:

- product
- price
- promotion
- place.

Product is the product or service that a business is hoping to launch or develop in the future. The idea for a new product or service will usually have come about through customer demand or intensive research carried out by the business. A lot of businesses today consider themselves to be customer led and therefore adapt their products and services to meet the demands of their customers.

Price is the amount of money that a business feels that they can easily achieve for the product or service being offered. There are many different pricing methods for launching a new product/service onto the market.

These include:

- **skimming** – the product is very new, and is placed on the market at a very high price. When it has established itself and become more popular the price will gradually begin to fall so that more and more people are able to afford it. A good example of this is DVD players.

- **competitive pricing** – a business launches its new product onto the market at the same price as all the other businesses selling a similar kind of product/service.

- **penetration pricing** – a business launches its product or service at a lower price than its competitors in order to gain some of their customers. It is trying to get a foothold in the market.

Promotion is the method the business is going to use to inform their target audience of the products/services they have on offer. Promoting a business is very expensive and therefore it must be targeted correctly otherwise it will achieve very little for the business. There are many different ways a business can advertise its products/services. Television is one of the most expensive but is able to reach a large number of people. Due to its high cost, television advertising is not realistic for the majority of small businesses and therefore they have to use a variety of other methods. Local radio is becoming increasingly popular but may still only be affordable to a medium-sized business which is fairly well established.

A small business may use promotional leaflets, business cards, advertisements in local newspapers and magazines. Another way to gain publicity is to try and get the launch of a new business or product/service reported in the local paper as a news article. This is known as public relations. An alternative way a local business can advertise is through the local sponsorship of football teams, school events, fêtes etc.

Place is the system by which the business gets its product/service to its customers. It could be as simple as the location of a retail shop or the location of the warehouse. It may involve more complex distribution networks. For example, a business may give its customer the choice of visiting one of their shops, having access to a catalogue and placing the order by telephone or from their website. With the growth in the use and access to the Internet a lot more people are purchasing goods and services online. Travel agents have seen a reduction in business as customers can now book direct with tour companies through the Internet.

> ### ACTIVITY
>
> Compile a suitable marketing mix for Megan and Richard's car washing and valeting business. Base your ideas on your local knowledge and any assumptions you need to make.

Finance

Another important factor to consider is the financial aspect of the business. It does not matter how good a business idea is, if the money goes out faster than it comes in the business will fail. It is therefore important that a business is able to keep accurate track of its finances.

Feasibility study

When a business is launched the first consideration has to be – is this financially viable? A feasibility study will allow the business to identify if the idea will generate sufficient income to cover costs. Obviously if it does not then the venture is not worth entering into.

Cash flow projections

One method of calculating the feasibility of a project is to complete a **cash flow forecast**. This will identify times when income could be less than potential expenditure. It will also allow the business to plan when it would be best to make large purchases.

A cash flow forecast is based on assumptions about how the product/service will behave within the market place. The cash flow will only ever be as accurate as the information that has been used to compile it. The accuracy of the cash flow predictions will have a direct link to the market research conducted by the organisation.

Table 2.5 shows Megan and Richard's cash flow forecast for their first four weeks of trading.

	Trading Preparation £	Week One £	Week Two £	Week Three £	Week Four £
Income					
Capital	2,000				
Bank loan	7,000				
Sales		700	700	790	790
Total income (a)	**9,000**	**700**	**700**	**790**	**790**
Expenditure					
Van	5,200				
Cold water washer	725				
Industrial vacuum cleaner	369				
Steam cleaner	325				
Cleaning materials		153	153	153	153
Advertising	200		20		20
Wages		600	600	600	600
Loan repayments		208			
Public liability insurance	15				
Motor expenses including insurance		75	75	75	75
General expenses	50	50	50	50	50
Total expenditure (b)	**6,884**	**1,086**	**898**	**878**	**898**
Opening balance (c)	0	2,116	1,730	1,532	1,444
Inflow/outflow (d)	2,116	(386)	(198)	(88)	(108)
Closing balance (e)	2,116	1,730	1,532	1,444	1,336

Table 2.5 *Squeaky Clean Cars' cash flow forecast for the first four weeks of trading*

ACTIVITY

Megan and Richard have asked you to complete their cash flow forecast for the next four weeks of trading from the information supplied below. The opening balance is the closing balance of week four above: £1,336.

In order to balance the cash flow at the end of each week Megan and Richard have added up all their income and this becomes (a). All the expenditure is then added up and becomes (b). The opening balance is the amount of money that the business has at the start of each week. In order to calculate the cash inflow/outflow (d) you take (b) away from (a). The closing balance (e) is calculated by adding the opening balance to the inflow/outflow. The closing balance of week one becomes the opening balance of week two. The figures in brackets are negative. More money has gone out than come in.

Week 5
The business has gained a further contract for a garage to supply their gold valet. Their sales will now consist of:
8 cars in total from the garages for the week on the gold valet
2 private cars in the week on the gold valet
3 cars per day at £30 per day for 5 days

Week 6
8 cars in total from the garage contract on the gold valet
4 private cars in the week on the gold valet
3 cars per day at £30 for 5 days

Week 7
Same as week 6

Week 8
6 cars in total from the garage contract on the gold valet
6 private cars in the week on the gold valet
3 cars per day at £30 for five days.

The expenses are the same as for the first four weeks of trading.
Advertising is £20 in weeks 6 and 8. The monthly instalment for public
liability insurance, and the loan repayment is paid in week 5.

Profit and loss account

Profit is the money that a business makes after it has deducted all its
expenses. In the case of Megan and Richard we can compile a simple profit
and loss account to include the trading preparation week and the first four
weeks of trading. The purchase of the cold water washer, vacuum cleaner,
steamer and van are not included in the profit and loss account as they are
fixed assets and would therefore appear in the balance sheet.

Fixed assets are items which have been purchased in order to run the
business. They will have a life expectancy of more than one year, for
example van, equipment and machinery.

If Megan and Richard decided to run their business as a partnership their
own wages would be known as drawings and would not appear in the
profit and loss account. However, if they decide to set up the business as a
private limited company they would be employees of the business and their
wages would appear in the profit and loss account.

The profit and loss account illustration below assumes that Megan and
Richard have formed a partnership and therefore it will not include their
drawings from the business.

Squeaky Clean Cars

Profit and loss account for the first four weeks of trading

	£	£
Sales		2,980
Less expenses		
Materials	612	
Loan repayment	208	
Motor expenses	300	
General expenses	250	
Advertising	240	
Public liability Insurance	15	
	____	
		1,625
		____
Net profit		1,355

ACTIVITY

Compile Megan and
Richard's profit and loss
account for the first
eight weeks of trading.
You will have to use all
the trading figures,
including those you have
calculated for the second
forecast cash flow.

This is the amount of profit the business has made before taking out the wages of the two owners. If we now deduct the wages of Megan and Richard we can see that the profit has been reduced to a loss of £1,045 as illustrated below.

Net profit   =   £1,355
Wages   £2,400

_____

Net loss   £(1,045)

Start up capital

Start up capital is the amount of money that the owner(s) put into the business to get it off the ground. If the owner has a car or computer equipment that they bring into the business, the value of these items will also be classed as the start up capital. Megan and Richard's start up capital consisted of the £10,000 they invested in the business venture.

Working capital

Working capital is the money that the business has available to pay its day-to-day debts. If we look at the cash flow of Megan and Richard you can see that after four weeks' trading they had £1,336 available to run their business. Their customers will pay as soon as the car is finished and therefore people will not owe them any money. The business will not have any debtors and they are unlikely to have people they owe money to (creditors). As a new business venture, suppliers are unlikely to offer them credit until they have established a reliable reputation. Squeaky Clean Cars' working capital will just consist of the money it has available in the bank to spend.

If a business has debtors and creditors, as it sells and buys goods and services on credit, these will also form part of the working capital.

Working capital is calculated by adding up all the current assets which consist of stock, debtors, bank and cash and taking away all the current liabilities, which include creditors and bank overdraft.

Human resources

If a business grows sufficiently the owner(s) may decide that they need to employ people to help them run the business. As soon as a business starts to consider employing other people they will have to consider the state of the labour market.

The labour market

The labour market consists of the people available to work. There are variations between the composition of the labour market within different regions of the country. It is widely recognised that there are certain skill shortages in the country but these may vary from area to area.

If a business is looking to employ someone who has a skill that is in short supply they may have to pay a higher wage rate in order to attract the person to come and work for them. On the other hand, if the business wants an employee to undertake basic tasks there may be a lot of people available to employ. Therefore the wage rate could be as low as the minimum wage.

In Unit 1 you learnt that the types of jobs people are now doing has changed over the last 30 years. There are far fewer people employed in the primary sector with the growth being in the tertiary sector.

Somerset vs Great Britain 2001 Broad industrial group	Somerset	GB	Percentage Somerset	GB
Agriculture, forestry, fishing	4,600	248,000	2	1
Energy and water	2,900	209,200	1	1
Manufacturing	34,400	3,603,300	18	14
Construction	5,600	1,148,500	3	5
Distribution, hotels & restaurants	58,000	6,175,000	30	24
Transport & communications	8,500	1,558,200	4	6
Banking, finance etc.	21,000	4,996,000	11	20
Public administration, Education, health	52,400	6,187,800	27	24
Other services	8,800	1,260,100	4	5
All industries and services	196,300	25,456,400	100	100

Table 2.6 *Labour skills in Somerset vs Great Britain 2001*   *Source: Annual Business Inquiry 2001*

If a business wanted to set up in Somerset they could use these figures to see what labour skills there were in the area. The largest percentage of the population in Somerset is employed in distribution, hotels and restaurants. If a business wanted to open a new hotel there would be a ready source of skilled labour available. In Somerset, banking and finance employ a lower percentage of people than the whole of the UK. If you wanted to open a new financial services company you may find there is a shortage of skilled labour. The new business would be faced with two choices. They could either employ and train people from the local area or advertise the position nationally and try and encourage potential employees to move into the area.

Tasks to be undertaken by the owner and any employees

In order for a business to run efficiently from day one the owner(s) must first decide what their own responsibilities will be within the business. They have to be very clear in their mind what exactly needs to be done and when this must take place. If more than one owner is involved then this becomes more of a complex procedure and many an argument will be avoided if this is clearly discussed early on. As the business grows, new demands will be made on the owner(s) and renegotiation of roles may have to take place.

ACTIVITY

Discuss as a group what you think would need to be done in order to run Squeaky Clean Cars? Remember it is not just cleaning cars , it also involves all the paperwork. Divide up the jobs between Megan and Richard.

Good organisation is essential

Employees

There is little point in a business deciding that it needs help if it then fails to identify clearly what type of help it actually needs. The first stage is to undertake a job analysis. This clearly identifies the tasks that need to be done. Once all the different tasks have been identified a job description can be drawn up. The job description is the document which is sent out to potential employees informing them of the job they are applying for. It is a general description of the level of responsibility of the job and tasks to be undertaken.

If job roles remain unclear the business will never run efficiently as everybody will be attempting to do the same thing. Not only will this be inefficient for the firm but it will also present a very poor image to the customers of the business.

Materials and equipment

This area was covered in Unit 1. Refer back to your notes to refresh your memory.

Materials and equipment are the items that a business needs in order to manufacture its product or supply the service to its customers. For example, in order to run a gym you would need cross trainers, cycles, tread mills etc. These items would all be classed as equipment

ACTIVITY

Megan and Richard's business has been running for two years now and they are about to expand. They have established five regular contracts and now feel they need help running the business in order to have a day off on Sunday!

Describe the general duties you think a new employee would undertake within the business.

Potential suppliers

If a business is manufacturing or selling goods they must ensure they always have sufficient stock. Stock is the materials or items a business has ready to be used or sold. Megan and Richard's stock would consist of wax, soap, polish, tyre dressing etc. In order to remain efficient, Megan and Richard must establish a good relationship with their suppliers. This will help ensure that stock arrives in time and any problems are quickly solved.

In any new business venture it is advisable to research as many potential suppliers as possible to work out which one will suit your business. Megan and Richard looked on the Internet and in the local telephone directory to find their potential suppliers. It is not necessarily the cheapest that always turn out to be the best. Quality has to be a major factor when considering the purchase of stock. If stock is cheap but of a very poor quality there might be high levels of wastage which in the long run will cost the business time and money. After a considerable amount of research, Megan and Richard decided to use just one supplier who would offer them all the products they needed in a monthly package.

Potential costs of required items

The research a business undertakes at its conception will help it gain accurate figures when it comes to the compilation of its cash flow forecast. If a business has researched how much its stock is going to cost and how long it will last, the figures used to produce forecast accounts will be accurate and the business stands a much better chance of survival. Due to lack of experience, Megan and Richard are not sure how long their supplies will last them. They do feel that they have overestimated the potential costs of their supplies in the cash flow forecast. However, they feel this is better than underestimating them.

Justification of what is required and why, including potential constraints

In business all costs must be clearly justifiable and this again is based on the accuracy of the research which was initially undertaken by the business. It is vital that at the beginning of the venture no money is wasted and all that is spent has the ability to earn profit either in the short or long term. It is no use a business having a new fleet of cars if they have no customers to visit.

All businesses will have constraints when they first start out. The major one is usually lack of money. Suppliers may also put constraints on them as a new business. For example, the business may not receive 30 days' credit as the business has yet to build up a reputation of being a reliable payer. This lack of credit may cause cash flow problems within the business as it has to pay for its supplies when it receives them but will probably have to allow their own customers 30 days' credit.

Type	Price £	Justification
Pain Cleanser (250 ml)	7.99	To ensure high-quality finish on all cars regardless of age.
Carnauba Wax (250 ml)	19.99	High-quality wax to ensure maximum shine for high-quality finish. To be used on Gold Valet
14 x 100% cotton towels + 14 sponges	14.00	To ensure that each car is washed and polished with high-quality products to eliminate risk of scratching cars
K300 Carnauba Speedwax (250 ml)	8.95	Quicker to use – remains high quality to be used on Silver Valet
Leather soap and conditioner	12.99	To use on leather upholstery
Leather Crème (250 ml)	14.99	To enhance the quality of leather upholstery. Used in Gold valet only
Crystal clear glass cleaner (250 ml)	9.99	To be used on all cars
Vinyl Dressing (250 ml)	12.99	To be used on all interiors to enhance finish

Table 2.7 *Squeaky Clean Cars' list of supplies and their justification for purchase*

Portfolio tip

This is a very large assessment objective. You need to ensure that you work through each section methodically. Clear referencing to your original research will enhance the quality of your overall grade.

AO4 The operational systems needed to make the intended business successful

This section will focus on the systems that are needed by a business in order to help it run efficiently.

How the product will be produced

In order for any business to start manufacturing a product in the most efficient and economical way it must first break down every task that has to be completed in order to have a finished product at the end.

It is usually quite surprising how many stages a product goes through before it is finished. If we take the example of making a cup of tea we can see that even a simple task is actually quite complex.

(a) Collect the kettle

(b) Fill it with water

(c) Plug kettle in

(d) Wait for it to boil

(e) Collect cup and saucer

(f) Place tea bag in cup

(g) When kettle has boiled pour hot water onto tea bag

(h) Leave it a few minutes to brew

(i) Remove tea bag

(j) Add milk and sugar as required.

As you can see making a cup of tea has been broken down into ten stages.

How the service will be provided

If a business is providing a service to its customers then there has to be a set procedure which outlines how the customer will receive the service and what they can expect from the service being offered.

Let us think about Squeaky Clean Cars. How will Megan and Richard provide the service? We can look at the different stages involved.

- Potential customers will make contact, probably by telephone.
- If it is a commercial contract, Megan and Richard will need to go and see the business to discuss the service they offer and their terms and conditions.
- Megan and Richard go to the customer's premises and provide the requested service.
- They will ask the customer to inspect their car to ensure the work has been completed to a satisfactory standard.
- They will invoice the customer and expect payment before they leave.

The level of service that Megan and Richard are going to offer their customers could be outlined in a promotional leaflet, business card or discussed directly with the customer. These methods would inform the customer of the service that Squeaky Clean Cars is offering, and would become the standard the customers could measure the service against.

How the product or service will be distributed

It is no good a business developing a wonderful new product if they have no idea how they are going to get the product to the customers.

Products can be distributed in many different ways:

- the business may sell their products to a wholesaler who then sells them on to an individual business who has direct contact with customers
- the business may try and make direct links with retail outlets in order to cut out the wholesaler

ACTIVITY

Outline the stages you think would be necessary to make a cheese and tomato sandwich.

ACTIVITY

Outline how you think the local leisure centre provides a service to members of the public.

● the manufacturer may sell direct to the general public. With the development of websites and Internet access, this is becoming much more popular with manufacturers directly targeting their customers.

Channels of distribution

A service can be taken to the customer or the customer may receive the service at a designated place. For example, a hairdresser can either offer his/her customers a visit to the salon or a mobile service where the customer is visited at home. The RAC offers different services to their customers. This includes taking assistance to them if they break down on the road, but they also have a complex website which allows people to join, find out about traffic jams and how to get to certain parts of the country. Customers receive this service by logging on to their computer at home or in the office.

Monitoring quality of product or service

Customers will only return time and time again if they can be assured they will receive the same quality of product or service each time they buy or use the service being offered.

Businesses are becoming increasingly more customer focused and this involves checking that the service being offered is consistent and meets the needs of the consumer.

There are four stages to quality control: prevention, detection, correction and improvement. Prevention tries to avoid problems occurring. Detection ensures that problems are noticed and resolved before the product reaches the customer. Correction is about putting right faults and discovering why the problem occurred in the first place; and improvement is ensuring that problems do not continually occur and the overall quality of the product is continually being developed.

Within manufacturing businesses there are different ways that a business can ensure that it is maintaining quality.

Quality assurance in action

ACTIVITY

As a group, discuss how Squeaky Clean Cars could deliver the same high-quality service every time they clean a car.

Total quality control

This is a process where everybody is made responsible for the quality of the item being produced. As the product moves along the production line, the employees at stage two check the work which was carried out at stage one. This encourages everybody to take responsibility for ensuring that their work is of the required standard.

It also ensures faulty goods do not make their way right through the production process and are rejected before the end of the production line.

Quality circles

A quality circle is a group of people who meet together to discuss and develop ideas where quality could be improved within the production process. It allows production line operatives the authority to make changes in order to improve the efficiency of the production line. It was one of the first developments which recognised that the men/women who worked on the production line often had a better idea of how production and quality could be improved as they had more experience of the processes involved than management.

Benchmarking

This is a system whereby a business compares itself with another business to find out how it could improve.

When a business only offers a service it can be more difficult to assess the quality of the service being offered. A lot of businesses spend time questioning their customers to check that everything is up to the expected standard. Restaurants and visitor attractions often have comment cards available for the general public to complete, asking for their comments on the standard of service experienced.

Businesses that maintain high standards are able to achieve ISO 9000. This award illustrates to customers that the business is producing reliable and safe products which have undergone stringent quality control checks.

Methods of raw material stock control

If a business does not have an efficient method of stock control it may run out of vital materials which will mean the whole production line will come to a halt. If this happens it will cost the business a lot of money and may even lose customers due to missed delivery dates.

Having too much stock can be as inefficient as having too little stock. If a business holds too much stock it will take up valuable storage space, and could deteriorate or become out of date over a long period of time. If a business has a lot of money tied up in stock it could mean the business will have cash flow problems until the stock has been sold.

In order to control stock levels a business needs to calculate three things:

- How much stock do they use each week?
- How long does it take to receive stock from the supplier?
- What is the minimum amount of stock needed?

Megan and Richard have probably ordered too much stock because, until the business becomes established, they were unsure of how much stock they would need each week and how quickly they would receive their supplies. They will now have to find somewhere to store this excess stock where it will not become damaged.

Example

Gateway Engineering manufactures small turbines for the aero industry. They use on average 250 of part D234 each week. Delivery time for the part is the next day. The business has decided that they will have a minimum stock of 300. Their production schedule is illustrated below.

	Week One	Week Two	Week Three	Week Four
Opening stock	300	300	300	300
Production	245	230	225	280
Balance	55	70	75	20
Re-order	245	230	225	280
Closing Balance	300	300	300	300

Table 2.8 *Production schedule for Gateway Engineering*

Production scheduling and service

Correct production scheduling is very important if a business is going to run efficiently. In order to do this it must ensure that it has broken down into simple steps every process that needs to be covered in order to either produce the product or deliver the service.

If Megan and Richard are going to run an efficient car valet business they are first going to have to work out every task that needs to be completed every day. They will have to work out in which order these tasks will need to be undertaken and by whom. They will need to ask themselves simple questions, for example:

- Do we wash the car before undertaking the interior clean?
- Do we need to wash the bodywork first and then the wheels?
- At what stage do we apply the dressing to the interior?
- When do we clean the windows?

They will also have to consider who is going to be responsible for the administrative side of the business and when during the day they will complete the paperwork. Will they tackle this job daily, weekly or monthly?

ACTIVITY

Discuss as a group how you think Megan and Richard could calculate how much stock they will need to keep.

Recording sales, purchases and payments

A business is only as successful as its ability to keep track of the money coming in and going out. There is no point having an excellent product or service that is selling really well if you have no idea of how much you have taken in sales or paid out on raw materials and expenses. A business will therefore need a system by which it can record all its income and expenditure.

The sales day book is a simple method by which a business can record all the sales it has made on credit. A credit sale is where the customer has received the goods or service and will pay later. The sales day book simply records the date, name of customer and amount of money owed (an illustration of the sales day book is on page 104 in Unit 3: Finance in business).

A purchase day book is exactly the same as the sales day book but just records the items the business has purchased on credit (see page 105).

A two column cash book (illustrated on page 106 in Unit 3) is a book of account which records all the money coming into and going out of the business. The two column cash book will record money that has come in as cash and through the bank account. All the incoming money is recorded on the debit side of the book (left-hand side) and all the outgoing money is recorded on the credit side (right-hand side) of the book. At the end of the month the cash book is balanced and this is the amount of money the business has available to spend.

ACTIVITY

Discuss as a group all the tasks you think Megan and Richard will have to complete in a day. What order do you think these tasks should be completed in?

Portfolio tip

You may find this assessment objective hard as you do not think that your venture will need any operational systems. If a business does not have any operational systems they limp along, and lack efficiency. Focus on what you need to do to ensure you get your product/service to your customer. You will soon begin to realise that all businesses do have operational systems.

AO5 Presenting a proposal to a key stakeholder

In order to achieve this assessment objective you are required to present your proposal to a key stakeholder. The first part of your planning for the presentation is to decide which key stakeholder you are going to present to. The choices are outlined below:

- banks or other financiers
- potential customers
- potential employees or colleagues
- potential shareholders or co-owners.

Each of the above stakeholders will have a slightly different interest in the business than the others. Before slanting the content of your presentation to your chosen stakeholder you will need to cover some general points within the content of the presentation.

Detailed preparation and a smart appearance are essential for a good presentation

Stakeholders

In order to catch your chosen stakeholder's attention you need to make sure that your introduction to your proposed business venture is very clear and interesting. You do not want to lose your audience within the first minute of the presentation.

Clearly outline what your proposal is and how it will meet the needs of your chosen **target audience**.

Target audience are the people the goods/services are aimed at. This could be young, old, female or male. Don't forget most men's toiletries are aimed at women as they are the ones who usually buy them!

The next part of the presentation should cover in general terms the business plan that you created in assessment objective 5. This will clearly outline how you intend to finance and run the business.

Depending on which stakeholder you have chosen you can emphasise the relevant points that will clearly illustrate the benefit of involvement for the potential stakeholder. Outlined below is the different type of information that each category of stakeholder may be interested in.

Banks or other financiers

These are the people who will be lending money to your new business venture.

Their major interest is going to focus on the financial stability of the business proposal. The bank or other financier will want to make sure that the new business venture will be able to make the required repayments on any loan made to it.

The information these stakeholders will be interested in is the forecast cash flow and profit and loss accounts. The figures used within these financial documents must be substantiated by the research you have undertaken and fully explained. A detailed description of how the figures were arrived at will appear more convincing when requesting a loan from an outside business.

Rather than presenting the whole set of accounts during the presentation itself it is usually better to use key figures such as gross and net profit within the presentation and give the stakeholder a copy of the accounts to study later.

Potential customers

These are the people you need to purchase your goods or service and hopefully become loyal and regular repeat customers.

Customers will be interested in the price of the product or service being offered and its availability as well as the quality of the product/service and how the proposed business venture is going to ensure quality is maintained.

Customers may also be interested in the long-term plans for the company so they are aware of the potential benefits that could be on offer in the future.

Potential employees or colleagues

Employees will have varied interests in the new business venture.

Prior to starting work for the business, potential employees will be interested in what their job will entail and their working conditions. They will want to know how they will fit into the organisation and if they will be able to progress through the business.

Before accepting a position within the company a new employee may want more information on the financial stability of the company. They may request information on the expected profitability of the company to reassure themselves that they will be paid and the new position offers them job security.

Colleagues will want to have an understanding of the **hierarchy** of the business: who will be their line manager, who they will have to report to and if they will have any people whom they will be in charge of. They may also want to have an understanding of the **culture** of the proposed business venture. Will they be able to share ideas with management and other employees and have a say in some of the decisions that are made? Will the business be run in an autocratic way with management making all the decisions and no consultation with the employees?

A hierarchy represents a tall organisational structure where authority flows from the top down. This type of organisational structure is often found in large organisations.

Culture represents the way people are treated within the business. Will the business encourage a relaxed but supportive environment where all employees are treated equally or is management totally in control with employees just being told what to do?

Potential shareholders or co-owners

These are the potential stakeholders you are hoping will invest money into the proposed business venture. In return for their investment in the business they will expect to have a share of the **profits**.

The profit paid out to shareholders is known as dividends. These are based on the number of shares a shareholder has in the company.

Shareholders or co-owners are going to be interested in the profitability and **liquidity** of the business. They will want to see the forecast profit and loss accounts and cash flow forecast. This will enable them to see if and when they will get a return on their investment.

Liquidity represents the money that is available to be spent within the business. Liquidity can be illustrated through the cash flow forecast.

The return on initial investment is likely to be small in the early days for a new business venture. Potential shareholders or co-owners will be interested in the long term future of the business. They will want to know if they are they likely to receive significant returns on their money in the future.

ACTIVITY

Which stakeholder are you going to aim your presentation at? Quickly jot down the information you think they will be interested in.

Presentation notes

A successful presentation is one that enthusiastically gets the information and message across to its audience. The presenter will have compiled slides which reinforce the message but do not distract the audience by containing too much information or animation. The presenter will be confident in their knowledge of the subject matter and be able to talk and maintain eye contact. They will require minimum prompts. Movement and use of body language will be natural and will also illustrate enthusiasm for the subject matter. In order to achieve a successful presentation, take into account the following points:

- make sure you know your subject matter and can talk confidently and knowledgeably
- don't put too much information on your slides or overheads
- put the detailed information onto a handout that can be given out either before or after your presentation
- use your bullet points as a reference to develop your ideas and thoughts throughout your presentation
- justify all your suggestions, for example refer back to your initial research
- make sure you have practised your presentation
- maintain eye contact with your audience
- move around, rather than standing like a statue.

Check your presentation against the bullet points. Are there any alterations you should make? If so – do so now!

Portfolio tip

The most important points when conducting a presentation are: know your subject matter and practise the presentation at least twice before you have to deliver it to your audience.

PORTFOLIO GUIDANCE

Your choice of business venture will be the lynchpin to this assignment. If you try and start a complex venture you do not know very much about you are likely to find collecting sufficient evidence for the assessment objectives quite difficult. It is best to choose a subject that you are familiar with and develop this into a potential business venture.

Assessment objective 1 is very important. It allows you to set the scene for the business. The more information you gather from your primary and secondary research the easier the remaining assessment objectives will be. In order to achieve the higher grades you will also need to refer back to this research in order to justify some of your ideas and recommendations that you use in the other assessment objectives.

Assessment objective 3 is very large and this needs to be worked through methodically, covering all the bullet points that are relevant to your chosen venture.

Assessment objective 4 is not as complicated as it first appears. A lot of the bullet points could be illustrated through the use of simple flow diagrams.

This unit clearly links to Unit 1 and Unit 3. Refer to these chapters in order to develop your knowledge and understanding.

SKILLS CHECK

1 What is the difference between primary and secondary research?

2 If you wanted to survey how many students travelled to school/college via public transport and their opinions of the service provided, what would be the best type of sampling method to use? Justify your reasons.

3 Think of two open and closed questions that could be applied to the survey outlined in (2) above.

4 Explain what would be the likely effect on people's disposable income if interest rates rise.

5 What is the difference between a bank loan and a bank overdraft? Justify one occasion when each would be used.

6 Describe how businesses compete against one another.

7 Explain why people choose to become sole proprietors. Describe the advantages of this kind of ownership.

8 Describe the term 'limited liability'.

9 Suggest and justify the benefits of becoming a limited liability company.

10 Explain the different elements of a SWOT analysis.

11 Explain how labour market trends affect the ability of a business to recruit staff.

12 Why is it important for businesses to maintain good contacts with their suppliers?

13 Outline the systems a business should put in place to record its sales, purchases and payments made and received from customers.

14 Explain the different interests of the following stakeholders:
(a) banks or other financiers
(b) customers
(c) employees or colleagues
(d) shareholders or co-owners.

Finance in business

Getting Started

A lot of people panic as soon as they see the word 'finance'. They think that unless they are excellent at maths they will not be able to tackle finance within a business context. This is not the case. Financial record keeping and decision making has very little connection with the ability to complete complex mathematical calculations. All the prior learning that you need up to this point is the ability to add, subtract and calculate percentages with the aid of a calculator.

Throughout life you will find the skills you learn within this unit useful. You will develop an awareness that will help you manage your own personal finances successfully, and understand the financial elements of starting up a new business.

To complete this unit successfully you will need to produce evidence to show that you understand the financial processes people go through in order to start up in business. Your work will focus on the financial aspects of starting up a business venture. You may choose to work on your own or as part of a group. If you choose to work within a group you must write up your evidence independently. You must produce evidence to achieve the seven assessment objectives that are outlined in the specification, and which are shown below. This unit is split into seven sections which match the assessment objectives and which contain information to help you achieve them.

This unit will cover

- AO1 Identify funding sources for the selected business activity or project.
- AO2 Identify a range of set-up costs for the selected business activity or project.
- AO3 Identify a range of running costs for the selected business activity or project.
- AO4 Estimate potential sales for the selected business activity or project.
- AO5 Identify break even point and profit margins for the selected business activity or project.
- AO6 Describe the range of financial operations carried out by a small business.
- AO7 Explain the function of financial statements prepared by small businesses.

AO1 Different funding sources

In this section you will learn about the different kinds of funding available to businesses. The more money you have in your pocket the more you are able to spend, and businesses are no exception.

Before any business can begin, the people involved must have sufficient funds to get the business up and running. A new business does not just require the funds to start up, but will also need sufficient funds to run for the first few months until the money starts coming in from its customers.

GLOSSARY

External funding:
External funding is money borrowed from people or institutions outside of the business.

Entrepreneur:
The entrepreneur is the person who has the idea and starts up the business.

Some businesses are able to start up without any **external funding**. The owners use their own money and therefore take all the risks. The **entrepreneur** may be lucky enough to have family and friends who will lend them money to start the business.

ACTIVITY

You are hoping to buy your first car. You have saved up a deposit of £750 but need a further £1,250 to get the car of your dreams. What would be the advantage of borrowing this money from your parents?

A car of your dreams?

People who decide to start up in business often have to look for additional funding from other sources. The person or institution lending the money will charge **interest**.

Interest is the amount of money that the lending organisation charges each month to allow the business to use their money.

Example:

When Gurvinder started up his own printing business seven years ago he borrowed £10,000 from the bank over five years at an interest rate of 4.2%. His repayments were calculated as follows.

£10,000 divided by 5 years = repayment of £2,000 per year. This is known as the capital repayment.

10,000 × 4.2% interest = total interest of £420 per year.

Total payable per annum = £2,420. Divide by 12 months of the year equals a monthly repayment of £201.67.

There are many different ways a business can raise the funds necessary to start up. We are going to be looking at some of the more common methods and the associated costs.

ACTIVITY

You are hoping to go on a tour of Europe next summer and have been wondering how to raise sufficient funds. One option is to take out a loan. You are thinking of borrowing £2,500 over 2 years at an interest rate of 5.5%.

(a) What is the capital repayment each year?

(b) What is the total interest charged each year?

(c) What are the monthly repayments?

One of the high street banks

The bank

The bank can lend businesses money by either allowing them an **overdraft facility** or **a bank loan**.

Overdraft

When a business has an overdraft it is spending money which belongs to the bank. The bank will charge the business interest on the borrowed money for the number of days it was borrowed.

GLOSSARY

Overdraft:
Overdraft money which belongs to the bank. The bank will charge the business interest on the borrowed money for the number of days it was borrowed.

Here is an example of a business's bank account.

Example of inflow and outflow of money from a bank account

Date	Inflow	Outflow	Balance
1 March			£500
3 March	£3,000		£3,500
5 March		£4,000	£500 overdrawn
6 March	£700		£200
8 March	£1,500		£1,700
10 March		£2,000	£300 overdrawn
12 March		£400	£700 overdrawn
20 March	£900		£200

1. How many days was the account overdrawn?
2. How much was the account overdrawn for on each occasion?

Example of interest calculations – overdraft

The Hi-Tec Engineering Company had £2,000 in their bank account on May 1. On 25 May they received their bank statement which showed they had been overdrawn by £1,000 for 10 days. This was due to the fact they had not received a cheque from a major customer for £4,000 as expected on May 15.

The interest rate on their overdraft is 4 per cent/per annum.

How much will it cost the company for the 10 days they were overdrawn?

Workings

$$\frac{£1,000}{100} \times 4 = £40 \quad \frac{£40}{365 \text{ days}} \times 10 \text{ days overdrawn} = £1.10 \text{ interest charged}$$

QUESTIONS

Pearsons plc received their bank statement on 5 June to find that a major customer had not paid them as agreed. Their account had been overdrawn for 20 days by £5,000. The interest on the overdraft is agreed at 4.5 per cent per annum. How much interest will they be charged?

Bank loan

A **bank loan** is an agreed amount of money lent from the bank to a business for a set amount of time.

The bank agrees to lend a business a set amount of money over an agreed time period, with regular repayments being made by the borrower. The agreement can include a fixed or variable rate of interest. A fixed interest rate is where the interest charged over the life of the loan will not change. A variable interest rate is where the rate of interest charged will go up or down according to the current interest rates being set by the Bank of England. This is known as the bank base rate.

Repayments are based on a business paying back the original amount borrowed plus the interest to be charged over the term of the loan. On the next page is a simple example.

Example of interest calculations – bank loan

You have decided to start up in business and need to borrow £5,000 to get your business venture off the ground. You have been looking around and discovered that the most suitable loan is one from the bank. You have been quoted an interest rate of 6.7 per cent. You think you will take the loan out over a period of 3 years. What you need to know now is how much this is going to cost you annually and monthly.

Calculations

$\dfrac{£5,000}{100} \times 6.7$ (rate of interest) = £335 is the interest charged annually.

$\dfrac{5,000}{3 \text{ years}}$ = £1,667 payable back each year of the loan.

Therefore each year you will pay back £1,667 plus £335 = £2,002
Your monthly repayments will therefore be:

$\dfrac{2002}{12}$ = £166.83 per month.

ACTIVITY

Susan has been thinking about starting up in business. She has undertaken extensive market research and is confident that her idea will be a best-seller. However, before she can get started she needs to borrow £15,000. Susan has investigated the possibility of taking out a bank loan. The bank has suggested an overdraft facility of £10,000 as an alternative to the bank loan. Susan is unsure what the difference is between the two. She has asked you to explain the following terms.

(a) What is a bank overdraft?

(b) What is a bank loan?

(c) How is interest calculated on an overdraft?

(d) How is the interest calculated on a bank loan?

If Susan takes out a bank loan it will be for £15,000 over two years. The interest quoted is 5.6 per cent.

(e) Calculate the capital repayments and interest payments on this loan.
   How much will the monthly repayments be?

If Susan uses the overdraft facility over the next twelve months she thinks she will be overdrawn approximately £8,000 every month. The interest rate will be 6.4 per cent.

(f) How much interest will Susan pay using the overdraft facility?

(g) Which method of borrowing do you recommend? Justify your recommendations using your calculations from (e) and (f).

What is the difference?

Grants

A grant is a sum of money that has been given to a business for a specified project or purpose. It will not have to be paid back. A grant will usually only cover part of the total costs involved, and could be between 15 per cent and 75 per cent. Grants to help businesses develop in the UK are available from a variety of sources and include:

- the government
- the European Union
- Regional Development Agencies
- local authorities or local councils
- Chamber of Commerce
- County Enterprise Boards.

Grants are linked to precise areas of business activity, such as exporting, new product development or training, or a specific industry sector. In addition, there are some grants linked to specific geographical areas which are in need of economic regeneration.

CASE STUDY

The Prince's Youth Trust

The Prince's Youth Trust was founded in 1976 by the Prince of Wales and offers practical solutions to help young people get their lives working. The Trust has been responsible for helping set up many young people in business when banks and other financial institutions have considered the proposed venture too much of a risk. The Prince's Youth Trust remit is to help people who are aged 18–30, are unemployed and have an idea for a business but are unable to raise the cash they need from other sources.

The Trust offers a start-up support which includes:

- a low interest loan of up to £4,000 for a sole trader or up to £5,000 for a partnership
- a grant of up to £1,500 in special circumstances
- a test marketing grant of up to £250
- ongoing business support and specialist advice such as free legal helpline
- ongoing advice from a volunteer business mentor.

You are eligible if you are:

- a UK resident aged 18–30
- unemployed or work less than 16 hours per week
- have not been able to get the funding you need from other sources
- have a good business idea and are ready to make it a reality.

Using the case study above, answer the following questions:

(a) When was The Prince's Youth Trust Founded?

(b) What is the main aim of The Prince's Youth Trust?

(c) What are the criteria to be eligible for a grant?

(d) Explain in your own words how you think that such an organisation can be of benefit to young people in today's society.

Partnership

From the work undertaken in Unit 1, can you recall what a partnership is? How many partners can it have? Spend a few minutes now looking back over your Unit 1 notes.

If a sole trader wanted to raise extra funds in order to expand their business they could consider taking on one or more partners. Each new partner would have to contribute a sum of money known as capital to the original owner in order to 'buy' into the business. The main advantage of this method of raising money is that there is no repayment to be made to external agencies. The business would now have more owners and this means that the profits have to be shared.

CASE STUDY

Graham's Garage

About ten years ago Graham started up in business with a small garage. When he started he only dealt with repairs to bodywork and spraying. He was not qualified to undertake mechanical repairs. It did not take long for the business to grow and he was being continually asked if he could undertake mechanical repairs.

Graham soon began to realise that he would like to expand the business but lacked the funds to do so. He found a new building to rent which had two workshops. He thought he could use one workshop for the body repair work and the other workshop for the mechanical work. He now had a couple of options. Should he employ a qualified mechanic or take on a partner?

He knew that his friend Jaymit, a qualified mechanic, was always talking about running his own business. Graham decided to ask Jaymit if he would like to invest some money into the business and become an equal partner. Jaymit jumped at the chance. With the money that Jaymit put into the business the partners were able to take on the new workshops and put in two new ramps.

Now answer the following questions.

(a) What are the financial advantages to Graham of going into partnership with Jaymit?

(b) What would be the financial disadvantages to Graham of going into partnership with Jaymit?

(d) Evaluate the importance of drawing up a Deed of Partnership to Graham and Jaymit.

Share issues

As you will recall from your work in Unit 1 there are only two types of businesses that issue shares. Can you remember which ones these are? Spend a few minutes now looking back on your notes from Unit 1.

Private limited companies

Private limited companies raise their initial start up capital by issuing shares to friends and family. People put in an agreed amount of money and, as a reward for their investment, they will receive a share of the company's profit in the way of a dividend. If the business does get into financial trouble it will only lose its initial investment, as the company has limited liability.

If a private limited company decided that it needed to raise more capital it would be able to sell some extra shares. The extra shares can only be sold with the full agreement of all the current shareholders. These shares are sold privately and are not available to the general public.

The advantage of issuing more shares is that the company is able to raise extra funding without needing external borrowing which will have to be paid off over a set period of time. If a business has to pay off a loan it may reduce the money it has available to run the business. The drawback of issuing more shares is that there are more owners to share the profits with.

CASE STUDY

Flowers For Every Occasion

Irene and Julie had been working for Flowers For Every Occasion for several years when the owner decided that it was time to retire. The two of them were suddenly faced with the thought of being out of work. Irene came up with the idea that they could buy the business from the current owner.

They decided that the best type of ownership for them was to become a limited company. However, with just the two of them they still did not have enough funds to pay the asking price. The bank did not seem very interested in lending them the required funds. Their answer was to offer shares in their new business venture to their immediate families. The company was set up with ten shareholders, each putting in £2,500.

Irene and Julie ran the business, receiving their normal salaries, and the remaining profits were shared between the ten shareholders at the end of each financial year.

Using the case study above answer the following questions.

(a) Explain why issuing shares to their immediate families was a good way of raising the capital necessary to start the business.

(b) Explain what the advantages and disadvantages would be if Irene and Julie decided to start up in a partnership and borrow the required capital from the bank. Focus your answer on financial issues.

Public limited companies

Public limited companies also raise their share capital through the sale of shares. However, they are able to sell their shares to the general public via the Stock Exchange.

If a public limited company decides it needs to raise more capital it will float some more shares onto the stock market. It will produce a prospectus which will tell the general public about the company and persuade them what a good investment it is. Anybody can buy shares on the London Stock Exchange and therefore public limited companies have many owners.

AO2 Set-up costs for the selected business activity or project

Every time you consider starting a new hobby or joining a new club you will have to consider the potential cost of doing so.

QUESTIONS

1 If you wanted to join the local gym how much do you think this would cost you on a monthly basis?

2 Would you need any new clothes before you could start?

3 If so how much do you think these will cost you?

When someone decides to start up in business they will have to buy equipment, computers, vehicles etc. before they sell or make their chosen product or service. These initial costs are known as **set-up** or **start-up costs**.

Businesses that provide a product will either manufacture or buy in the product from another business and sell it on to customers. Other businesses which sell a service, for example a dentist, a hairdresser or an accountant, all sell their knowledge and skills to their customers for payment. Due to the diverse nature of business activity all businesses have very different start-up/set-up costs.

Outlined on the following page are the general set-up costs for businesses.

GLOSSARY

Start-up or set-up costs:
The amount of initial spending to start up in business.

Buildings

Industrial parks are designed to meet the needs of businesses

Some very small sole trader businesses trade from their own homes, but many businesses have their own premises. A lot of businesses can be found on industrial parks that have been built specifically to meet their needs. Industrial parks are often built with good access to main roads. This is to help the business transport its products to and from its customer base.

A major consideration for a business when it decides to set up is how much are the premises going to cost? Will the owners be able to afford to buy or rent the premises and still make a profit? Will the business have sufficient funds to cover the rent or mortgage repayments in the first few months? Premises that are considered to be in a **prime location** will command a much higher sales price and rents will also be considerably more expensive.

Prime location is a location that is ideal for the particular business. The site may have excellent road access, a local airport and a highly trained workforce living within the locality.

CASE STUDY

Parvinder's Dream

Parvinder has always wanted to run her own clothes shop. She has undertaken lots of market research and decided to focus on selling new and second-hand ball gowns and formal wear. She knows this is a growing market that includes young people who attend school and college proms. Her main concern is where she can locate her business on a restricted budget. She has found two small shops in her local town, but each has its own problems. The first is situated in the high street but the rent is going to be

£12,000 a year. Parvinder is not sure that her sales initially would be large enough to pay the rent and still make a profit. The second location is a small side road away from the main town centre. The rent on this shop is only £5,000 per annum. The problem is that Parvinder is not sure if enough people would walk past the door in order to attract sufficient trade.

Her final option is to rent a small section of a factory and try and promote the business on a mail-order basis. The rent for the factory is only going to be £100 per month.

1 **How much will the annual rent be on the factory?**

2 **If Parvinder tries to launch her business on a mail-order basis what other financial costs will she have to consider?**

3 **If Parvinder were to locate her business in the side street what other financial costs would she have to consider to ensure that customers know of her existence?**

Furnishings

Shut your eyes for a few moments and picture your bedroom. Identify and write down all of the items of furniture that you have in your bedroom. Identify any extra furniture that you would like in your bedroom or any that you would like removed. Will the items of furniture you have identified make your bedroom a more pleasant environment for you?

Different businesses will have many different pieces and types of furniture. What they choose to buy is guided by the:

- budget available
- function that it is required to do.

The furnishings that a business purchases can often reflect the image it portrays to its customers. The Marriott Hotel has the same furnishings in all its hotels. This is their **corporate image**.

Furniture can also make a big difference to the working environment of employees. If they are supplied with a nice desk, comfortable chair and sufficient storage space they will often be able to work more efficiently.

Would you like to work here?

Machinery

Businesses that manufacture products will have to purchase machinery in order to complete the manufacturing process. The trend over the past 30 years is to replace labour on production lines with technology. The Ford Motor Company's production lines are almost all automated and run by complex robots. Robots can work 24-hour shifts and do not get tired. They are also unlikely to make mistakes. However, the initial cost is usually large. To update the production line at Swaythling, Ford spent over £15 million. In a stark contrast, Kipling Cakes production line is still labour intensive.

Machinery in action

ACTIVITY

Look at the picture above and identify how much you would need to spend in order to improve the working environment.

ACTIVITY

As a group, identify your nearest manufacturing business. Think of the type of machinery that they use on a daily basis.

Fixtures and fittings

The next time you go into a shop, stop and look at the way the clothes, food, footwear, CDs and DVDs are displayed for the public to purchase. The shelving, stands, racks and display boards are all known as fixtures and fittings.

Whilst it is important for a business to have the correct fixtures and fittings, if it spends too much money when starting up, this could seriously affect its cash flow. It is better for a new business to purchase the basic requirements until they have established their customer base and have a secure income. When the business comes into profit it can then start developing its fixtures and fittings.

ACTIVITY

Using the Internet, research the cost of the fixtures and fittings you would need to start up a newsagent.

Computers play a major part in businesses

Computer equipment

Computers are now part of everyday life. By using simple computer software any business can present a professional image. It can produce its own letterheads, letters, purchase orders, invoices etc. Computer technology enables businesses to keep in touch with customers through websites and email. Access to the Internet has enabled businesses to tap into a much larger customer base, and opened up the possibility of expansion.

Large businesses can purchase complex computer software which enables them to run their whole business venture from simple purchasing of initial stock, stocktaking, producing final accounts through to keeping detailed records of their customers.

ACTIVITY

As a group, identify all the computer equipment that your school/college uses in order to run efficiently. If you can, identify the types of software that are used.

Vehicles

Some businesses will need vehicles in order to conduct their business. A lorry may be needed for distribution, a sales person will need a car to visit customers around the country and a van may be required by a florist to deliver flowers. The type of vehicle chosen will depend on the job that it is required to do. A courier firm may find motorbikes more efficient for document delivery in busy city centres whereas the building industry would use many different vehicles e.g. cranes, dumper trucks and earth movers.

ACTIVITY

Find out the cost of the following types of vehicle. You can choose a specific make:
- car
- small van
- large van.

CASE STUDY

Elderly care

Gail, Tejal, Simon and Anthony all worked in the National Health Service, specialising in the care of the elderly. They recognised there was a gap in the market for a private nursing home that was able to look after elderly patients who needed specialist nursing care. They decided to focus on those patients who were recovering from hip replacements, heart attacks, strokes etc. The idea was not to offer long-term care but to offer a place to stay and recover. They found a suitable house on the outskirts of town, situated in about half an acre of beautiful gardens. The house was on the market for £750,000. The four of them now need to work out all the other set-up/start-up costs.

1 What will be the cost of the furnishings you think the partners will need to purchase?
2 What will be the cost of the fixtures and fittings you think they need to purchase?
3 The partners are not sure what type of computer to buy. Explain to the partners what types of computers are currently available and their potential cost.
4 The partners are unsure whether to purchase a car to be used within the business. Research how much a car would cost the business. Recommend and justify whether you think this is a necessary expense.

Portfolio tip

You are required to identify and estimate a range of set-up costs for your selected business. In order to achieve the higher grades you will need to justify your choices.

AO1   Business running costs

In order to live we all have to spend money. We have to eat, drink, buy clothes and pay for somewhere to live. These could be identified as our personal **running costs**.

QUESTIONS

1 What are your normal running costs?
2 Make a quick list of what you have spent your money on so far this week.

All businesses have running costs, but these will vary depending on the type of business. The most common are outlined in the following section.

ACTIVITY

Look in local newspapers and the Internet to find out the cost of renting an industrial building in your area. Compare this with the rents in other parts of the country.

ACTIVITY

As a group research the business rates being charged by your local council. This will vary according to the location of a business.

ACTIVITY

A close friend of yours has just qualified as an accountant and is about to start their own business. They have asked you to outline the kind of services they will need to pay for on a regular basis. Undertake some research to find out what these services are likely to cost on a monthly basis.

Rent

Once a business has decided on its location it must then decide if it can afford to buy its own premises. If the business cannot afford to buy its own premises it will use premises owned by someone else and pay rent. Rent can be paid weekly, monthly, every three months, every six months or even yearly. If the premises chosen are in a prime position, have good road links, are close to customers, and have a good reputation, the rent is likely to be much higher than property located in a less popular area.

Rates

All premises are subject to local rates. Residential property pays council tax and businesses pay business rates, which are based on the size of the building, facilities and location. Rates are paid annually to the local council and are used to provide local services, which include the emergency services, education and public transport. Rates can be paid annually or on a monthly basis.

Services

Services include a mixture of expenses which are necessary in order for a business to function effectively. Businesses need electricity for heat and light, power for machinery and telephones and Internet access to communicate with their customers and suppliers. If a business has to make use of vehicles it will incur expenses such as MOTs, road tax, petrol and repairs. The business will also need stationery and postal charges in order to communicate with customers and suppliers.

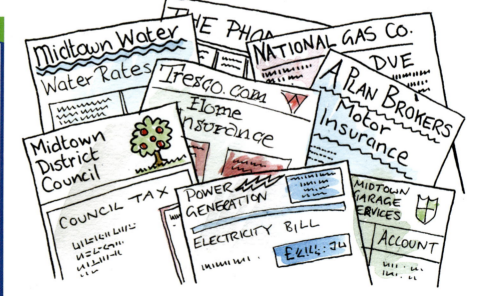

Bills, bills, bills!

Insurance

Insurance is when you pay another person/organisation to secure a risk. For example, if you own a car you are required to purchase car insurance with the minimum coverage of third party, fire and theft. You pay the insurance company a set amount of money and if you cause damage to another person's vehicle or property your insurance company will compensate the person who is making the claim against you. If your car is stolen or catches fire, the insurance company will pay you the value of the car. Businesses have to have business use added to their car insurance. This will often increase the premiums. Premiums are calculated on a risk factor. Young male drivers are considered high risk and therefore their car premiums are the most expensive. The more powerful the car you drive, the higher the premium will be.

In businesses, car insurance and employers' liability are compulsory by law. Employers' liability provides the business with cover for injury, disease, or death sustained by employees and arising from employment within the business. By law the minimum legal liability is £2,000,000 and a certificate of employer's liability must be displayed at each workplace. Public liability insurance protects the business against claims to pay damages to members of the public as a result of activities of the business. If a business owns its own premises it will also need buildings insurance. This covers the business if the building were to be burnt down and destroyed. A business will also require contents insurance which covers all the fixtures, fittings and stock which is stored within the building.

I am so glad nobody was hurt but I wish I was insured!

Why we need insurance

ACTIVITY

You are considering starting up a business as a part-time gardener. You will not have any employees and you will work in your customers' gardens. You will own a van and have all your own gardening tools. You will remain living at home with your parents. What will be the cost of the insurance cover you will need to purchase?

Materials

Any business that manufactures a product will need to buy in the **raw materials** to make their chosen product. In order to manufacture transit vans at Swaythling, the Ford Motor Company has to purchase many different types of raw materials. These include sheets of steel, which are compressed to manufacture the main body of the vans, plastic for interiors, engines, seats, screws and bolts, paint and many other parts.

Raw materials are the items needed to manufacture a product. For example, in order to manufacture a chair, the raw materials required would be wood, screws, glue, varnish etc.

You are having three friends round tonight and want to make a pizza with mushrooms, onions, tomato, cheese and olives.

Labour

As a business expands the owner(s) may no longer be able to cope with the demands of the customers and will therefore need to employ people in order to remain efficient and competitive. An employee will be given a **contract of employment** which outlines their **wage**, working conditions, hours of work, rate of pay, sickness and holiday benefits. As soon as a business employs people it will incur the following costs:

- wages
- taxation
- national insurance.

Taxation is the amount of money that is deducted from an employee's wage and paid to the government.

Taxation is set at different levels, depending on factors such as how much a person earns.

A single person has a personal allowance of £4,745 for the tax year 5 April 2004 to 4 April 2005. This is how much money they are allowed to earn before they have to pay any tax. The next £2,020 earned will be taxed at 10 per cent. From £2,021 to £31,400 will be taxed at 22 per cent and over £31,400 will be taxed at the higher rate of 40 per cent.

As soon as an employee earns over £79 per week they are required to pay **national insurance** to the government. This payment goes towards health care and old age pensions.

Corporation tax is the tax that a limited business would have to pay on its profits. The main rate of corporation tax is 30 per cent. For companies with taxable profits between £50,000 and £300,000 the small companies' rate of 19 per cent applies. The starting rate is zero for businesses with taxable profits of £10,000 or below.

Did you know?

All employees must be issued with a contract of employment within 16 weeks of starting work. The contract sets out their terms and conditions of employment, for example their working hours, rate of pay etc.

Did you know?

As at July 2005 the national minimum wage for workers over 22 years is £4.85. For employees aged 18–21 years the rate is £4.10, but both will increase in October 2005.

CASE STUDY

Local deliveries

Peter has decided he wants to start up in business on his own. His passion in life is driving and so he has decided to start up a local delivery company. He has purchased a Mercedes van at a cost of £5,000 plus VAT and advertised his services in the local newspapers on a Thursday as it is 'business night'. This cost him £75 per week. Upon further investigations, he knows that his van does approximately 5 miles per litre and he is expecting to travel at least 350 miles per week. The most recent diesel price is 80.4p per litre. He also needs to insure the van for commercial use which is going to cost a further £1,500. Road tax is £160 per year. The only other cost Peter can think of is his mobile telephone which he estimates will cost him approximately £25 per week.

1 What was Peter's initial start-up cost?
2 How much did the Mercedes van cost Peter including VAT?
3 How much will Peter spend on diesel each week?
4 Make a list of all Peter's estimated running costs.
5 How much will he spend each week on running costs?
6 Why was Thursday the best day for Peter to advertise his business?
7 Why does Peter need to insure his van?
8 Are there any other running costs that Peter has not considered?

Portfolio tip

In order to achieve this assessment objective you need to identify, estimate and recommend a range of running costs for your chosen business activity. In order to gain the higher grades your costs will need to be realistic and fully justified.

AO4 Estimating potential sales

Sales consist of the goods or services that a business sells to its customers. It is important for businesses to make realistic estimations about how many products or how often its services will be purchased by their **target market** in order to estimate their potential sales accurately.

The target market is the people whom the product/service is aimed at. For example, the sale of modern music is aimed at the teenage market.

Target markets can be grouped in many different ways. Potential buyers can be classified by gender, age, family size, income and social status. It is very important for a business to aim its products at the right classification of customer otherwise they end up not making any sales. It would be foolish to try and sell roller skates to old age pensioners!

Methods of estimation

Estimation based on research of potential customers/demand

A business will undertake **market research** in order to discover who their potential market will be and what the potential sales could be.

Market research is undertaken by a business to find out the buying habits and needs of the general public.

Primary market research is conducted by the business.

Secondary market research is carried out by an independent organisation and used by other businesses.

You will recall from your work in Unit 2 there are two types of market research. Can you remember what they are? Spend a few minutes now looking back on your Unit 2 notes.

A business will use primary research in order to establish the following points:

- who their customers are
- how often they will purchase the product/service
- how much they are prepared to pay for the product/service.

Once a business has found out this information it will enable it to estimate the value of its potential sales.

Estimation based on performance of similar product/services

Another useful tool to use when trying to identify trends in sales figures is for a business to look at how a similar product/service has performed in the market. A lot of businesses produce a number of products. For example, Cadbury's produce a wide variety of chocolate bars. If it decided to develop a new cereal bar which was linked to a healthy eating campaign, it may research how well a competitor's cereal bar is performing in the market. Cadbury's may also refer back to its own statistics and compare potential sales against a similar product.

A business may also refer to secondary research that has been undertaken by other organisations. The government produce a wide variety of statistics through the Office of National Statistics (ONS) which are freely available to members of the public. For example, if the Caravan and

Camping Club wanted to open a new caravan park they might refer to statistics on holiday trends to find out how many people still take holidays in the UK and the most popular areas of the country.

Trade associations represent the interests of the member companies and therefore collect statistical data on the state of their industry. The Society of Motor Manufacturers and Traders collects production and sales statistics for the UK car market. Trade Associations are listed in a directory called Trade Associations and Professional Bodies of the United Kingdom (Published by Gale Research, 13th ed. 1997).

Market intelligence reports such as Keynotes, Mintel and Retail Business include data on market size by volume and value, market shares, sales trends and forecasts.

National newspapers such as the *Financial Times* report daily on business affairs world wide.

All of these sources could be used to help a business identify possible trends in consumer spending.

CASE STUDY

Year Book

You have been given the task of interpreting some market research that has been conducted within the school. Research had been undertaken into the possibility of producing a Year Book for the Year 11s. The results showed that 98 per cent of pupils would be prepared to buy a Year Book. 20 per cent of them would pay between £6–£8 and 80 per cent would pay between £3–£5. There are currently 250 students in Year 11.

(a) How many pupils have stated they would be interested in purchasing a Year Book?
(b) How many students do you think would actually purchase the Year Book?
(c) Identify the price you think should be charged for the Year Book. Justify your answer.
(d) Estimate the potential sales revenue for the Year Book using the assumptions you have made in (b) and (c) above.

Sales, estimates/targets for given situations

If the business has conducted accurate market research it will be aware of the potential demand for its product(s)/service(s). Armed with this information the business should be able to estimate accurately how much it will receive from customers over a set period of time.

In order to calculate sales accurately, the business will need to know the following information:

- how much the customer will pay for the product(s)/services
- how often they will purchase the product(s)/services.

Single product

If a business sells just one product it is very easy to calculate its potential sales. It will multiply the sales price by the number of potential customers.

Example

Eddie produces custom-made pedal cycles. He builds them to special order. He is able to make two bikes per week which retail at £420 each. Eddie is going to take four weeks' holiday a year and, in order not to overestimate his potential sales, is going to allow for three quiet weeks in his first year. His estimated sales are as follows:

52 weeks – 4 weeks' holiday – 3 quiet weeks
= 45 weeks per year $\times$ 2 bikes = 90 bikes
90 $\times$ £420 per bike = £37,800 sales income per year.

QUESTIONS

Sam and Joe run their own window-cleaning business. They have one standard price of £15 per house. They are able to clean 12 houses a day.

1 Calculate Sam and Joe's daily and weekly sales.

2 Calculate their annual sales. They will work 48 weeks a year.

Small range of products

If a business sells more than one product, the procedure to calculate sales will be exactly the same as for a single product but will have to be calculated for each individual product.

Example

Florence runs her own pottery business and sells three different types of pots:

- small pots £12
- medium pots £16
- large pots £23

Florence has estimated she will sell 10 small pots, 8 medium pots and 12 large pots per week. What will be her weekly sales?

$10 \times £12 = £120$
$8 \times £16 = £128$
$12 \times £23 = \underline{£276}$
Total sales £524

If Florence manufactured and sold her pots for 42 weeks of the year her annual sales would be:

42 weeks $\times$ £524 = £22,008

QUESTIONS

Ken sells garden furniture and is planning to work 40 weeks a year. Based on his primary and secondary research, Ken has calculated that he can manufacture and sell the following furniture on a weekly basis:

  3 × garden tables – £120 each
12 × garden chairs – £22 each
10 × garden planters – £14 each.

1 What will be the value of Ken's sales each week?

2 What will be the value of Ken's sales per month?

3 What will be the value of Ken's sales per year?

Multiple products

When a business sells a wide range of products, the process of estimating sales becomes much more complex. If a large supermarket were considering opening a new store in your area they are unlikely to try and work out how many cans of baked beans, loaves of bread, tins of dog food etc. are going to be sold each week. They would simplify the process by looking at their sales figures for similar areas. They would consider the location of the store, the floor area, and the number of residents living in the locality and then calculate their potential sales on the number of people they think will visit the store on a weekly basis multiplied by average spend.

Example

A well-known supermarket is considering opening a new branch in your area. The board of directors have looked back over past sales trends and estimated that the average number of customers per week will be 15,000. From past experience they know that the average spend will be £82 per week.

Weekly sales = 15,000 × £82 = £1,230,000.
Annual sales = 52 weeks × £1,230,000 = £63,960,000.

Did you know?

Supermarkets often have targets for how much each square metre of the store should earn on a daily basis. Average spend is calculated by taking the total sales figure over a set period and dividing it by the number of customers who shopped in the store.

QUESTIONS

Since leaving school Yasmin has worked in a garden centre. She has just been offered the opportunity to start up her own garden centre. The garden centre will sell a wide range of products. Yasmin needs to estimate her potential weekly, monthly and yearly sales.

Based on her previous experiences, she has come up with the following information. She is expecting to serve on average 200 customers per week.

She thinks that on average customers' spending patterns are reflected in the information below.

- 50 people would spend approximately £25 per visit
- 25 people would spend approximately £40 per visit
- 125 people would spend approximately £15 per visit.

1 Calculate the average spend.
2 Calculate Yasmin's estimated weekly sales based on average spend.
3 What would Yasmin's annual sales be? Assume the garden centre is open 50 weeks a year.

Portfolio tip

In order to achieve this assessment objective you need to clearly illustrate how you have estimated your potential sales. You must include evidence of all your calculations including justification.

AO5 Break even point and profit margins

One of the most important aims for a business is to make a profit. It is vital that a business is aware at what point in production it will cover all of its costs and break even. The next unit produced or customer served is the point where the business begins to make a profit.

Fixed costs

Fixed costs are the costs that do not change regardless of the level of production or service provided.

Consider the following. The local music shop rents its shop premises for £25,000 per year. The rent paid will not increase or decrease according to the number of CD, DVDs or videos it sells.

Fixed costs include rent, rates, electricity, gas, rental of telephone. The rental charge on the telephone is considered to be a fixed cost as it will not change regardless of the number of telephone calls made.

ACTIVITY

As a group identify the fixed costs of your school/college.

Variable costs

Variable costs are costs that do change with the level of production or service provided.

Example

A mobile DJ will incur petrol costs according to how far the business has to travel. If the business does not have any bookings the petrol expenses will be very low. If the business has 'gigs' booked which are a long way away then petrol costs will increase.

Variable costs will include power to run machinery, fuel costs for transport, raw materials required to manufacture products and telephone calls. Variable costs will differ according to the type of business being conducted.

Wages can be either a fixed or variable cost. If an employee is paid a salary this would be classified as a fixed cost. However, if the employees' wages are directly related to the production or provision of a service then their wages would be considered to be a variable cost.

ACTIVITY

Consider your local supermarket. What do you think are the fixed and variable costs of running the supermarket?

CASE STUDY

Polly's Petals

A close friend of the family, Polly, is in the process of starting up her own florist business. In order to secure a loan from the bank she needs to calculate her break even point. Polly has no knowledge of business and therefore does not know where to start with the calculations. She has come round to see if you can shed any light on what all these different terms mean. She wants you to help her with the following points:

- what are fixed costs?
- what are variable costs?
- how does she calculate her sales income?

In order to help you explain these points you have ascertained the following information concerning how she is going to run the shop.

She will rent the shop premises at an annual rent of £6,000 which will be paid monthly. She will order her stock of flowers on a daily basis to ensure freshness. She will hold some stock e.g. ribbons, wire and these will be replaced as and when required. To start with she is going to be the only person working within the business. She will have a van which will be used to deliver flowers to customers. The shop is equipped with electric heating and a telephone. She will also have a mobile telephone so that she can be contacted when she is out and about delivering flowers. She has purchased a computer to be used within the shop to keep a record of all her customers and financial records.

She has estimated that the average spend within the shop will be £15 and she is hoping to serve at least 25 people a day. The shop will be open six days per week.

Using the case study explain and give examples of the following:

(a) fixed costs

(b) variable costs.

Estimate Polly's potential sales revenue for the first year of trading.

Sales income (revenue)

This is the amount of money a business has taken in sales. This is not profit because no expenses have been deducted from the amount.

As we have seen in assessment objective 4 the sales income of a business is the price of the product times the number of products sold over a set period.

Break even

There are a number of ways that break even can be calculated. In this next section you will learn how to calculate break even using the formula and by drawing a graph.

Figure 3.1 *The concept of break even*

How to identify break even point using the formula

$$\text{Formula} = \frac{\text{Fixed costs}}{\text{Contribution}}$$

Contribution = Sales price (per unit) − Variable costs (per unit)

When you calculate break even the answer will not always be a whole number. If this is the case, round your final calculation up to the nearest whole number. In order to break even you cannot sell part of a unit.

Example

A business manufacturing picture frames called Picture Frames for All Occasions has calculated that its annual fixed costs are £25,000.

The variable costs per picture frame are 75p and each picture frame sells for £2.00. It currently produces 35,000 picture frames per year.

Contribution therefore = £2.00 − 75p = £1.25

$$\frac{25,000}{1.25} = 20,000 \text{ picture frames need to be manufactured and sold in order to break even.}$$

Drawing a break even chart (graph)

In order to draw a break even graph successfully you will need a sharp pencil, a long ruler, and graph paper. Many a student has missed the break even point due to having the wrong equipment to complete the job successfully.

On the graph you will be plotting the fixed cost line, the total cost line and the sales revenue line.

Total costs are calculated by adding together the fixed and variable costs. Sales revenue is calculated by multiplying the number of items sold by the sales price.

The revenue is shown on the *y*-axis and the number of products sold on the *x*-axis.

Using Picture Frames for All Occasions you need to complete a table which will enable you to plot these figures on to your graph.

On the graph on the following page you will see the following points marked.

Break even – this is the point in output and sales where all of the costs have been covered.

Loss – this is the area where the business has yet to cover all of its costs.

Profit – this is the area where the business has covered all its costs and each extra unit manufactured and sold will start to earn profit.

Margin of safety – this is the area between the current level of output and the break even point.

ACTIVITY

Using the figures below, calculate the break even point for High Flying Engineering Ltd. They want to know the break even point for unit 287. They currently manufacture 2,500 per year. The business has calculated their costs as follows:

Fixed costs – £19,500 per annum. Variable costs £16 per unit and they sell for £55 each.

No. of Picture Frames sold	Fixed Costs (FC)	Variable costs (VC) (0.75 × No. produced)	Total Costs FC + VC	Sales Revenue (£2 × No. sold)
0	25,000	0	25,000	0
5000	25,000	3,750	28,750	10,000
10,000	25,000	7,500	32,500	20,000
20,000	25,000	15,000	40,000	40,000
30,000	25,000	22,500	47,500	60,000

Table 3.1

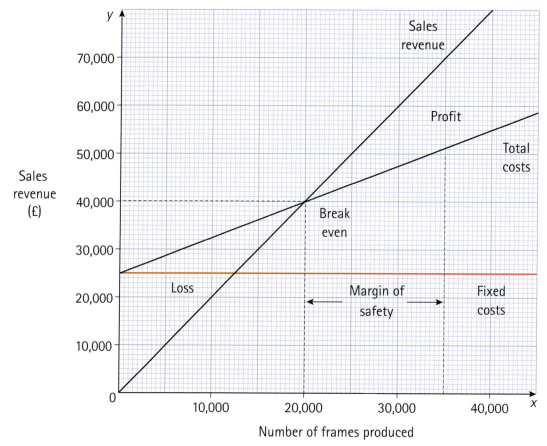

Figure 3.2 *Break even chart for Picture Frames for All Occasions*

Profit margin

The profit margin illustrates how much profit a business is making measured against its sales. The higher the profit margin the better the business is performing. It is calculated using the following formula.

$$\text{Profit margin} = \frac{\text{Operating Profit}}{\text{Sales Income}} \times 100 = \text{percentage}$$

Operating profit is the final profit of the business. It is calculated by taking all the expenses of the business away from the sales income.

How to calculate profit using contribution

In order to work out the profit margin of a business you will first have to work out their operating profit. There is a quick method of doing this using contribution and fixed costs.

Can you remember how contribution is calculated? If not, take a few minutes looking back over your notes.

How does it work?

Contribution per unit is multiplied by the number produced. The fixed costs are then deducted from this figure. The remaining amount is the operating profit of the business.

Let us go back to our example of Picture Frames for All Occasions.

Each picture frame made the following contribution:

£2.00 – 75p = £1.25 multiply this by the 35,000 the number produced = £43,750 less the fixed costs of £25,000 gives an operating profit of £18,750.

Sales revenue = £2.00 × 35,000

Manufactured = £70,000

The profit margin would be:

$$\frac{18{,}750}{70{,}000} \times 100 = 26.78\%$$

For every picture frame manufactured and sold the business makes 25p operating profit.

Factors influencing profit margin

There are many factors which can affect the profit margin of a business. Outlined below are some of the more common factors. Throughout the following illustration Picture Frames for All Occasions will be used. Below is a quick reminder of the figures to help you work through the examples.

- Annual fixed costs £25,000
- Sales price of picture frames £2.00
- Variable costs 75p per picture frame
- Normal production 35,000 per year
- Break even point 20,000 picture frames
- Operating profit margin 25 per cent

Pricing strategy

The higher the price a business charges for their goods and services the higher its profit margin will be, as long as **expenses** are maintained at the same level. Expenses are the costs of running the business.

Example one – the price of the picture frames increases to £2.50

Contribution = £2.50 – 75p = £1.75

$$\text{Break even} = \frac{25{,}000}{£1.75} = 14{,}286 \text{ picture frames}$$

The break even point has reduced by 5,714.

Profit margin

Contribution = 35,000 (number produced) × £1.75 = £61,250

less fixed costs £25,000

Operating profit £36,250

$$\frac{36{,}250}{87{,}500} \times 100 = 41.43\%$$ profit margin has increased by just over 14% (number produced times by sales price)

ACTIVITY

Using the figures supplied for High Flying Engineering Ltd calculate the operating profit and profit margin.

Example two – the price of picture frames decreases to £150

Contribution = £1.50 − 75p = 75p

$$\text{Break even} = \frac{25,000}{75p} = 33,334 \text{ picture frames}$$

The break even point has increased by 13,334.

Profit margin

Contribution = 35,000 × 75p =	£26,250
less fixed costs =	£25,000
Operating profit =	£1,250

$$\frac{1,250}{52,500} \times 100 = 238\%$$
(35,000 produced by sales price £1.50)

Urgency of required break even point

Until a business reaches break even point it is losing money. No business can withstand losses for long periods of time. Smaller businesses are less likely to be able to withstand losses and need to reach their break even point as quickly as possible.

There are different ways this can be achieved.

- A business can raise the price of its goods which will increase the contribution the product makes towards covering fixed costs. However, if the price is too high the number of customers may fall. This scenario was illustrated in example one.

- A business can try and reduce its variable costs. This in turn will also increase the contribution the product makes towards fixed costs. There is a danger in using cheaper suppliers. The products may be of an inferior quality and the business could experience high levels of wastage as a result.

Example three – the variable costs of the picture frames could be lowered to 50p per frame

The new break even point is illustrated below.

Contribution = £2.00 – 50p = £1.50

$$\frac{25,000}{1.50} = 16,667.$$ The break even point has been reduced by 3,333 picture frames

The profit margin has also increased by just over 14% as shown below.

Operating profit = £1.50 × 35,000 = 52,500 – fixed costs 25,000 = £27,500

$$\frac{\text{Operating profit}}{\text{Sales income}} = \frac{27,500}{70,000} \times 100 = 39.29\%$$

Competition

If a business faces stiff competition it may choose to launch its product at a lower price than its competitors. The lower the sales price the lower the profit margin will be. If a business has launched a product which is unique and there is little or no competition the selling price could be high. This will mean the business will have high profit margins.

This is illustrated in the example used for pricing strategy.

Fixed and variable costs

Fixed and variable costs are expenses and will therefore affect the profit margin of a business. If these costs increase and the business does not pass these increases on to the customer, profit margins will fall. If the business passes these costs on to the customer, profit margins will remain the same. If fixed or variable costs decrease, profit margins will increase.

The lowering of variable costs is illustrated in **example three** under the section urgency of required break even point.

Example four – fixed and variable costs increase

If Picture Frames for All Occasions has an increase of fixed costs to £30,000 and variable costs rise to 80p the break even point and profit margin would change as illustrated below.

Contribution = £2.00 – 80p = £1.20

Break even = $\dfrac{30,000}{£1.20}$ = 25,000 picture frames needed in order to break even.
An increase of 5,000 frames

Profit margin

Operating profit = 35,000 × £1.20 = £42,000 – fixed costs £30,000 = £12,000

Operating profit/Sales income × 100 $\quad\dfrac{12,000}{70,000}$ × 100 = 17.14%

A decrease in profit margin of 2.9%

Example five – fixed costs decrease, variable costs remain the same

If Picture Frames for All Occasions has a decrease in their fixed costs to £20,000, the break even point and profit margin would change as illustrated below.

Break even = $\dfrac{20,000}{£1.25}$ = 16,000 picture frames. A reduction of 4,000 picture frames

Profit margin

Operating profit = 35,000 × £1.25 = £43,750 – Fixed costs £20,000 = £23,750

$\dfrac{\text{Operating profit}}{\text{Sales income}}$ × 100 $\quad\dfrac{£23,750}{£70,000}$ × 100 = 33.93% an increase of 13.93%.

ACTIVITY

Sophie has decided to go into business manufacturing motifs that can go on to T-shirts overalls etc. After extensive research she has calculated that she can sell each motif for £1.50 each. The variable costs are 25p per motif and her fixed costs are going to be £6,000 per year. She has estimated production and sales to be 1,200 per month.

1 Calculate the break even point.
2 Plot the break even graph.
3 Calculate the possible operating profit and profit margin.

For the first six months everything went really well. Sophie has just had some bad news. Her rent on the unit is going to increase by £2,000. She is unsure how this will affect her break even point and profit levels.

1 Calculate the new break even point.
2 Calculate the revised operating profit and profit margin.

Sophie is considering raising the price of the motifs to £1.75 each. How will this affect her break even point and profit margins?

1 Calculate the new break even point.
2 Calculate the revised operating profit and profit margin.
3 Advise Sophie of the problem she could encounter if she did choose to raise her prices.
4 Recommend to Sophie what you think she should do.

PORTFOLIO GUIDANCE

In order to achieve this assessment objective you will need to identify and describe the break even point either through the use of calculations or by drawing break even graphs. You will need to clearly state how the break even point and profit margin could be altered using the bullet points outlined above. You must include all your calculations, clearly describing any assumptions you have made.

AO6 The range of financial operations in a small business

No matter how good a business idea is the business is likely to fail unless there is sufficient control over the money flowing in and out. Cash flow is crucial to a business's survival. Think how many times you have wanted to go out but have had insufficient funds to do so!

Tracking financial performance

The majority of people go into business with the aim of making money. There is little point in continuing if at the end of every month the business has spent more money than it had coming in. All businesses, whether large or small, need to have systems in place in order to keep track of their finances.

In order to track financial performance, a business must first decide what documents and books of account to use. Below is a flow diagram to show the flow of documents between two companies. Westons of Warwick want to order some garden tools from Tools R Us.

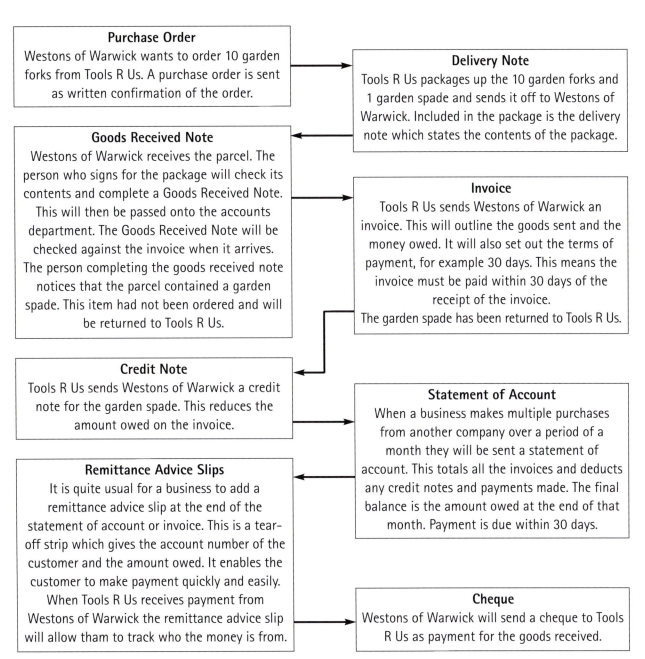

Purchase Order
Westons of Warwick wants to order 10 garden forks from Tools R Us. A purchase order is sent as written confirmation of the order.

Delivery Note
Tools R Us packages up the 10 garden forks and 1 garden spade and sends it off to Westons of Warwick. Included in the package is the delivery note which states the contents of the package.

Goods Received Note
Westons of Warwick receives the parcel. The person who signs for the package will check its contents and complete a Goods Received Note. This will then be passed onto the accounts department. The Goods Received Note will be checked against the invoice when it arrives. The person completing the goods received note notices that the parcel contained a garden spade. This item had not been ordered and will be returned to Tools R Us.

Invoice
Tools R Us sends Westons of Warwick an invoice. This will outline the goods sent and the money owed. It will also set out the terms of payment, for example 30 days. This means the invoice must be paid within 30 days of the receipt of the invoice.
The garden spade has been returned to Tools R Us.

Credit Note
Tools R Us sends Westons of Warwick a credit note for the garden spade. This reduces the amount owed on the invoice.

Statement of Account
When a business makes multiple purchases from another company over a period of a month they will be sent a statement of account. This totals all the invoices and deducts any credit notes and payments made. The final balance is the amount owed at the end of that month. Payment is due within 30 days.

Remittance Advice Slips
It is quite usual for a business to add a remittance advice slip at the end of the statement of account or invoice. This is a tear-off strip which gives the account number of the customer and the amount owed. It enables the customer to make payment quickly and easily.
When Tools R Us receives payment from Westons of Warwick the remittance advice slip will allow tham to track who the money is from.

Cheque
Westons of Warwick will send a cheque to Tools R Us as payment for the goods received.

Figure 3.3 *Flow of documents between Westons of Warwick and Tools R Us*

Books of original entry used to record financial transactions

It is normal for a business to allow its customers 30 days' credit. This means that the customer receives the goods and pays for them at a later date, usually the end of the month. A business need to set in place a system whereby it can check which customers have paid and those who have not. A customer who owes the business money for goods or services received is known as a **debtor**.

In order to record credit sales a sales day book is kept. This will record the date the invoice was issued, the name of the customer, the net amount, the VAT charged and the total due.

A business has to become VAT registered if its turnover is over a limit set by the government. The limit is reviewed and increased by the government at regular intervals.

How to calculate VAT

VAT is currently set at 17.5 per cent. To calculate how much VAT would be charged on £20:

$$\frac{20}{100} \times 17.5 = £3.50$$

Total to be charged £20 + £3.50 = £23.50

Below is an example of a sales day book for Black Horse Catering Ltd which provides catering for special events, for example weddings and 18th birthday parties.

The business is owned and run by Wayne and Jayne.

ACTIVITY

Using the sales day book supplied record the information below for Black Horse Catering Ltd. The figures given are net. You will have to calculate the VAT and totals.

2 July
Mr Singh: £829.00

6 July
Mr & Mrs Fatima: £230

15 July
Horsham Cycling Club: £2,821

20 July
West Bay Mothers Union: £482

24 July 24
Mr & Mrs Jarvis: £592

Date 2004	Customer	Net £	VAT 17.5% £	Total £
2 June	Mr & Mrs Hugh	326.00	57.05	383.05
9 June	East Side Sailing Club	2,458.00	430.15	2,888.15
21 June	Hightown Golf Club	3,712.00	649.60	4,361.60
30 June	Total	6,496.00	1,136.80	7,632.80

Table 3.2 *Example of a sales day book*

At the end of each month the columns are totalled. When these invoices have been paid they can be ticked off. The business has a record of its monthly turnover, how much VAT it owes, and who has not yet paid for goods or services received.

A business will also need a system whereby it can record what it has spent buying goods or services. This is known as the purchase day book. A business's suppliers are known as **creditors**. These are people the business now owes money to because it has had the benefit of goods or services with the promise that it will pay for them within 30 days.

Below is an example of the purchase day book for Black Horse Catering Ltd.

Date 2005	Customer	Net £	VAT 17.5% £	Total £
3 June	Wines UK Ltd	438.00	76.65	514.65
10 June	Damion Butchers Ltd	129.00		129.00*
17 June	Gales Ales Ltd	1,723.00	301.53	2,024.53
22 June	The Finishing Touch Ltd	152.00	26.60	178.60
26 June	Macro	827.00		827.00*
30 June	Total	3,2689.00	404.78	3,673.78

*Note there is no VAT charged on the purchase of food. However, the business is legally required to charge VAT on external catering contracts.

Table 3.3 *Example of a purchase day book*

The purchase day book is totalled at the end of each month enabling the business to monitor how much it has spent and to whom it still owes money.

ACTIVITY

Using the purchase day book supplied record the information below for Black Horse Catering Ltd. The figures given are net. You will have to calculate the VAT and totals.

6 July Macro: £481 (don't forget no VAT)

10 July Damion Butchers: £173

15 July Gales Ales Ltd: £625

21 July Wines UK Ltd: £721

29 July Finishing Touch Ltd: £78

Recording incoming and outgoing money

A business will also need a system to record the money it receives from its customers (debtors) and payments it makes to its creditors. This is known as the two column cash book.

Below is a copy of Black Horse Catering Ltd's two column cash book. The figures are taken from its sales and purchase day books for June. It has received and made all payments within the 30 days allowed.

	Debit (In)				Credit (Out)			
Date 2005	Details	Cash	Bank	Date 2005	Details	Cash	Bank
(a) 1 July	Balance	150.00	1,289.00	(c) 3 June	Wines UK Ltd		497.03
(b) 2 July	Mr & Mrs Hugh		383.05	(c) 8 July	Damion Butchers Ltd		129.00
(b)10 July	East Side Sailing Club		2,888.15	(c) 11 July	Petrol	30.00	
(b) 20 July	High Town Golf Club		3,712.00	(c) 18 July	Gales Ales Ltd		2,024.53
				(c) 24 July	Finishing Touch Ltd		178.60
				(c) 27 July	Macro		827.00
				(c) 30 July	Printer cartridge	29.00	
				(d) 31 July	Balance b/d (f)	91.00	4,616.04
		(e) 150.00	8,272.20			(e) 150.00	8,272.20
(g) 1 August	Balance c/d	91.00	4,616.04				

Notes

(a) 1 July balance is the money that the business has available to spend at the beginning of the month. The business had £150.00 cash and £1,289.00 in the bank.

(b) 2 July, 10 July and 20 July on the debit side (in) are all payments which have been made to the business for services received.

(c) These are payments made for goods or services supplied. All payments made by the business are recorded on the credit (out) side of the cash book. You can see that there were two payments made with cash – petrol and the printer cartridge.

(d) Wayne and Jayne will want to know how much money they have left at the end of each month. They will need to balance their cash book. To do this they need to follow the procedure outlined below:

  (i) Add up all the money that has come into the business including the opening balance

 (ii) Record this figure at the bottom of the cash book and carry it across to the credit side (e)

(iii) Deduct all the money that has been spent (credit) and this will give you the balance bought down (b/d) (f)

The balance is then carried over the debit side of the cash book. This becomes the opening balance for August (g).

Table 3.4 *Two column cash book*

ACTIVITY

Complete the two column cash book for the Black Horse Catering Ltd assuming that all payments made and received are the same as the sales and purchase day books you completed above for July. Make up your own suitable dates in August. Use the proforma supplied on page 120.

The opening bank balance is £4,616.04 and cash has £9,100
Two cash payments were made in the month – 5 August, petrol £37.00, and 28 August, stationery £16.57. One cash payment was received for £187 from Hugh Jones on 25 August.

Balance the cash book at the end of the month.

I wish I'd kept on top of the paperwork ...

Cash flow forecast

A cash flow forecast is produced to enable a business to predict what its future income and expenditure will be. A business will be able to see if it has sufficient cash to meet all its expected expenditure. It will highlight if the business needs to organise a bank overdraft or even a short-term loan. A cash flow forecast is often used by businesses to see if they can afford to purchase large items of equipment, and if so, at what point in their financial year. If someone is starting up a new business it is often a useful exercise to see how much initial money they will need to be able to survive the first few months. If a business needs to borrow money from the bank it will also complete a cash flow forecast as part of its business plan. A cash flow is an illustration of the money flowing through a business over a period of time. This is not the same as profit.

Black Horse Catering Ltd is considering the purchase of a new vehicle. However, it is not sure how much it can afford. Wayne has found a nice Peugeot Partner van which would be ideal for £6,500. He has decided to produce a cash flow forecast for the next six months to find out:

(a) how much spare cash will be available and

(b) how much will need to be borrowed in order to make the purchase.

Cash flow forecast for six months ended 28 February 2005

	September	October	November	December	January	February
Income	£	£	£	£	£	£
Sales	6,000	4,500	5,000	6,750	3250	4,250
(a) Total Income	6,000	4,500	5,000	6,750	3,250	4,250
Expenditure						
Purchases	1,800	1,350	1,500	2,025	975	1,275
Motor expenses	120	120	120	120	120	120
Rent on premises	500	500	500	500	500	500
Wayne & Jane salary	2,000	2,000	2,000	2,000	2,000	2,000
General expenses	100	100	100	100	100	100
(b) Total Expenditure	4,520	4,070	4,220	4,745	3,695	3,995
Opening Balance	3,400	4,880	5,310	6,090	8,095	7,650
(a–b) Inflow/Outflow	1,480	430	780	2,005	(445)	225
Closing Balance	4,880	5,310	6,090	8,095	7,650	7,905

Notes
The opening balance is the amount of money in the bank at the start of the forecast.
The inflow/outflow is calculated by deducting (a) the total income from (b) the total expenditure. If this is a negative amount the figures are placed in ( ).
The closing balance is found by adding the opening balance to the inflow/outflow.
The closing balance of September becomes the opening balance of October etc.

Table 3.5 *Cash flow forecast*

You can see from the cash flow, the month with the largest closing balance is December. If the owners of Black Horse Catering Ltd decide to purchase the van in December their closing balance would reduce to £1,595. They would have to consider if this left them with sufficient funds to run the business. Below is an updated extract of the cash flow forecast for December, January and February which includes the purchase of the van in December.

	December	January	February
Income	£	£	£
Sales	6,750	3,250	4,250
(a) Total Income	6,750	3,250	4,250
Expenditure			
Purchases	2,025	975	1,275
Motor expenses	120	120	120
Rent on premises	500	500	500
Wayne & Jane salary	2,000	2,000	2,000
Purchase of Van	6,500		
General expenses	100	100	100
(b) Total Expenditure	11,245	3,695	3,995
Opening Balance	6,090	1,595	1,150
(a–b) Inflow/Outflow	(4,495)	(445)	225
Closing Balance	1,595	1,150	1,375

Table 3.6 *Cash flow forecast (extract)*

At the moment it appears that the business will have sufficient money to fully fund the purchase of the van. However, Wayne and Jayne are aware that they are often quieter through March and April. Rather than committing themselves to a long-term loan they have decided to put together a further cash flow forecast for the next three months to see if they become overdrawn. If they do have a negative bank balance for one month they could negotiate a bank overdraft.

ACTIVITY

Using the figures below produce Wayne and Jayne's cash flow forecast for the three months ended May 2005. The opening bank balance for March is the closing balance for February, assuming the van was purchased in December. Use the proforma on page 121 to fill in your forecast.

Sales for March £3,700, April £4,200 and May £5,000

Purchases for March £1,110, April £1,260 and May £1,500

Motor expenses £150 per month

Rent £500 per month

Wages £2,000

General expenses £100 per month

Documents used for issuing requests for payment

Wayne and Jayne will need standard documents to issue to customers which will request payment.

The first document used to request payment is a pre-printed standard document known as an **invoice**. It states the name, address, telephone number and email address of the business. If the business is VAT registered, the VAT number must also be included on the invoice. All invoices must be dated and numbered consecutively so that the business can track that all sales have been invoiced and recorded correctly.

Black Horse Catering Ltd

Unit 6 Westwood Way
Fenshaw
Lincolnshire
LX34 7YB

Telephone: 0238 987 564
Email WayneJayne21@aol.com

Invoice number: 00765

Date: 16 May 2004

VAT Reg: 0865 8353 9871

Address of customer:

Mr & Mrs B Parkes
Green Side Cottage
West Lane
Fenshaw
Lincolnshire
LC54 9PM

To:

Provide catering for 120 people at £12.50 per head

Terms: 30 days net	Net	
		1,500.00
	VAT	
		262.50
	Total	
		1,762.50

Figure 3.4 *Example of an invoice used by Wayne and Jayne in their business.*

ACTIVITY

Design your own invoice or use the one on page 122 for Wayne and Jayne and complete it with the following details:

Date as today
Invoice number: 00766
Customer details: Lincolnshire Gardeners Club
Buffet meal for 248 people at £7.50 per head
Bar bill £2,400

If a business deals regularly with another business it may not pay on the receipt of individual invoices. It will wait until it receives a **statement of account** at the end of the month. This document itemises all the goods/services that have been received and any payments that have been made. The final balance is the amount due. The business is then allowed 30 days to pay this final balance.

As Wayne and Jayne usually only deal with 'one off' customers they are unlikely to use statements of account. However, they do buy regularly from several suppliers and are likely to receive statements of accounts from them. Let us look at an example of a statement of account being received from Wines UK.

Wines UK Limited
120–122 Hyth Way
Fenshaw
Lincolnshire
LX28 7HD

Account: 90272

Date: 1 June 2005

To: Wayne & Jayne's Catering
Unit 6 Westwood Way
Fenshaw
Lincolnshire
LX34 7YB

Date	Description	Debit	Credit	Balance
				690.00
1 June		72.00		762.00
3 June	Invoice No. 00692		690.00	72.00
5 June	Cheque received	380.00		452.00
15 June	Invoice No. 00721	1,290.00		1,742.00
29 June	Invoice No. 00846		600.00	1,142.00
30 June	Cheque received			1,142.00
30 June	**Closing Balance**			

Figure 3.5 *An example of a statement of account from Wines UK Ltd*

You can see from the above example that at the beginning of the month Wayne and Jayne owed Wines UK Ltd £690.00. They received goods on 3, 15 and 29 June. They made payments on 5 and 30 June. This meant that on 30 June they owed Wines UK Limited £1,142.00.

ACTIVITY

Design your own statement of account or use the one at the end of the unit for Finishing Touch Limited which is another supplier to Wayne and Jayne. This company supplies ribbons, balloons, napkins etc.

The following transactions took place throughout the month of June 2005. The opening balance on 1 June was £2,345.

They supplied Wayne and Jayne with goods on the following dates:
16 June Invoice Number BCD149 – £192.00
22 June Invoice Number BCD298 – £150.90

Wayne and Jayne made payments by cheque to Finishing Touch on the following dates:
2 June – £2,345
29 June – £162.90

(a) How much do Wayne and Jayne owe Finishing Touch on 30 June?

In order to speed up payment from customers, businesses often attach a remittance slip to the end of their statement of account. The remittance slip is a tear-off slip which contains the details of the customer.

The following is the example of the statement of account sent to Wayne and Jayne. It has a remittance slip attached.

Wines UK Limited
120–122 Hyth Way
Fenshaw
Lincolnshire
LX28 7HD

Account: 90272

Date: 1 June 2005

To: Wayne & Jayne's Catering
Unit 6 Westwood Way
Fenshaw
Lincolnshire
LX34 7YB

Date	Description	Debit	Credit	Balance
				690.00
1 June				762.00
3 June	Invoice No. 00692	72.00		72.00
5 June	Cheque received		690.00	452.00
15 June	Invoice No. 00721	380.00		1,742.00
29 June	Invoice No. 00846	1,290.00		1,142.00
30 June	Cheque received		600.00	1,142.00
30 June	**Closing Balance**			**1,142.00**

Remittance Advice

From: Wines UK Ltd
120–122 Hythe Way
Fenshaw
Lincolnshire
LS28 7HD

Customer Account No.: 90272

Date of Statement: 30 June 2005

Cheque Number ....

Amount Enclosed ....

Date of Payment ....

All cheques made payable to Wines UK Ltd

Figure 3.6 *An example of a statement of account plus remittance slip*

In order to pay Wines UK Limited, Wayne and Jayne just have to tear off the remittance advice and attach it to their cheque.

Documents used in receiving payments

If a business receives payment on delivery of the product or service they will be issued with a receipt. This is proof that payment has been made. Black Horse Catering Ltd will issue its customers with an invoice at the end of the evening and may receive payment before they leave. It would then issue its client with a receipt to acknowledge that payment has been received.

When you pay for an item you will receive a written receipt

Documents used in making payments

There are a number of ways that a business can pay its creditors. The most commonly used one is a cheque. Increasing in popularity is the use of electronic data interchange (EDI). Cash as a method of payment is slowly decreasing in popularity.

ACTIVITY

Use the blank cheque on page 123. Make it out to Wines UK Limited for the amount Wayne and Jayne owe them. Use today's date.

The cheque

A cheque is a safe way of making payments through the post. The person who writes the cheque is known as the drawer and the person to whom the cheque is to be paid is the payee.

Figure 3.7 *An example of a cheque*

The amount to be paid is written in words in the main body of the cheque and in figures in the box on the right-hand side. The cheque is crossed a/c payee. It can only be paid into the bank account of the person to whom it has been made payable.

A business can also make payments to another business via the use of electronic data interchange (EDI). For example, if Wayne and Jayne wanted to pay Wines UK Ltd via EDI, all they have to do is inform their bank of Wines UK Ltd's bank account number and the date they wish the payment to be made. The money would be taken out of Wayne and Jayne's business bank account and transferred to the business account of Wines UK Ltd. This is a very fast and secure way to pay creditors or bills.

Cash can also be used to pay creditors. However, it should not be sent through the post. Due to the high security risk of cash, very few businesses hold large amounts of cash for any length of time. It is therefore not a common method of payment for many businesses.

Wages and salaries

Salaries

A salary is a set amount that a person will be paid over a twelve-month period. The figure will be divided by the twelve months of the year and the employee will receive 12 equal instalments. For example, a Sales Director's salary has been agreed at £36,000 per year. This means that his/her monthly payment before tax and insurance will be £3,000 per month. A salaried employee will get paid the same amount each month regardless of the number of hours worked. They are not usually entitled to overtime payments.

Wages

Payments made to employees who are paid by the number of hours they work are called wages. An employee who receives a wage will usually be paid a fixed amount per hour, for example £6.30, and will work a set number of hours per week known as their basic hours. Any additional hours may be payable at an overtime rate. For example, an employee's rate of pay is £6.50 for a basic working week of 38 hours, overtime is paid at time and a half. If they worked 42 hours how much would they receive?

38 hours at £6.50 = £247.00

4 hours at £9.75 = £39.00

Total wages = £286.00 gross pay.

ACTIVITY

Wayne and Jayne have so many bookings throughout July and August they have decided to take on a student for the summer period. They are going to pay them £5.50 an hour. If they work on a Sunday they will get £6.90 per hour. Calculate the wages for the new employee from the figures supplied:

Week One – 25 hours Monday to Saturday, 6 hours on Sunday

Week Two – 35 hours Monday to Saturday

Week Three – 27 hours Monday to Saturday and 4 hours on Sunday

Week Four – 42 hours which includes 7 on Sunday.

AO7 Financial statements prepared by small businesses

Profit and loss account

The profit and loss account calculates two profits. The **gross profit** is the amount of profit made from trading less the costs directly incurred through trading. For example, a supermarket's gross profit will be calculated by deducting all the purchases it has brought in for resale from the value of its sales. **Net profit** is also known as operating profit and is calculated by deducting all the business's expenses from the gross profit. For example, a supermarket would include all the wages, rent, electricity, stationery and any other expenses it incurs.

Why does a business need to calculate profit?

The owners of a business will use the profit and loss account for the following reasons.

As a measure of profitability

The profitability of a small business is usually calculated on a yearly basis. It provides a measure for the owners of a business. It enables a business to assess if:

- it has made a profit or loss
- if the profit or loss was more or less than last year
- what products/services were most successful.

In order to make plans

Based on the information gained from the compilation of the profit and loss account a business will be able to start making plans for the future. These could include the following:

- is the business making sufficient profit to continue?
- has the business been doing so well that now is the time to expand?
- could the business afford to take on more employees in order to lighten the owner's workload?
- what has been the best selling product or service?
- does the business need to consider developing the products/services they provide in order to retain customers?

In order to borrow from external sources

If at any time a business needs to borrow from external sources, the profit and loss account will form part of the business plan presented to the provider of external funds, for example, the bank. In order to borrow money, a business will usually need to provide copies of previous profit and loss accounts as well as their most current one. This is so that the organisation lending the money can calculate the risk. The external organisation will also be able to look at previous profit and loss accounts to see if there is a trend – is the business experiencing an increase or decrease in profitability?

The tax authorities

It is a legal requirement for all businesses to submit accounts to the Inland Revenue so that an assessment of the tax and national insurance liability can be made.

The type of business ownership and size of turnover will govern what kind of accounts have to be submitted by the owner(s). A very small trader with a turnover, at the time of writing, of less than £15,000 a year does not have to submit formal accounts. Sole traders and partnerships pay income tax. However, limited companies pay corporation tax as they are taxed in their own right as a separate legal entity. Limited companies are required by the Companies Act to submit full accounts to the Inland Revenue.

Balance sheet

The balance sheet is a picture of a business's wealth at a moment in time. It contains the assets and liabilities of the business. The balance sheet will include the following headings:

Fixed assets are items the business owns, for example, buildings, vehicles, machinery and equipment.

Current assets are items and debts due to the business which can be turned into cash relatively quickly. Current assets include stock, debtors (customers who owe the business money for goods/services received), bank and cash.

Current liabilities include creditors (people the business owes money to for goods or services received), and if the company has one – bank overdraft.

Long-term liabilities are loans from a third party which will last longer than one year. For example, a bank loan over 5 years would be classed as a long-term liability.

Capital includes the money that the business was started with and profit that has been accumulated through trading and been retained within the business.

The value of the business can be calculated by using the balance sheet.

Why businesses need to produce balance sheets?

The owners of a business will produce the balance sheet for the following reasons.

A measure of the business's value

The owners can calculate the value of their business by adding up all the assets and subtracting the liabilities. The difference is the value of the business. This can be a useful measure if the owners wanted to sell the business. It gives the owners and potential buyers a value from which a sales price could be negotiated.

In order to make plans

The balance sheet illustrates the **working capital** of the business. This is the difference between the current assets and current liabilities. If a business has more current assets than current liabilities it would have a good working capital ratio. This means that they have sufficient funds available to meet their immediate debts. A business that does not have adequate funds to meet its debts will soon find itself with cash flow problems.

   The balance sheet will help a business identify any problems that they may have. For example, a business may be holding too much stock. Excess stock means the business has money tied up doing nothing. This situation could hinder the business making payments to the suppliers because it has been unable to sell its stock in order to raise the required funds. Once a cash flow problem has been identified the business should be able to start making the necessary changes. Another problem that could be illustrated in the balance sheet is that the business has too many debtors, customers who still owe them money. This could be rectified by the introduction of a credit control system. Somebody in the company would have to take over the responsibility of chasing customers who have not paid their bills within the 30 days allowed.

In order to borrow from external sources

The balance sheet also forms part of the business plan which is presented to external lenders of finance if a loan is being sought. It illustrates if the business has sufficient fixed assets to secure the loan. External sources look at the balance sheet to see how much the fixed assets of the company are worth. If they are worth more than the value of the loan required, the fixed assets can be used as security. For example, if a business wanted to borrow £20,000 and they had buildings worth £120,000, the lender of the loan would be reassured that if the business got into financial trouble they would get their £20,000 back by making the business sell their buildings.

Cash flow forecast

A cash flow forecast predicts the income and expenditure of a business over a set period of time. A cash flow forecast is compiled to identify when a business may experience high or low levels of income and expenditure. A cash flow forecast is a prediction and is only as accurate as the figures that have been used. Most businesses will compare their cash flow forecasts with actual results to see how good their predictions were.

Why does a business need to produce a cash flow forecast?

The owners of a business will produce a cash flow forecast for the following reasons.

As a measure of liquidity

The cash flow will illustrate to a business when they are likely to have cash flow problems. This means that they may have insufficient funds in the bank to meet all the business's required expenditure in a certain month. By identifying possible months where there could be a problem, a business can take the necessary steps to arrange a short-term loan or bank overdraft.

To make future plans

A cash flow forecast can be used to estimate not only sales but when a business can afford to make additional expenditure. The business may wish to purchase a large item of machinery and the cash flow forecast will help them decide which month this could best be afforded. It could also help a business decide whether they have sufficient funds to undertake a large marketing campaign? It could help a business identify areas of high expenditure so that remedial action can be taken.

In order to borrow from external sources

The cash flow forecast is the third financial document that would be presented within the business plan. External financial agencies would be able to see from the cash inflows and outflows whether the business could afford to make the required repayments. For example, if you had approached the bank for a loan which had repayment costs of £200 per month the bank would check the cash flow forecast to see if the business actually had £200 spare every month to meet these repayments.

ACTIVITY

Explain to Megan and Richard the function of a profit and loss account, balance sheet and cash flow forecast.

PORTFOLIO GUIDANCE

Assessment objective 7 is the theory of why small businesses keep financial statements. In order to achieve the higher grades you will have to explain in detail the function of financial statements. To enhance your evidence, this could be directly linked to your own business venture.

The most important decision you make when starting this unit is the type of business venture that you are going to do. It is best to keep it simple and based on a subject which you are familiar with. You will need to undertake some detailed research in order to estimate start-up and running costs. If the quality and accuracy of your research is good it will enable you to calculate break even and profit margins easily. If you are creative, assessment objectives could offer you scope to design some financial documents that could be used within your own business venture. Finally, you will have to understand why businesses have to keep final accounts.

SKILLS CHECK

1. Identify the different types of funding that could be used to launch a new business, stating their advantages and disadvantages.

2. How would you raise the following funds? Outline your reasons.
   (a) Over the next two months your expenditure will be £200 more than your income. However, by the third month you will have sufficient funds to cover all your expenditure.
   (b) You need to raise £25,000 to buy a new piece of machinery which will increase the profit of your factory by at least £8,000/year.
   (c) You are 20, and have been unemployed for the last 18 months. You have just designed a new gadget which will greatly enhance the lives of people with arthritis. All you need is a grant for £5,000 to £8,000 to get the business idea started.

3. What are set-up costs?

4. Why are computers so vital to all businesses – large or small?

5. Explain the different methods businesses can use to estimate sales.

6. What is the difference between fixed and variable costs?

7. What is the formula for break even?

8. How do you calculate profit margin?

9. Why is it vital to keep track of business financial transactions?

10. What is a statement of account?

11. What is the difference between gross and net profit?

12. What is a cash flow forecast?

14. Give the main reasons to produce a profit and loss account.

Blank documents for use with exercises

Sales day book

Date 2005	Customer	Net £	VAT 17.5% £	Total £

Two column cash book

Debit (In)   Credit (Out)

Date 2005	Details	Cash	Bank	Date 20x4	Details	Cash	Bank
1 August	Balance	91.00	4,616.04				

Purchase day book

Date 2005	Customer	Net £	VAT 17.5% £	Total £

Cash flow forecast

	March £	April £	May £
Income			
Sales			
(a) Total Income			
Expenditure			
Purchases			
Motor expenses			
Rent on premises			
Wayne & Jane salary			
General expenses			
(b) Total Expenditure			
Opening Balance	1,375		
(a–b) Inflow/Outflow			
Closing Balance			

Invoice

<table>
<tr>
<td colspan="3" align="center">

Black Horse Catering Ltd

Unit 6 Westwood Way
Fenshaw
Lincolnshire
LX34 7YB

Telephone: 0238 987 564
Email WayneJayne21@aol.com

</td>
</tr>
<tr>
<td colspan="2">

Invoice number:

Date:

</td>
<td>VAT Reg: 0865 8353 9871</td>
</tr>
<tr>
<td>*Address of customer:*</td>
<td colspan="2">To:</td>
</tr>
<tr>
<td>Terms:
30 days net</td>
<td>Net</td>
<td></td>
</tr>
<tr>
<td></td>
<td>VAT</td>
<td></td>
</tr>
<tr>
<td></td>
<td>Total</td>
<td></td>
</tr>
</table>

Statement of account

Finishing Touch Limited   High Street
Fenshaw
Lincolnshire
LS27 5YH

Date:

To:

Date	Description	Debit	Credit	Balance
1 June	Balance			£2,345

Cheque

Date _____	**Kesteven Bank plc**		61-01-48
_____	Main Street		
	Fenshaw LX34 8NN		Date _____
_____	Pay _____	A/C PAYEE ONLY	
_____	_____		£
	_____		For and on behalf of
			BLACK HORSE CATERING LTD
£ _____			Signature _____
000877	Cheque No.	Branch sort code	Account No. Transaction code
	000877	61-01-48	47311605 02

Getting Started

Communication is the process by which information is exchanged between two or more people. We all use communication in our everyday lives and we use many different methods to enable us to do so.

In this unit, you will look at the ways we use to communicate and will concentrate specifically on those used in business, rather than those you use in your everyday lives. However, your knowledge and day-to-day experiences of communication will be very useful.

This unit will cover

- AO1 Produce a variety of different written communications for specific purposes, using appropriate formats and conventions.
- AO2 Use appropriate research methods to obtain information for a specific purpose.
- AO3 Use email for communication purposes.
- AO4 Use a range of verbal communication methods suitable for specific situations.
- AO5 Review the advantages and disadvantages of communication using technology.
- AO6 Analyse the impact of the continuing development of ICT as a tool for communication in business and society.

AO1 Different types of written communication

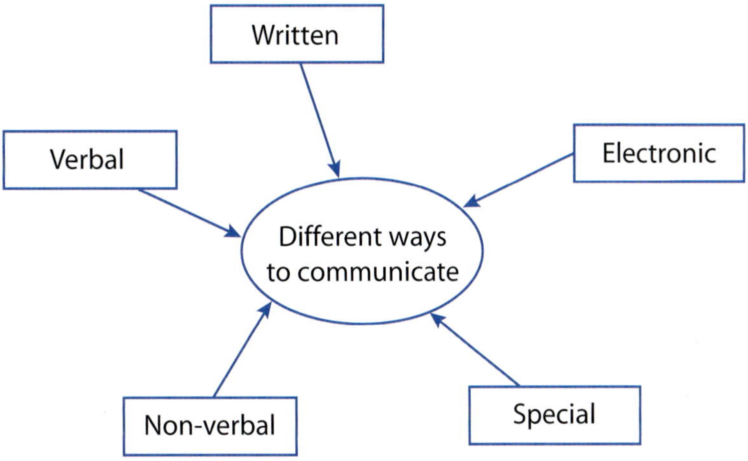

Figure 4.1 *Methods of communication*

Figure 4.1 lists various methods of communication. Think of all the ways you use to communicate with others. How many can you think of?

In your portfolio, you will need to provide evidence of various written documents that you have prepared. We will start by looking at the written communications that are used in business.

Examples of written forms of communication are:

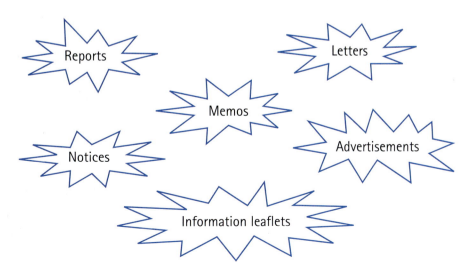

Figure 4.2 *Written forms of communication*

Effective written communication

For communication to be effective, two very important aspects must be considered.

- When composing the communication, you must consider the person you are communicating with. For example, a message to your boss would be very different from one to a friend or colleague. When you write to your boss, the presentation and the tone and language used would be very much more formal than if you were writing to a friend.

- The content of the communication must be correct – the grammar, vocabulary used and spelling must be accurate.

The communication cycle shown below enables us to see how the process works:

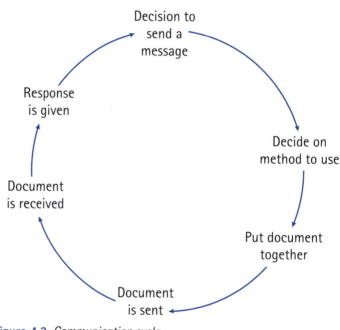

Figure 4.3 *Communication cycle*

Written communication guidelines

You may find these guidelines of help to you when using written communications.

1. Always have a clear aim for writing your message – this will help you to express yourself clearly.

2. Ensure your structure is clear and that you use a logical layout, making it as easy as possible for the reader to understand and follow your message.

3. The style of writing you use must be appropriate for the reader.

Structure of written communication

People who write stories will tell you that a good story should have three qualities:

a beginning

↓

a middle

↓

an end

Figure 4.4 *Structure of written communication*

Written communications are very similar.

Beginning

Start by thinking about something that is already known to the reader. For example, if you are replying to a letter, start the reply by saying something like '*Thank you for your letter of ...*'.

Middle

This is where you present all the information you wish to communicate. Try to ensure you do this in a clear and logical order – put each point of information into a separate paragraph. In a report, paragraphs could be presented as bulleted points if there is a great deal of information to be included.

End

This is where the summing up is presented. You would end a report by including recommendations and conclusions. In a letter or memo, you might wish to add a comment such as that you are looking forward to meeting someone. Some useful phrases which are often used to end a document are:

In conclusion, (report)
I look forward to meeting you. (letter)
Please contact me if you need any further details. (memo)

Presentation of written communications

In this unit we will also look at how different written communications are normally displayed. You should use word-processing software to produce all the documents you prepare for your portfolio. When using a computer, the way we present them is known as **formats and conventions**.

Reports

Reports are used for many different purposes in business; for example to provide information regarding an accident or incident, to detail the findings of research or to give progress of work in hand.

Portfolio tips

- *Find somewhere quiet to compose your communication.*
- *Always use plain English, be courteous and ensure you use the correct tone for the person receiving the communication.*
- *Keep to the point – don't be tempted to stray into discussing other details which are not relevant.*
- *Think about the person who will be reading the report.*

CHARACTERISTICS	STRENGTHS	WEAKNESSES
Have standard layouts used to: • request information • record facts clearly and objectively • interpret information and make conclusions • present suggestions • provide information for making decisions and taking action.	Structured information presented in a standard format Logical sequence Easily recognised by all readers Standard format makes easy reading	If badly prepared can be difficult to understand content

Table 4.1 *Strengths and weaknesses of reports*

The structure of a report should be as follows:

- main heading
- introduction – to inform the reader what the report is about; what information is being provided
- logical sequence for the content – how information was obtained, summarising the information (body of report should be divided into sections with topic headings)
- conclusions
- recommendations
- date report was produced should be included (may be inserted as a footer or added at the end of the text)
- page numbers should be inserted
- index of the report (if required)
- appendices (if required).

Main heading ——————➤	**QUARTERLY REPORT OF THE CHIEF EXECUTIVE**
Topic heading ——————➤	**Introduction**
Introductory ——————➤	I am delighted to be able to report that the Company has had a very
paragraph (possibly	successful three months' trading. This report sets out the new appointments
Terms of Reference)	that have been made, as well as new business that has been achieved and a
	look ahead to the future for our Company.
Topic heading ——————➤	**New Appointments**
Procedure and ——————➤	James Michael Kerry and Suranne Mitchell joined the Company at the
Findings	beginning of the year. James is our new Sales Manager and Suranne our
	new Head of Recruitment. We welcome them.
	–continuation of body of text here–
Conclusion ——————➤	**Conclusion**
	In conclusion, I would like to thank all the directors for their encouragement
	and all our wonderful staff for their hard work and dedication over the past
	few months.
Recommendations ——————➤	I would, therefore, recommend:
Date report produced ➤	[Today's date]
Page numbering ——————➤	1

Figure 4.5 *An example of a report*

ACTIVITY

1   Draft a short report outlining what you hope to achieve after your studies
    are complete. Explain in your report how your studies will help you in your
    future career. Ensure you set out your report in the correct format and use
    normal conventions as detailed above. Print a copy and save.

2   On completion of your report, read it through and answer these questions:
    a) Does the report show that it was planned carefully before writing?
    b) Does the introduction explain the subject and purpose of the report?
    c) Does the layout of the report make sense?
    d) Are the items in the report in the order of importance?
    e) Has all the important information been included?
    f) Is there any unnecessary information?
    g) Could the report have benefited from diagrams, drawings or
        illustrations?
    h) Does the report do what it was intended to do?

3   When you have answered these questions, recall your report and amend as
    necessary. Print a copy and save.

Portfolio tip

In your portfolio, you should include an example of a short report and this should be displayed on plain A4 paper. Correct formats and conventions will be required and you will need to take these into consideration when planning your report.

Memos

Memos are informal notes that are normally used by people within a business to communicate with each other. Memo is the shortened form of the word memorandum.

CHARACTERISTICS	STRENGTHS	WEAKNESSES
Have standard layouts including today's date	There is always a written record	Need to be delivered by someone
Less formal than a letter	An efficient and easy method of communication within a business	Slower than emails
No address, salutation, or complimentary close		
Informal language used		
Usually not signed, but can be initialled		
Used to request or to provide information		
May also be used to give an instruction		

Table 4.2 *Strengths and weaknesses of memos*

MEMO

TO	Natasha Simpson
FROM	Lawrence Adebayo
REF	LA/499
DATE	[Today's date]

Memo headings {TO, FROM, REF, DATE}

Subject heading → NEW STAFF

Body of memo, using single line spacing for paragraphs →

Further to our discussions last week, I would be grateful if you could devise an induction course for the staff due to start work with us on the 1st of next month.

I enclose a copy of the training materials that Roni put together before she left the company. These may be of use to you.

Enclosure → Enc

Figure 4.6 *An example of a memo*

ACTIVITY

1 Using a word processor, key in the memo headings (To, From, Date, Ref). Save as temp.mem so that you can use this template again.

2 Recall the file temp.mem and key in the memo below. Ensure you use the correct layout – as shown on the previous page. Print a copy and use Save As to store your memo, ensuring that you can use the memo template again.

> To Head of Year   From Year 11 students   Subject Canteen facilities
>
> We held a meeting of all Year 11 students today. The purpose of our meeting was to discuss the facilities provided by the canteen and ways in which these could be improved.
>
> We are holding a meeting in Room 49 on Wednesday of next week and would be grateful if you could attend. Please could you let us know when you will be available during that day.

3 Using the memo template, file temp.mem, send a memo to your tutor explaining the main differences between a memo and a letter. Print a copy and use Save As.

Letters

Letters are probably the most widely used form of business communication. Businesses use letters to communicate, usually externally with another business but occasionally also to communicate with employees, such as in disciplinary matters where privacy and confidentiality is vital.

CHARACTERISTICS	STRENGTHS	WEAKNESSES
Produced on printed letterheading	There is always a written record	Cost of overheads (lighting, heating, computers etc.)
Have standard layouts including today's date	Can easily be filed for future reference	Cost of executive's time
Portray a company's image		Cost of word-processor operator's time
Formal language used		Cost of mailroom staff
Used to		Cost of postage
● request or to provide information		
● provide a reference or offer a job		
● to make or respond to a complaint		
● attract potential customers or participants.		

Table 4.3 *Strengths and weaknesses of letters*

Portfolio tip

In your portfolio, you should include an example of a letter, using correct formats and conventions. Any letters that you produce should be displayed on letterheaded paper. You may use a pre-printed letterheading or you may prefer to use a template. An opportunity to prepare your centre's letterheading is given in the text – you will be able to save this and use it again and again. You would normally include your name in the complimentary close and sign the letter yourself.

Letterheading	**COOMBE FLOWERS BY POST** PO Box 2244 Guernsey Channel Islands TEL: 01481 963104 FAX. 01481 963105
Reference →	Our ref AC/203
Date →	[Today's date – day, month, year]
Name and address of person receiving letter (addressee) →	Mr K M Partridge 151 Fore Street TORQUAY Devon TQ12 4SS
Salutation →	Dear Mr Partridge
Subject heading →	YOUR ORDER NO 203
Body of letter – using single line spacing for paragraphs →	Thank you for your order and cheque for £34.50 received this morning. We are delighted to inform you that your order will be despatched by first class post today. As requested, I am enclosing a copy of our latest brochure. Please let me know if I can be of any further help to you.
Complimentary close (space for signature) →	Yours sincerely
Name of writer → *Job title* →	Arabella Coombes *Partner*
Enclosure →	Enc

Figure 4.7 *An example of a business letter*

ACTIVITY

1   Using a word processor, prepare your centre's letterheading. Be sure you include the details given below. Use any font styles/sizes and any other features you would like to include, such as clip art etc. Save your letterheading as a temp.let so that you can use it again.

Name of centre

Full address

(including postcode)

Telephone number

Fax number

Email address (if appropriate)

Website address (if appropriate)

2   Recall the file stored as temp.let (the letterheading you have just prepared). Key in the letter given below, displaying it in the style shown on the previous page of this Unit. Use Save As to store the letter, using a suitable file name. Use of Save As will also ensure you can use the letter heading again.

> Letter to: Mrs Rajinder Siraj   Chief Executive
> Siraj Products PLC   229 Port Street EXETER
> EX1 2PZ   Use Our ref JM/Kmp Subject Heading:
> New Contract
>
> Dear Mrs Siraj
> Thank you for your fax received today.   I am
> enclosing our new colour brochure, as well as a list
> of our charges.
>
> If you would like to visit our premises and see the
> cars we use, I would be very happy to arrange
> this.
>
> Yours sincerely
>
> James Matthews
>
> Owner

Notices

Notices come in all shapes and sizes. They are used to display information and can be seen on noticeboards in shops, offices and a wide range of venues such as company display boards, canteens, community halls, police stations, pubs, nightclubs, libraries and local shops etc.

CHARACTERISTICS	STRENGTHS	WEAKNESSES
Used to catch people's attention	Colour fonts can be used to very good effect	May take time to design and produce, depending on complexity
Usually no larger than one sheet of A4 paper	Clever use of coloured and stylised paper (such as embossed) can be very effective	Limited in scope by size of paper
Varied styles and formats may be used	An easy way to communicate a message to many people	
Information must be displayed clearly	Fairly inexpensive way to get the message across	
Imaginative use of fonts styles/sizes and word art, drawings, clip art etc.		
Used to provide information		
Used to attract potential customers or participants		
The date the notice was first displayed is usually inserted (as a footer using a small font size)		

Table 4.4 *Strengths and weaknesses of notices*

Portfolio tip

In your portfolio, you should include an example of a notice, in which you should display the text with as much variety of emphasis as you can, such as font styles/sizes; word art; colour; pictures (clip art), etc. You should try to ensure that the notice fits onto one sheet of A4 paper.

THE SPECTACULAR SHAOLIN MONKS

WILL BE VISITING YOUR AREA NEXT MONTH

Shaolin Kung Fu and Tai Chi Show

Various Dates, Times and Venues

All shows start at 7.15 pm

TICKETS FROM £4.00

(reduced prices for senior citizens and children)

WATCH OUT FOR MORE INFORMATION IN YOUR LOCAL PRESS

Figure 4.8 *An example of a notice*

ACTIVITY

Using a word processor, prepare a notice of a sports event (or similar) in your area. Ensure you keep the information on one sheet of A4 paper. Use your imagination to conjure up a colourful notice which will attract attention. Print a copy and save.

Leaflets

These may be information or promotional leaflets. Both types are used to display information – to tell people about a product, service or similar. Leaflets can be simple one-sided, or 2-sided, or more complex 2- or 3-tier. A simple one-sided A4 leaflet will be sufficient for your portfolio.

CHARACTERISTICS	STRENGTHS	WEAKNESSES
Used to inform people of a product or service or similar	Colour fonts can be used very effectively	May take time to design and produce, depending on complexity
May be limited to one sheet of paper, but often reverse of sheet(s) are also used and folded to make booklet	Clever use of coloured and also stylised paper (such as embossed paper) can be very effective	
May be produced as an A4 landscape brochure, with detail on all sides as a folder	An easy way to communicate a message to many people	
Varied styles and formats may be used	Cheap to produce	
Imaginative use of fonts styles/sizes and word art, drawings, clip art etc.	Are often distributed as inserts in magazines, newspapers etc.	
Used to attract potential customers or participants		

Table 4.5 *Strengths and weaknesses of leaflets*

GINSENG
CHINESE TAKEAWAY

163 Main Street
Exeter

All meals can be ordered by telephone

01392 176176

FREE HOME DELIVERY
(within a 3-mile radius
minimum order £7.00)

OPENING HOURS

Sunday to Thursday: 5.00-10.30 pm
Friday and Saturday: 5.00-11.00 pm

7 days a week including
Bank Holidays

Figure 4.9 *An example of a leaflet*

ACTIVITY

Using a word processor, prepare an information or promotional leaflet for an event for a community organisation in your area. Remember to include all the details required, such as date, time, venue etc. and contact details (name, and telephone number etc). Print a copy and save.

Advertisements

Wherever you go, you will see plenty of examples of advertisements. They may be straightforward informative adverts in a local newspaper , a small advert in the corner shop selling an unwanted gift or a business advertising a job vacancy.

Portfolio tip

In your portfolio, you should include an example of an advertisement. Display your advertisement so that it attracts attention – use word art, colour, different font styles and sizes and pictures (clip art) etc. You should try to ensure that the advert fits onto one sheet of A4 paper.

CHARACTERISTICS	STRENGTHS	WEAKNESSES
Used to inform people of a product or service or similar	Colour fonts and paper can be used very effectively	May take time to design and produce, depending on complexity
May be very short but should be no more than one side of A4 paper	Display is crucial – to ensure advert is eye-catching	
Care is needed to ensure information is correct and not misleading in any way	An easy way to communicate a message to many people	
Varied styles and formats may be used	Fairly inexpensive to produce	
Imaginative use of font styles/sizes and word art, drawings, clip art etc.	Can be used in a variety of ways, such as newspapers, noticeboards etc.	
Used to attract potential customers or participants		

Table 4.6 *Strengths and weaknesses of advertisements*

FOR SALE
FORD SIERRA COSWORTH 4 × 4
K Reg

75,000 miles
Full service history
All the usual Cosworth refinements including:
Leather interior, Radio & CD player
Electric windows, sunroof and mirrors

£4,250 *ono*

TELEPHONE 01626 142334

Figure 4.10 *An example of an advertisement*

ACTIVITY

Using a word processor, prepare an advertisement selling a PlayStation 2 (or similar item). Ensure you include all the details that a prospective buyer would want to know in order to be tempted to buy. Print a copy and save.

Portfolio tip

In order to provide the evidence required in your portfolio for this assessment objective, you will need to produce a variety of different written communications for specific purposes.

The formats and conventions adopted (such as layout, language and fonts) should be appropriate for the purpose for which they will be used, such as requesting and providing information, giving instruction or attracting potential customers or participants.

AO2 Appropriate research methods to obtain information

In our everyday lives, we often carry out research in one form or another. For example, when you decide to go to see a film at the local cinema you need to find out at what time it is showing and when.

The main methods of research that we will be looking at in this unit are:

- Internet searches and website navigation
- verbal questioning/interviewing
- surveys and questionnaires
- paper-based reference materials

In your portfolio, you should provide evidence of research you have carried out to find out some specific information. This entails three stages:

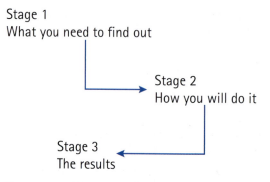

Stage 1
What you need to find out

Stage 2
How you will do it

Stage 3
The results

Figure 4.11 *The stages of research*

You will need to carry out research using a particular source, such as the Internet, and you will need to use other sources for your research, such as textbooks, questioning, surveys etc. When you have thought about exactly what you are searching for and the source you will use, you then need to consider how you will use the information you find in your searches. For example, you could include the information in a document such as a report, memo, or letter or you may list the website addresses you have visited and a summary of the information you found. Whatever information you need, you must be sure that you follow the process step-by-step.

You may be able to find some of the information in your classroom e.g. books, textbooks, reference books, timetables, Yellow Pages, CD-ROMs, magazines, newspapers, journals, leaflets, brochures, catalogues etc. You may be able to use the Internet in your centre. However, it may be necessary for you to go outside the classroom to find reference resources and your local library is sure to be able to help you.

Internet searches and website navigation

The **Internet** is an extremely valuable source of information. It is a worldwide system of networks linking millions of computers which is why it is also called the **World Wide Web**. Using the World Wide Web is known as **website navigation**.

The World Wide Web contains a very large number of locations called **websites**. These provide information about a company or organisation or on a subject or topic and contain photographs, images, text, graphics etc. Websites are located on computers in schools, colleges, homes, offices and a multitude of places all over the world. The computers are linked by telephone lines and/or optical cables. Many people spend time searching the World Wide Web and this is often known as **surfing** the web and browsing websites.

Figure 4.12 *Internet research*

To explore the World Wide Web you need to use a **browser**. This is an application that is designed to enable you to look at websites. There are several browsers that you can use. Well-known browsers include Microsoft's Internet Explorer and Netscape. However, there are others including those especially designed for people with disabilities, such as the visually impaired.

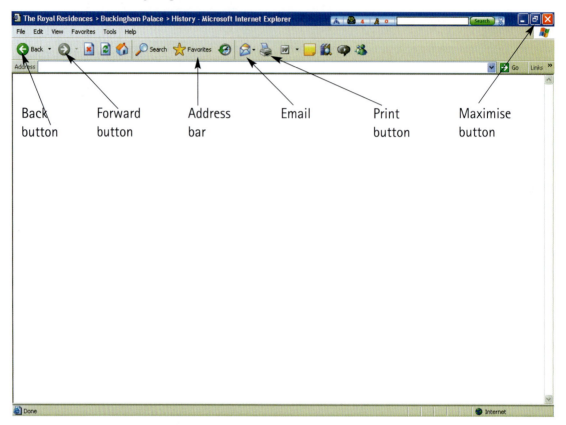

Figure 4.13 *Using Microsoft's Internet Explorer browser*

If you intend to use computers at your training centre, your tutor will be able to tell you how to go about this, but if you are intending to browse on your home computer, you will need to subscribe to an **Internet Service Provider** (ISP) and to have a modem and connection via a telephone line. Once you are connected, you can load the browser and you are then ready to start.

An Internet service provider is a company that provides connections to the Internet.

Structure of a website

A website consists of various pages and these are linked so that you may go from page to page easily. Links may be underlined words or buttons (often called hover buttons, control buttons or hot spots).

When you pass the mouse pointer over a link, it changes its appearance. If you then click on the link, you will move to another page within that website.

Website navigation

If you know the website of the organisation or company you wish to look at you can simply type the website address. For example, the website address for a well-known bookseller, Amazon, is **www.amazon.co.uk** Try this now.

1. Ensure you are connected to the Internet by clicking on the browser on the desktop (be sure to ask your tutor for guidance if you are not sure).

2. The browser may fill the entire screen but it is more likely that it will appear as a small window. You can expand the window by clicking on the maximise button at the top right-hand corner of the window – see Figure 4.13

3. On the address bar (see Figure 4.13), key in www.amazon.co.uk

4. Press the **Enter** key.

5. The **home page** for Amazon's website should now appear. The home page is the introductory, welcome page which then links to other pages.

6. Click on one of the links – this will take you to information concerning that topic.

7. To go back to the home page, you can either click on **home page** or you may click on the **Back** button (see Figure 4.13).

8. Click on the **Forward** button – it will take you forward again (see Figure 4.13).

9. Explore the site by clicking on different hyperlinks and then clicking on the Back and Forward buttons.

Internet searches

If you are not certain of the exact details of a website address, you can use a **search engine** to help you find what you are looking for. There are many search engines but the most popular are:

AltaVista   = www.altavista.com
Ask Jeeves = www.ask.co.uk
Google   = www.google.co.uk
Lycos   = www.lycos.co.uk
Yahoo   = www.yahoo.com

Some search engines are UK-based and some are American. If you are looking for something that is based in the UK, it is easier to use a UK search engine. These are easily recognised by the **UK** part of the website. A website ending with **.com** is usually an American **com**pany.

Try searching now: we will search the Internet for the Buckingham Palace website.

1. Ensure you are connected to the Internet.

2. Key in the website address of one of the search engines, for example www.ask.co.uk

Did you know?

Be very careful that you enter website addresses accurately as any errors in keying may result in an error message and you will not gain access to the website you are looking for.

3. Press **Enter**.

4. The Ask Jeeves website should now appear.

5. The cursor should already be positioned in the **Search** box.

6. Key in **buckingham palace** (capitals not necessary).

7. Click **UK web results** (this ensures you restrict your search to the UK only).

8. The screen will change while the search is being carried out.

9. On the new screen, a list of websites will appear: click on 'The Royal Residences – Buckingham Palace'

10. The Buckingham Palace website should now appear and you should be able to see a photograph of the Palace.

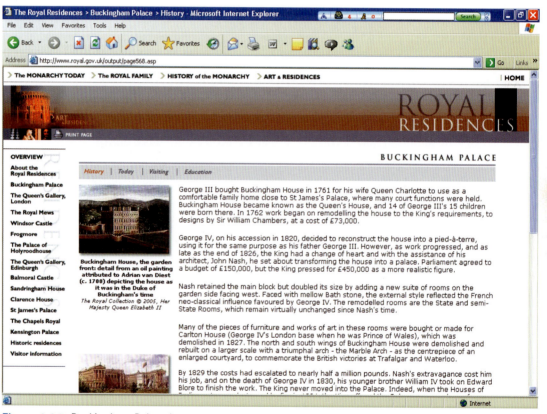

Figure 4.14 *Buckingham Palace home page*

Now search the Palace website for some information on its history:

1. Click the hyperlink **History**

2. The screen should change again and some information regarding the history of the Palace should appear:

Portfolio tip

In your portfolio, you will need to produce evidence of the searches you have made, with the results. You may list the website addresses of the websites you visited or you may print a page of a website.

CASE STUDY

Pia's Pizzas

Pia Piaggio has been running Pia's Pizzas in your town centre for over five years. At present, Pia's is a restaurant that seats 22, the majority of the customers being young people and families. She prides herself on the quality of the food she serves. Everything is home-made on the premises and she has built up an excellent reputation. People come quite long distances and repeat trade is high. However, competition in recent months has become much stronger, with the opening of a fish and chip shop and two curry houses in the same street. Pia's takings are down and she is considering what she can do to improve business.

Pia is considering offering a takeaway service. The town is large and there are many people living in the suburbs and nearby small villages. Pia feels she has the kitchen space and might have to consider taking on more kitchen staff, but otherwise she doesn't think she would have difficulty in handling the extra work a takeaway would involve. At present, all her staff are young, mostly students who work part-time.

Pia intends to offer free delivery within a five-mile radius of the restaurant to start with. She can then see how successful that is before she decides whether she could charge for delivery. She thinks it would be a good idea to employ young people to deliver the pizzas. She wants to buy or lease three scooters no bigger than 50 cc, painted in the same bright red colour she uses for her business.

In order for her to be sure of the legal requirements, Pia has asked you to research the rules and regulations regarding learners riding scooters.

1 Using the Internet, research the laws relating to the riding of 50 cc scooters by learners – you should bear in mind that government departments often refer to scooters as mopeds.

2 You should find out the following information:
    – What is the minimum age for a person to ride a scooter?
    – What test or tests must be passed before a person can ride a scooter on a road?

3 On completion of your research, prepare an information leaflet for Pia, giving the results of your research.

4 You should also attach a list of the website addresses of the websites you visited during your research and the information you found. This could be presented in a simple table with headings such as:

Websites visited	Brief summary of information found

Verbal questioning/interviewing

When one person asks another person questions face-to-face, this is called an **interview**. During that interview, the person will use questions to find out the information he or she requires. Interviews, however, may involve more than two people, such as an interview panel when several people may interview one person in order to fill a job vacancy.

An interview in process

You have probably seen people with clipboards in shopping malls questioning others. Companies often use this method to find out what people like or don't like about their products. The person conducting the interview will have been given specific questions to ask in order to get the views of the people being interviewed.

Questioning and interview techniques

In your portfolio, you will need to include evidence of research you have done by interviewing one or more people in order to find out some specific information.

Step 1
Before you start an interview, think carefully about the questions you need to ask in order to obtain the information you are looking for.

Step 2
Carry out the interview – be sure that you listen carefully to what is being said and accurately record responses.

Step 3
Once you have carried out your interview, asked your questions and recorded your responses, you need to think about how you will produce the results of your interview.

Example of an interview/questioning
You are going to interview a colleague who uses your centre's library. The aim of the interview is to find out:
- what he/she likes about the library
- what he/she does not like about the library
- one change he/she would like to see.

Think about the questions you would ask and have some paper handy, with a clipboard, if possible, to record the responses. You will find it easier to have word-processed questions – leave plenty of space for you to record the responses. You can then simply write down the answers to your questions as your colleague answers.

You may need to ask the permission of the librarian or other person in charge before you start the interview. Ask your tutor for help with this.

If your centre does not have a library, you may wish to consider using your local library. You must, however, ask your tutor for permission before you leave the building and you may need to ask the Chief Librarian for permission before you start.

The questions could include:
- How long have you been using the library?
- What would you say are your main reasons for using it?
- What other resources in the library do you use?
- What aspect of the library do you particularly like and use regularly?
- What aspect don't you like?
- What one change would you like to see made to the library, such as more books, computer use etc?

The next stage is to consider how to produce the results of the interview. In your portfolio, you should include the results of your interview in a word-processed letter or memo (or you may decide another document may be more suitable, such as a leaflet).

Prepare a memo to your tutor including the results of your interview.

Your mum is finding it difficult to remember appointments and family birthdays and anniversaries. She has heard about electronic diaries and has asked you to find out about them. She wants to spend no more than £35. Ask colleagues or staff at your centre in order to find someone who uses an electronic diary. Conduct an interview with that person to help you find out everything possible about electronic diaries. Prepare and produce a notice for your mum, with all the relevant information she needs to help her decide whether or not to buy an electronic diary.

Surveys and questionnaires

A **survey** is similar to an interview in that it is used to find out information needed from people. Surveys, however, are usually conducted using several people, rather than one or two as with an interview.

Whether you decide to use a **questionnaire** will largely depend on where you will be conducting the survey. It may be more appropriate in some circumstances to question people and record their responses yourself. For example, people in a restaurant or pub would probably not be willing to complete a questionnaire. However, if you conduct a survey of people at work, they would be able to sit down and would be more likely to complete the questionnaire themselves (or to take it away to complete it). A logical step-by-step process should be followed:

Step 1
What you want to learn

↓

Step 2
Who you will survey and where it will be conducted

↓

Step 3
How you will conduct the survey

↓

Step 4
Create a questionnaire (if appropriate)

↓

Step 5
Pre-test the questionnaire and amend if appropriate

↓

Step 6
Conduct the survey – record responses or get people to complete the questionnaire

↓

Step 7
Analyse the data and produce a report or similar with the analysis

Figure 4.15 *Step-by-step procedure for conducting surveys*

Example of a survey/questionnaire

You are on work placement, helping Mrs Marina Ambrose, the Catering Manager at Bradbury Products. She has asked you to conduct a survey of ten people to find out if they are satisfied with the canteen facilities and quality of food served. She would like some comments from customers on changes and improvements they would like to see (you may wish to use your centre's canteen in order to carry out this survey). Prepare and produce a word-processed questionnaire to use in your survey. An example of how the questionnaire could look is shown below:

QUESTIONNAIRE

Canteen Facilities at (Bradbury Products)

1. Name (optional) _____

2. How long have you been using this canteen? _____

3. How would you rate the facilities? (tick one of the following options)
   - ❑ Excellent
   - ❑ Good
   - ❑ Fair
   - ❑ Poor

4. How would you rate the food? (tick one of the following options)
   - ❑ Excellent
   - ❑ Good
   - ❑ Fair
   - ❑ Poor

5. What changes would you recommend to improve the facilities? _____

   _____

   _____

6. Is there any food and/or drink you would like to be able to purchase that is not available at present?

   _____

   _____

   _____

Signed: _____   Date: _____

Figure 4.16 *An example of a questionnaire*

On completion of the survey, prepare and produce a short report for your tutor (acting as Mrs Ambrose) giving her the results of the survey. Save the report on a floppy disk (if possible) and use the file name Survey.1 (this is very important, as you will need easy access to this file later in this unit).

Steps 1 and 2

You need to survey 10 people who use the canteen at your centre (Bradbury Products) to find out whether or not they are satisfied with the facilities (the service, furniture, equipment etc), as well as the food and drinks served, and changes and improvements they would like to see.

Steps 3 and 4

You will use a survey and will compile a questionnaire.

Step 4

Compile the questionnaire – think about what should be included in this.

Step 5

Before you use it for real, test the questionnaire – ask a colleague to complete it for you. Depending on how easy or difficult it was to complete, you may wish to amend the questionnaire before printing the number of copies you will need (approximately 10 to 15).

Step 6

Although you have been asked to conduct the survey, before you start you should inform your tutor (acting as Mrs Ambrose) of the date and time you propose to do it.

Step 7

Analyse the results. You may do this in a number of ways. You may wish to use charts or graphs or to simply present the findings in a word-processed document.

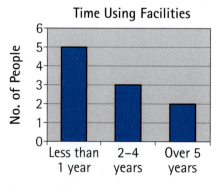

Figure 4.17 *Research results 1*

Figure 4.18 *Research results 2*

Figure 4.19 *Research results 3*

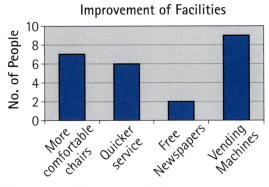

Figure 4.20 *Research results 4*

FOOD/DRINK PEOPLE WOULD LIKE TO BE ABLE TO PURCHASE

9 people   more hot drinks, such as chocolate, cappuccino

8 people   more variety in food available, such as curries, Mexican food

7 people   more fresh fruit and vegetables

4 people   better selection of salads, especially in hot weather

Figure 4.21 *Research results 5*

Finally, prepare and produce a report for your tutor (Mrs Ambrose) including the results of your survey (see Figure 4.22). Use appropriate software, formats and conventions in your report. You should attach a copy of the questionnaire you prepared for the survey to the report.

REPORT ON CANTEEN FACILITIES (AT BRADBURY PRODUCTS)

Introduction

A survey of 10 people was carried out on Wednesday and Thursday of last week (insert actual dates of survey). All the people surveyed were those who said they regularly used the canteen facilities at Bradbury Products.

Survey

A questionnaire was compiled and this is attached. People in the survey were asked how long they had used the canteen, how they rated the facilities (furniture, service, utensils, etc.) and how they rated the food (hot and cold including drinks). They were also asked to recommend any improvements that could be made to the facilities and to indicate any food or drink they would like to be able to buy that is not available at present.

Results of survey

The results of the survey were produced as charts and these are attached.

They show that 5 people surveyed had been using the canteen for less than 1 year, 3 for 2 to 4 years and 2 for over 5 years.

Rating of the facilities was 3 excellent, 5 good, 1 fair, and 1 poor.

Rating of the food served was 2 excellent, 4 good, 3 fair and 1 poor.

Five of the people surveyed said they would like the service to be quicker, 7 said the chairs should be more comfortable, 2 would like free newspapers and 9 would like vending machines.

Conclusions

Most of the people surveyed seemed happy with the facilities, although all complained that the chairs were not comfortable and the 5 females surveyed said the edges of the chairs were very rough and they frequently damaged their clothes. All agreed that the service was too slow, especially at the busy lunch time. Of those surveyed, 9 said they would like vending machines and 2 would like free newspapers.

Recommendations

Facilities

1. The chairs in the canteen should be examined and perhaps the carpenter could do something to make the edges less rough. This might be a cheaper option than replacing all the chairs.

2. Perhaps consideration could be given to staggering the lunch time. Instead of everyone having 12.30 to 1.30 for lunch, some could go at 12.15 and others at 12.45. This would ensure that people are served quicker and their food would therefore be hotter.

3. Free newspapers would not be so easy as there are so many and everyone has different tastes. Also, people might walk off with them so it would be difficult to ensure they are available all day.

4. Consideration could be given to installing one vending machine with a variety of snacks, sweets and cold drinks. People would, then, still have access to different foods and drinks when the canteen closes at 2.30 pm. If it is successful, perhaps another vending machine giving hot drinks could be considered.

Food and drink served

1. It might be possible to have special food days. Perhaps once a month the canteen could serve food from a specific country in the world, such as Italian, Indian, Mexican etc. A suggestion box could be situated near the door to the canteen for people to suggest foods they would like to eat, or to sample.

2. The provision of a drinks vending machine might be cheaper than providing a large variety of hot drinks which have to be served by staff. People could help themselves, whether the canteen was open or not. The company could consider providing these free of charge, or make a small charge.

3. At present, the canteen only provides hot food. This might be because there are no refrigeration facilities to store salads etc. In hot weather, salads are very popular but the provision of facilities to cater for these might be too expensive.

4. To enable people to buy fresh fruit and vegetables, these could be displayed in baskets next to the till.

(Date report produced)

Figure 4.22 *Report of research results*

ACTIVITY

Working in groups of 3, survey 8 to 10 people to find out what gym they use. You want to find one or two local gyms that cater for people of all ages and provide a wide range of cardiovascular and weight-training equipment. You should prepare a short questionnaire to enable you to carry out the survey.

On completion, produce a notice displaying all the information you think is essential for one of the gyms. Use appropriate software, formats and conventions in your notice.

Paper-based reference materials

These may be:

- textbooks
- newspapers and magazines
- journals
- leaflets, brochures, catalogues (including CD-ROMs)
- reference materials such as timetables, directories etc. and other books

Paper-based reference materials

Although the Internet is widely used and gives access to a great deal of information to a large number of people all over the world, the largest amount of information to be obtained is still held on paper. There are so many sources of paper-based reference materials that can be used that it is only possible here to include the major ones. You may also have access to guides and information pamphlets available in your area that deal with local issues such as tourist information, history, street maps, museums etc.

Textbooks, magazines, newspapers, journals

A variety of textbooks may be available to you which will give advice, guidance and information on a wide range of subjects.

Many businesses and organisations issue a large range of magazines, journals, booklets and information factsheets. These include:

- the Royal Mail
- government departments such as the Department of Trade and Industry and Inland Revenue
- financial institutions such as banks.

The 'quality' newspapers, such as *The Times*, the *Daily Telegraph* and the *Guardian* include information as well as articles on business and finance that may be useful in your studies.

Leaflets, brochures and catalogues

Company leaflets, brochures and catalogues

Suppliers use brochures and catalogues to tempt people into buying their goods or to use their services. They are often very colourful and extremely detailed.

You may be able to pick up various leaflets, brochures and catalogues of products in shops and stores. These are very useful for giving up-to-date information, especially with regard to electronic items, which can change so quickly as technology develops.

Books, reference books, timetables

There are so many of these that it would need a very large room indeed to house them all. Libraries enable access to a wide range of these and training centres will have some to help in your studies such as Yellow Pages, directories, dictionaries, thesauruses, road maps, street plans, restaurant and hotel guides, information about local tourist attractions etc.

Real business

In order to provide the evidence required in your portfolio for assessment objective 2, you will need to display excellent research ability and you should include each research method used e.g. Internet searches, surveys and paper-based reference materials.

ACTIVITY

Working in pairs, use a variety of paper-based reference sources to find out the following information:

- the telephone number of the local Citizens Advice Bureau
- the full name, address and postcode of your local council
- the difference between the word 'complimentary' and the word 'complementary', giving one example of each word in a sentence.

On completion, you should work together to prepare and produce a memo displaying the results of your research. You should use appropriate software, formats and conventions.

AO3 Use email for communication purposes

We have looked at written communication – now we will look at electronic communication. In this assessment objective, you will:

- create and edit email messages
- send and receive email messages
- send attachments to email messages.

You will need access to an email application if you have not used email before. To enable you to send an email you must be connected to the Internet. Ask your tutor for details of how to access an email system for your studies. For the purposes of this assessment objective, we will use Microsoft Outlook Express. However, if you do not have access to this particular system, any email system may be used so long as it enables you to receive, create, edit and send messages and also send attachments to email messages.

Folders are used to store different items – the ones you will be concerned with are:

- Inbox – this folder stores an email that has been received.
- Sent Items – this is where all your emails that have been sent are stored.
- Drafts – this folder is very useful for storing messages that are not yet ready for sending.

Before you start, you also need to ask your tutor for details of the email address that you may use for your studies. You will need to know to whom you should send messages and from whom you will receive messages. For example, it may be possible for you to send messages to another student (or to a work colleague), or to your tutor and to receive messages from them.

Create and send an email message

1. Click on the Outlook Express icon (or ask your tutor for guidance on gaining access to email if your system is different).
2. Ensure you are connected to the Internet.
3. Click on the **Create Mail** button on the toolbar.
4. On this screen, you should be able to see your email address in the **From** box
5. The cursor should be in the **To** box.
6. Key in the address of your colleague in the space in the **To** box. Be very careful to enter the email address accurately. If it is not absolutely accurate, the email will not be delivered.
7. Move the cursor to the **Subject** box and key in the words: First email
8. Move the cursor to the **message area**.
9. Key in the following message:
   This is the first time I have sent an email message. Please would you reply so that I know it all works and I can see what happens when I receive a reply.
   Many thanks
   (your name here)
10. Check to see if you have made any mistakes. Use the spellchecker to help you. Correct any errors, using the delete key and mouse etc. (in the same way as you would on a word-processing program).
11. Double-check that the email address is absolutely accurate.
12. When you're happy that everything is accurate, click on the **Send** button.
13. Now check that the email has been sent by clicking on the **Sent Items** folder – you should see the email address listed of the person to whom you sent the email.

Your message should look something like Figure 4.23.

Figure 4.23 *An email message*

Receiving emails

1. When you open Outlook Express, any emails that have been sent to you by other people will appear in your Inbox.

2. The list of messages displayed will give you details of who the message is from, the subject and date and time it was sent.

3. In the previous activity, you sent an email to your tutor and asked for a reply. The reply should be listed in your Inbox.

Creating, saving and editing email messages

One of the major disadvantages of using email is that you may send a message to someone before you have really thought it through and, once sent, it cannot be retrieved. It is possible to create an email and save it so that you can look at it carefully and edit it before sending. To do this:

1. Ensure you are connected to the Internet.

2. Click on the **Create Mail** button on the toolbar.

3. The cursor should be in the **To** box.

4. Key in the email address of a colleague or friend in the space in the **To** box.

5. Move the cursor to the **Subject** box and key in these words:
   Opening Hours of the Motor Museum

6. Move the mouse pointer to the **message area**.

7. Key in the following message:
   The opening times of the Motor Museum are 8.30 am to 7.30 pm every day.
   (your name here)

8. Check to see if you have made any mistakes – use the Spellchecker to help you. Correct any errors you may find.

9. Click **File**.

10. Click **Save**.

11. Click on the X at the top right-hand corner of your screen to remove the message from your screen.

12. Now move the mouse pointer to the **Drafts** folder and click on Drafts.

13. The email should be in this folder.

14. You have now been told that the opening times have been changed. Double-click on the message in the Drafts folder, maximise the screen and edit the message as follows:
    Change 8.30 to 9.45 and 7.30 to 6.30 pm and add these words at the end of the message:
    except Christmas Day and New Year's Day.

15. Check that your name is still visible and that you have made no errors.

16. Click **File** and then click **Save** to save it to your **Drafts** folder.

17. Your message should look like this:

    The opening times of the Motor Museum are 9.45 am to 6.30 pm every day except Christmas Day and New Year's Day.
    Your name here

18. Right-click on your message in the Drafts folder and select **print**. The Print menu will appear – click **Print**.

19. Check again that your message is accurate. When you are sure that it is, click **Send**.

ACTIVITY

- Prepare an email to a colleague. Inform him or her that the opening ceremony for the new nightclub in town will take place on Wednesday of next week at 9.30 pm. Insert your name at the end of the message.
- Save this message to your Drafts folder.
- Print a copy of the message.
- You've just heard that the ceremony has been moved to another day. Amend the message that the ceremony is now to be held on Friday of next week at 10.00 pm. Ask your colleague to reply to ensure that he or she has received it.
- Check and amend any errors, then print a copy of the amended message.
- Check again for errors, then send the email.
- Receive the reply and print it.

Send attachments to email messages

Email messages are usually fairly short. However, it is very easy to send a lot of information by email by using attachments. The attachment facility enables you to attach other documents such as reports, images, photographs, maps, spreadsheets, graphs etc.

Example of a file attachment

Mrs Marina Ambrose, Catering Manager for Bradbury Products, has told you that, unfortunately, she cannot find the report you produced for her (see page 150). She has asked you to email this to her as she needs it urgently for a meeting. To do this:

1. Insert the floppy disk on which you stored the file: **Survey.1** (the report you saved – see page 148).

2. Create a new message to your tutor (acting as Mrs Ambrose).

3. Use the subject: *Survey Report*.

4. Key in the message:
   I'm attaching a copy of the report. Hope it's useful.
   Your name here

5. Click **Insert**.

6. **File Attachment** click.

7. The File Attachment menu drops.

8. Now go to the **Look In** box – you will see a drop-down arrow on the right. Click on this and select 'A' drive. Then click on **Survey.1**.

9. Once you have the file name **Survey.1** in the Look In box, click **Attach**.

10. The filename of the attachment will appear next to **Attach:** in the header.

11. Now click on **Send**.

Your email message should look similar to Figure 4.24.

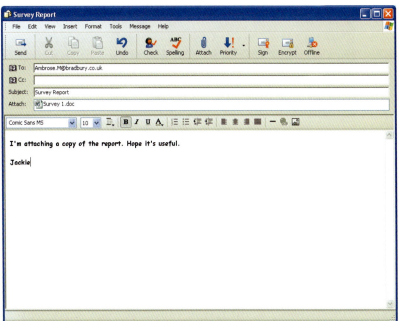

Figure 4.24 *An email message plus attachment*

AO4 Verbal communication methods

We all use verbal communications every day. Some people refer to these communications as oral rather than verbal but they are the same thing – people are talking to each other. When we talk to someone, when we discuss something, when we take part in a meeting or an interview and when we talk to someone on the telephone – we are using verbal communication.

In this assessment objective, we will be looking specifically at:

- informal discussions
- formal presentations
- formal debates.

Discussions

Discussions are very useful in all kinds of situations. They may be very formal (such as those held at managerial level in a business) or may be informal (such as those held between colleagues at school, college or at work). We will be looking particularly at informal discussions.

Face-to-face discussions

Face-to-face discussion

Face-to-face discussions can include anything from talking to one other person to a large meeting where lots of people talk together. Discussing something face to face enables you to see the way people are using their bodies to express themselves (e.g. the way in which they may wave their arms around or use gestures when making a point). Their posture may indicate to you that what they are saying does not match how they appear. Whether they are willing to keep eye contact is also an indication of how they are feeling. This non-verbal communication, or **body language** as it is known, can be very useful.

Face-to-face discussions can also be useful in obtaining immediate feedback and response from the person (or persons) taking part.

The tone and style of communication used in a discussion is likely to be informal and casual. This will help ensure that the discussion is held in a relaxed atmosphere so that participants will want to take an active part.

Think about the following in a discussion:

- Choose your words carefully – try to ensure that the words you use are appropriate to others in the discussion and be polite.
- Use appropriate body language – try to make others feel at ease.
- Speak clearly and calmly – to ensure that people can understand what you are saying.
- Always ensure you listen carefully to what people are saying – don't be tempted to rush them.

Before a discussion can take place, you will need to consider:

1. The reason for the discussion – what it is you intend to discuss.

2. The people who will form the discussion group.

3. Where and when it should take place.

4. Being responsible for controlling it.

5. Appointing one of the group to take notes of the important facts during the discussion and, most importantly, to write down the result of the discussion – what was agreed and, perhaps, what was not.

ACTIVITY

1 Working in groups of three, search the Internet for your favourite football team. Each member of the group should use a different search engine to search for a different football club (ensure you decide on this aspect before you start). Print the information from at least one of the pages of each website visited.

2 On completion of the search, discuss the results with the group, one of whom should be nominated as reporter to take notes of the discussion and particularly to note the outcome. You should use this discussion to help you decide on which search engines may be particularly useful to you, and your fellow students.

3 You should then prepare a short report for your tutor that indicates clearly the results of your research and discussion. Use appropriate software, formats and conventions in your report.

Remote discussions

Many communications these days are made remotely

Remote discussions are those that are not face to face. We take part in remote discussions every day when we call someone on the phone.

One of the main difficulties with remote discussions is that you cannot see the person you are talking to and so cannot gauge their body language. You can only hear the tone of their voice and the words they are using. When you are talking to someone you know very well, this is relatively easy but it is not so easy when it is someone you don't know.

Think about the following when using the telephone

- Prepare everything in advance – check the name of the person you are calling, their telephone number and extension number if appropriate.
- Have pen and paper handy – to make notes etc.
- Prepare a list of the questions you want to ask, if appropriate.
- Make notes of any information you obtain during the discussion and be prepared to ask questions if you are not certain about anything.
- Always ensure you listen carefully to what the other person is saying – don't be tempted to interrupt him/her – you could be speaking over each other and both will lose part of the discussion.
- Be polite and make sure the language you use is appropriate to the person you are talking to.
- Always speak clearly.

Conferencing

Conferencing is used by businesses, both inside and outside their premises. For example, employees working in other countries of the world cannot take part in face-to-face discussions because these would be very expensive, in both travel and accommodation costs, as well as lost time. Conferencing allows people to hold meetings and enables them to work together as though they were sitting together in the same room, using the same computer. A major advantage of conferencing is that people are often more focused on the topic to be discussed, rather than talking about other, unrelated things.

Videoconferencing

Many businesses use videoconferencing to enable employees, suppliers and customers to meet, without physical contact. An all-in-one video conferencing system includes a camera, visual display, speakers, cables and a microphone. Videoconferencing enables people to conduct a meeting where they can hear and see everything that is happening. It is an ideal way for those in various parts of the world to 'meet' – it can link people between up to six locations and has a variety of options on how the pictures from the different sites are displayed on the screens.

Webconferencing

A webconference enables a person to communicate so that they can see and hear everything that takes place. Webconferencing enables a face-to-face meeting to be held, without actually meeting in the same location. One person controls the presentation from his or her desktop while other participants can access it via the web. The system uses communication tools such as a computer and web browser and enables participants to view documents and PowerPoint presentations, share applications, chat, view whiteboard presentations and also to amend documents. Webconferences are secure and have numerous uses including training, legal conferences and various consultancy events.

Teleconferencing

As its name implies, a teleconference enables people anywhere in the world to hold a discussion via their telephone and several people can be linked wherever they may be, even via their mobile phone. It is, however, an audio conference only – participants are not able to see each other. This can be a problem if one of those taking part is trying to describe a particular product, which could perhaps be more easily solved if all the participants could clearly see the product.

Formal presentations

A formal presentation

When we hear the word 'presentation' we often think of computer software, such as PowerPoint, which is available to help someone to give a professional presentation to sell a product or explain statistics etc.

As part of assessment objective 4, you should prepare and deliver a 5-minute presentation to a group of at least three people. You will need good skills for the preparation and delivery of the presentation. Remember: practice makes perfect.

The topic should be related to information you have previously researched. You may use any aids to help you and may prepare slides on a computer if you wish. Slides prepared in this way can help you produce an interesting presentation, with the use of colour, sounds and animation. You may prefer to use other aids such as audio/video recordings, notes, handouts, overhead projector transparencies etc.

You should provide any presentation notes and prompt cards that you used as well as copies of your slides and also audio and/or video recordings and any other presentation materials you used.

A witness statement from your tutor will also be required as a contribution towards the assessment of your performance.

When you are conducting a presentation, think about the following:

- preparation – when you have carried out your research and know what you want to say, make a plan of how you will present it and in what order. Good preparation is essential for a successful presentation

- structuring your presentation – start at the beginning by introducing your subject and telling the people you are making the presentation to (the participants) what you intend to talk about; in the middle section, give the facts (and statistics if appropriate) clearly; don't be tempted to rush, even though you may be nervous; finish the presentation with a summary of the facts and the findings from your research

- if you intend to use presentation slides, consider producing audience notes – all participants will then have a printed version and this will help them to follow your presentation

- before you give your presentation, have a rehearsal – ask a colleague to help you with this

- just before the presentation, look at the audience and be sure to pace the presentation according to who is there; use language, tone and style appropriate to the audience, speak clearly, raise your voice if necessary but do not shout.

CASE STUDY

Bayview Hotel

Mr and Mrs Donovan have owned Bayview Hotel for six years. The hotel is situated in a lively holiday resort in the UK, overlooking the bay, and is open for the summer months only. A number of full-time and part-time staff are employed. The hotel is small and offers bed, breakfast and evening meal, mainly to families.

Mr and Mrs Donovan's daughter, Carly, is a keen windsurfer and is eager to set up her own watersports business in the town. She has discussed the possibility with her parents who are keen to support her. Carly has discovered that a beach hut is for sale which could be used for her new business.

Her parents think it would be good for business to be able to offer inclusive watersports holidays. However, the variety of watersports is bewildering and they are not sure which would be the most appropriate for a UK seaside resort.

You are a family friend and Mr and Mrs Donovan know that you are studying for your OCR National in Business. They have asked you to help them to make a decision on which watersports should be offered.

1. Using the Internet, research the websites of UK watersports businesses. You need to find out what watersports are offered in the UK and what prices are charged for these activities.

2. List the websites you visited and include a brief summary of the information you found.

3. Prepare and deliver a 5-minute presentation to the owners (or colleagues acting as Mr and Mrs Donovan).

4. You may use any form of presentation e.g. you may wish to consider using an appropriate software package to help you prepare and deliver your presentation.

5. Practise your presentation beforehand.

6. Print your slides (if appropriate) and include your notes, handouts, audio/video recordings etc. as evidence of your presentation.

Formal debate

You may have heard of 'debates' on the television or radio. For example, the House of Commons operates on a daily basis by MPs holding a number of debates.

The House of Commons holds debates

A debate is a structured argument. It consists of two opposing views. Debates in business are normally held at senior levels of management. They enable people to give their point of view and to exchange opinions. Debates can be held at a fast pace and the language used is often very formal. The use of appropriate body language is crucial to a person taking part in a debate. Voices can be raised as part of the process of making a point. Normally, only one person at a time would speak; others would wait their turn. It is often necessary to limit people's time to ensure everyone has a chance to give their point of view.

Portfolio tip

In order to provide the evidence required in your portfolio for assessment objective 4, you will need to demonstrate very good competency in an informal discussion or formal presentation or debate.

You will need to provide your presentation notes, prompt cards, handouts, copies of your slides (if appropriate), audio and/or video recordings etc. in your evidence and to submit a witness statement from your tutor.

Tips for debates

- Set the rules before the debate starts. For example, how long will each person be given to speak? Who will keep a check on the timing? You may wish to ask someone, perhaps your tutor, to help by acting as 'referee'.

- Only one person should be allowed to speak at one time.

- Remember to speak clearly and use your voice to help emphasise a point.

- Use body language to help you express yourself.

- Keep to the topic being debated – don't be tempted to start talking about unconnected issues.

- When all the speakers have had their say, the audience should be asked to vote for one of the views.

ACTIVITY

Work with fellow students to organise and take part in a debate. Do not be too ambitious – a small debate with a group of approximately 15 to 20 participants should be sufficient.

You should be prepared to act as one of two lead debaters (speakers) – you and your colleagues will need to choose the other main debater. The group should then discuss the subject they wish to debate. This could be a topic of national interest or something that is relevant in the local neighbourhood or perhaps of interest within your school or college. It should, however, be of interest to the majority of those taking part – the audience as well as the speakers.

The two main speakers should decide which view they will support and pick their 'teams' – about 4 in each team would be ideal. These will be people who will speak in support of the views of each of the main speakers

The remainder of the group will act as the audience – to listen to the debate and to vote when the debate has concluded.

Before the debate, you should carry out research using as many resources as possible, including the Internet. Be thorough – you will feel more confident if you have lots of valid facts and information to back up your case. You should also consider the topic from the opposing side – what are the arguments opposing your views likely to be?

On conclusion of the debate, take time to consider what went well and what was not so good. What would you do differently at the next debate?

AO5 Review the advantages and disa[dvantages] of communication using technolog[y]

In this assessment objective, we will **review** the types of communication that use technology and the advantages and disadvantages of their use. You will need to consider the following issues:

- costs of investing in ICT (installation, training, maintenance)
- speed of access
- ease of access
- format of data.

In your portfolio, you will need to describe in detail the advantages and disadvantages of communication using technology.

Firstly, think about the types of communication that use technology. Some of these are:

- mobile phones
- email
- personal digital assistants (PDAs).

This list is by no means complete and as technology becomes ever more smart and technical, you will be able to add more communication tools to this list.

Mobile phones

Some advantages of mobile phones are:

- employees can keep in touch at all times
- staff have easy and quick contact with customers – those who are out on the road can be contacted by customers; for example, if a member of staff has made an appointment to meet a customer and has been held up, the employee can make a mobile phone call directly to explain the circumstances and re-book the appointment if necessary
- many mobile phones are now fitted with WAP (wireless application protocol) – this enables people with mobile phones with WAP to gain access to the office intranet, browse the web, check their emails and to do some shopping

advantages

e phones enable people to
n touch – they are
ally useful in
ncies and give many
who use them a feeling
ity, that they can call
contact friends when
re they want to.

A mobile camera phone

Some disadvantages of mobile phones are:

- they can be expensive to buy, especially those that offer photography and WAP capability
- businesses may be paying a great deal of money by enabling their staff to have instant and quick communication but some employees may be tempted to abuse the system
- the various packages are confusing and, if people do not choose their mobile phone service carefully, they could find it is a very expensive way to communicate
- mobile phones can be very intrusive and people can become frustrated when they are used in public places because of the constant ring tones as well as being forced to listen to someone's else conversation.

Email

Some of the advantages of email are:

- it is very fast – messages are received almost immediately after they have been sent
- it enables people to ask a question and receive a response in a very short space of time, without having to wait for the post
- messages can be saved and referred to again and again
- less expensive than telephone calls, faxes or couriers
- enables you to send one message to lots of people with one press of a button
- files can be attached to an email message
- saves on printing costs – including ink, paper etc.
- it is possible to prioritise a message by flagging it as an urgent message – to ensure the person receiving it will deal with it immediately

- enables you to receive a receipt that an email has been received safely
- more secure than a telephone call, especially a mobile phone call.

Some of the disadvantages of email are:

- you can only send an email message to someone who has an email account
- some research has shown that employees can waste a great deal of time by emailing each other
- staff rarely talk to each other any more – they email each other, even though they may be sitting next to one another
- easy access means that inappropriate messages may be sent – once sent, they cannot be retrieved
- costs of training staff to use email efficiently
- email attachments can contain viruses
- cost of purchasing and installing anti-virus software
- it is not possible to send packages by email
- users can be bombarded with junk mail.

Personal digital assistants (PDAs)

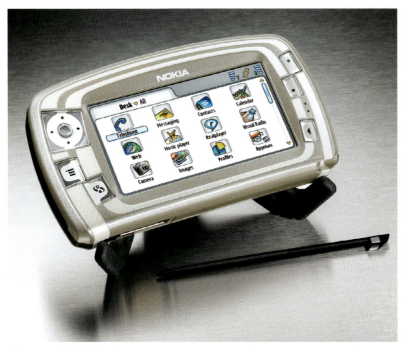

A personal digital assistant

Personal digital assistants are small fully-functional computers that you can hold in one hand – they are about the size of a small calculator. They can help to organise your life by providing an electronic diary and many other functions and are designed to complement desktop or laptop computers, not to replace them.

There are two sizes of PDAs – hand-held and palm-sized. Hand-held PDAs are larger and use a miniature keyboard, usually in combination with touch-screen technology. Palm-sized PDAs are smaller and lighter. They have smaller screens and rely on stylus/touch-screen technology and handwriting recognition programs for data entry.

PDAs use operating systems that are not as complex as those used by PCs. They do not have hard drives but store basic programs in a ROM (read-only memory) chip. Data is stored in the device's RAM (random access memory).

Some of the advantages of PDAs are:

- large number of functions such as address book, daily planner, to-do lists, memo pads, calendar, project lists, expense reports, calculator etc.
- more advanced PDAs have Bluetooth capability which means they can be used as mobile phones and can send and receive emails
- small, easy to store in a pocket or bag
- enable easy access to the Internet while away from the home or office computer.

Some of the disadvantages of PDAs are:

- cost of initial purchase and possible upgrades
- cost of maintenance including batteries etc.
- cost of training users
- easy target for thieves
- loss of data and organiser if PDA is lost.

ACTIVITY

Working in groups of three, research the advantages and disadvantages of communication using mobile phones. You should use as many types of research as possible.
- On completion of the research, each group should discuss the findings and prepare and produce a word-processed list of their findings.
- Each group should then prepare and deliver a five-minute presentation, using the findings from their research, to the whole class.
- On completion of all the presentations, the class should discuss the presentations and evaluate performances, slides etc., as well as the advantages and disadvantages of communication using technology.
- This discussion should also give you feedback to help you in future presentations.

Portfolio tip

You should use as many types of research as possible, including the Internet, as well as technical magazines, such as those aimed at computer users, and the websites of telephone and Internet service providers.

CASE STUDY

Brigham's Bakery

Joseph Brigham started the business in 1912. It is still owned and run by his family – Joseph's granddaughter is the Chairman, the Chief Executive is his eldest grandson and five other grandchildren are Directors.

Brigham's produces high-quality home-made cakes and biscuits including farmhouse fruit cakes, flapjacks, shortbreads and mince pies (at Christmas and New Year). The ingredients used are pure and natural – there are no preservatives and colourings are not used. The firm is very proud of the fact that they have recently been awarded two major prizes by the industry.

Their head office is situated in Reading in Berkshire. The products are made in several small factories in Reading, Bristol, Manchester and Aberdeen. A member of the family supervises each factory. The customer base is increasing all the time and deliveries are made to companies, universities, hospitals and tourist venues all over the UK.

The directors are hoping in the very near future to be able to provide biscuit bars to tourist outlets in Singapore and Malta. There has been a great deal of interest from these countries and Brigham's hope that this is just the beginning of their involvement overseas.

1 Using the Internet, research the advantages and disadvantages of the use of email as a means of communication for Brigham's Bakery.
2 Prepare and produce a report that includes your findings. Use appropriate software, formats and conventions in your report.
3 List the websites visited and a summary of the information found.
4 Email your report and the list as email attachments to your tutor.
5 Ask your tutor to reply to your email.

Portfolio tip

In order to provide the evidence required in your portfolio for assessment objective 5, you will need to describe in detail the advantages and disadvantages of communication using technology, including costs of investment, speed and ease of access and format of data.

AO6 The ICT as a tool for communication in business and society

In this assessment objective, you will analyse the impact of the continuing development of ICT as a tool for communication in both business and society. In your portfolio, you should include an analysis for a particular type of communication and how the continuing development might impact on business. You should also consider how the development of this communication might impact on society (on people). Your analysis should be extensive, giving as much detail as possible and should include the impact of the following:

- broadband Internet access
- mobile communications
- networks
- the home workstation
- access to communication services via television.

Technology is changing rapidly and new products are being tested and developed all the time. To ensure that you can give an accurate and detailed up-to-date account of the impact of the continuing development of ICT, you will need to do extensive research:

- Internet – consider using several search engines to help you find the websites of companies who are manufacturing/selling products, websites of users and technical experts.
- Technical (including computer) magazines and journals – these are a very good resource for up-to-date information on what is happening and how things are changing.
- Newspaper articles – there are many interesting and informative articles (in daily and Sunday newspapers) produced by journalists who are specialists in the field.
- Shops – go into shops selling these products, ask questions of the sales staff, look at the products, question customers, pick up brochures and catalogues.
- Ask users – one obvious source often not thought about is to ask people who use the products; you may find people coming out of shops are happy to give you information.

Broadband

Broadband is the latest in high-speed Internet access technology. It can deliver Internet access at speeds hundreds of times faster (at least 256 kilobytes per second) than a traditional dial-up modem (approximately 56 kilobytes per second) can provide.

Broadband offers these benefits:

- convenience – your computer is always connected to the Internet. You will have to log on to your Internet Service Provider but once you have done this, you stay connected
- speed – you can download web pages, files, images, photographs and films and music at a fast rate – almost instantly
- sending and receiving emails is very fast
- you can use the telephone at the same time as the Internet. This means that people will not get the engaged tone every time they try to contact you by phone and you will be able to make calls while online.

ACTIVITY

You should explore ways in which the continuing development of broadband could impact on business and society. Carry out research to find out the main features and the research and development being carried out to develop the use of broadband.

Consider implications such as teleworking, hot desking, e-commerce, the provision of television services so that people can watch programmes on their computers and the impact broadband may have in the future, for example, all UK patients should be able to book their hospital operations via their doctors' computer terminals.

Some of the implications should include the impact on jobs. For example, if people can download films to watch on their computer, will they still want to go to see a film at the cinema? Will this result in cinemas closing? Could this lead to job losses? If people can watch television on their computer, will they stop buying televisions? What would be the implications if this happened?

In future, many other implications may become obvious as the technology expands and more and more uses are found for broadband.

Mobile communications

Mobile communications include mobile phones, laptops and personal digital assistants (PDAs). As technology advances, you will be able to add to this list.

Mobile phones

These offer access to communication virtually everywhere. There is very good coverage in the UK and coverage throughout the world improves day by day.

You should consider the recent developments that have taken place. For example, inventors have been looking at a credit card sized mobile phone, totally disposable. These disposable phones may now be available. If they are, what are the implications for business – for example, for manufacturers of PDAs and mobile phones, as well as those who make and sell phone cards? What would be the implications for society – for example, would parents be happier for their children to have a mobile phone of this size?

Another consideration could be the wire-free (wi-fi) technology, which enables people to communicate using their laptops and mobile phones. A wireless network will also enable a desktop computer to connect to a laptop so that they can share a broadband connection and all files on each of the computers.

M-commerce (mobile commerce), using mobile phones, is also developing. It is intended that this will provide a mixture of information with individual users being able to use different applications for specific purposes. Some of the features include:

- mobile banking: e.g. services offered by SMS (Short Message Services) – sending short text messages, or WAP – enabling Internet browsing
- alerts: e.g. news, traffic and weather reports, stock market prices, flight times
- spontaneous shopping: e.g. buying a book from a website using voice-enabled browsing
- location related services: e.g. provision of maps, traffic updates, restaurant and hotel services and local advertising – once the Global Positioning System (GPS) is widely available
- streaming media: e.g. videos transmitted over the Internet to PDAs and mobile phones.

ACTIVITY

What would be the impact on business and people (society) of the above features?

Laptops

A laptop

Technology has advanced to such an extent that it is possible to surf the net on the move. As well as connecting your mobile to your laptop, via wi-fi technology, it is now possible to connect your laptop to your computer without wires trailing everywhere. Broadband is not essential, but will enable you to get better access. Wi-fi also enables you to connect to the Internet and to access emails, using your laptop.

Personal digital assistants

The use of personal digital assistants (PDAs) has grown enormously over the last few years. With Bluetooth, it is possible to use PDAs as mobile phones, to send and receive email messages, to view photographs and to download music. As a tool for communication, its use is likely to continue. However, you should consider researching tools that might supersede PDAs such as the digital pen which can write or draw and send an email. Everything from sketches, diagrams to application forms, delivery notes and graphical emails can be transmitted. Handwritten notes can be sent to any computer and meeting notes can be made and stored instantly.

Another aspect that you could research is ICR (intelligent character recognition) which can change handwriting into text. For example, a van driver makes a delivery, the delivery note is signed with a digital pen and this is then instantly emailed to the office where the invoice is compiled and sent out immediately, thus speeding up the payment for the goods.

Networks

A network is a number of computers that are connected, enabling them to communicate with each other. The network software can be part of the operating system or it can be software designed specifically to manage a network.

The benefits of using networks include being able to share other facilities such as printers and modems and to share information and files, which will also save costs.

Continuing developments in networks could include:

- the use of satellite, radio or microwaves to provide links
- network cards
- point-of-sale terminals used in retail outlets
- use of intranets within a business
- maintenance of stock levels and control – electronic data interchange etc.

Your research must be confined to the impact of the continuing development of ICT as *a tool for communication.* Don't be tempted to stray into writing about other ICT developments that are not related to communication.

Your research could focus on the ways in which networks can be used to communicate and how they are likely to develop in the future. You may find it particularly helpful to research how a business uses a network to communicate. It may be possible to interview a staff member of a local business who has good knowledge and experience of networks. You should bear in mind that your research should include how communication using networks may continue to develop.

If it is difficult to gain access to a business that uses networks, you may be able to base your research on a network used in your school or college. Your tutor will be able to advise and help you in contacting the appropriate person dealing with the administration of the network.

As well as users, consider how the networks could impact on the customers of a business, or parents and students attending the school or college.

Your research should include a wide variety of resources, including the Internet, and should enable you to analyse the impact of the continuing development of networks as a tool for communication in business and society.

Home workstations

Many people are now able to work at home, thanks to the advances in technology. More people now work outside their company's premises than ever before and as technology advances still further, the numbers of home workers will increase. Most computers will enable people to access their company's computer network in a secure and safe working environment. So long as the computers have anti-virus software and firewalls, communication by this means should be safe and secure.

ACTIVITY

You should consider how home computers may evolve further and the impact on people, as well as business, of these changes. Do some research on features that are available on computers, such as removable media (DVDs, CDs etc.). You should give some thought to the size and power of home computers – what developments are there in relation to these issues? Another possible feature to research might be the purchasing of a system with components such as sound and video integrated on the motherboard – how would these impact on business and society?

Access to communication services via television

Interactive television offers so many facilities that they are too numerous to list. Some of the main ones that could be used as a tool for communication are:

- t-commerce (television commerce) – customers see a product and order it straightaway
- home banking
- videoconferencing
- instant messaging

Portfolio tip

In order to provide the evidence required in your portfolio for assessment objective 6, you will need to produce an extensive analysis of the impact of ICT as a tool for communication in business and society.

- email
- high-speed telephone line services
- broadband.

You may find it helpful to conduct research on the websites of the major television companies, such as ITV, BBC and Sky.

Please also bear in mind that, when this book was written, some of the features described above were in the research and development stage. As time has progressed, the features may not have been developed, perhaps because costs were too high, or the features were not appropriate. In your research, you must endeavour to find out what is being developed and include full details on the results of your findings in your portfolio.

SKILLS CHECK

On completion of this unit, can you:

1. Produce a variety of written communications, using appropriate software, formats and conventions – these include reports, memos, letters, notices, information leaflets and advertisements?

2. Use a variety of research methods, including the Internet, verbal questioning/interviewing, surveys and questionnaires, and paper-based reference materials to obtain information for a specific purpose?

3. Use email for communication purposes – receive, create, edit and send email messages and attach files to emails?

4. Communicate with people verbally – informal discussions and formal presentations and debates?

5. Review the advantages and disadvantages of a variety of communication methods which use technology?

6. Analyse the impact of the continuing development of ICT as a tool for communication in business and society?

Working with people in business

Getting Started

Throughout your life you have been developing the skills necessary to work with other people. Since starting school you have been required to obey rules and comply with important legislation such as health and safety. You may already have a part-time job or taken part in a work experience placement. Within these two situations you are required to work alongside other employees and follow the rules set out by the business. These skills are further developed when you enter the world of work full-time.

To complete this unit successfully, you will need to produce evidence to show that you understand how to recruit, organise and develop people and the importance of motivating and organising people within a business. You will learn about legislation and its importance within the workplace. You will also gain an understanding of how employer and employee relations can affect the performance of a business. You will need to produce evidence to achieve the six assessment objectives that are contained in the specification and which are shown below.

This unit will cover

- AO1 Investigate employer and employee co-operation and show how this affects business performance.
- AO2 Investigate and explain job roles in business.
- AO3 Illustrate the stages of the recruitment process.
- AO4 Describe staff development programmes in two selected businesses.
- AO5 Describe employment protection, health and safety and equal opportunity legislation.
- AO6 Show, using examples, how disagreements between employers and employees arise and are resolved.

AO1 Workplace co-operation and how this affects business performance

'A happy workforce is a motivated workforce'. A wide range of motivational theorists have undertaken detailed studies of people at work in order to find out what actually motivates people, and how this is linked back to the degree of employer and employee co-operation within a business.

Links between motivation and employer and employee co-operation

Motivation is the level of desire and drive a person has to complete a set task. A motivated employee is interested and enthusiastic about their job. A person's motivation can be affected by many different situations, some of which may not be directly related to the workplace. People are motivated by different factors which can vary depending on the task being undertaken.

ACTIVITY

Write down what motivates you to come to college and what would motivate you to go to work. Are your two lists very different?

Motivational theorists

Motivational theorists have spent the last 100 years studying people to try and discover what motivates them, as owners of businesses wanted to find out how to get the most out of their workforce in order to increase **productivity** levels. Even today, organisations are trying to establish what motivates the modern workforce.

GLOSSARY

Productivity: Represents the amount a workforce produces in a set amount of time

F. W. Taylor

Originally it was considered that pay was the sole motivator of people in the workplace. F. W. **Taylor** believed this to be so. However, the major criticisms of his work were concerned with the fact he did not consider the social side of work.

Douglas McGregor

Douglas McGregor came up with two theories which were based on how managers treated their workers. His first view was **Theory X**. This was based on managers who felt that they had to organise the work of employees, tell them exactly what to do and used money as the main motivator. In order to ensure workers continued to remain focused and productivity stable, threats of the sack and demotion were used. There was no consultation between workers and managers. **Theory Y** was based on managers who believed that workers were able to organise their own work, could be given responsibility and were not motivated solely by money. The managers were able to organise the work in order to allow workers to take responsibility for their own jobs and be consulted in decisions concerning their work.

The type of environment which is described by Theory X would probably not be a very pleasant place to work. There would be a lot of conflict between employers and employees.

Abraham Maslow

Abraham Maslow demonstrated a hierarchy of needs. Maslow believed that the lower-level needs were not motivators but were essential in order to improve people's everyday lives. The higher-level needs were the ones that drove people to take on challenges and stretch their intellectual ability.

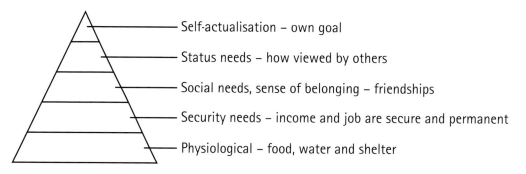

Figure 5.1 *Maslow's hierarchy of needs*

- The first level of need is **physiological**. We all need food, water, clothes and shelter, and for these we need money. Everybody needs to be able to earn money in order to survive in today's world.

- The second level of need is **security.** Employees need to feel secure within their job. They want to know their job is safe and they will be paid regularly. People who are paid solely on a commission basis lack the security of a regular pay packet and may not achieve this level of need.

- **Social needs** are met when an employee works within a happy team, is able to mix with colleagues and establish friendships within the workplace. This constitutes the third level of need.

- People often strive to have **status** and to be seen by others as having achieved 'a good job', with plenty of material possessions, and a good standard of living. This is the fourth level of need.

- The final level of need is **self-actualisation.** An employee is continuing to achieve in order to meet individual intellectual goals.

The principle behind the hierarchy of needs is that people must achieve the lower levels before they can work their way up the triangle. It is therefore the job of an employer to make sure that their workforce is able to meet these needs throughout their working life. If they are able to do so it will help maintain good working relationships between employees and employers.

Frederick Herzberg

Frederick Herzberg decided that employees considered there were positive and negative aspects to their working lives. The positive aspects could be considered as motivators and the negative aspects could cause conflict within the workplace and ultimately cause motivation to decrease. The positive motivators are:

- achievement
- nature of work
- recognition
- responsibility.

The negative aspects are called **hygiene factors** and defined as:

- company policy and bureaucracy
- working conditions
- salary
- job security
- status
- relationship with peers.

Herzberg felt that if the hygiene factors were not met satisfactorily, employee and employer relationships could break down and ultimately result in a de-motivated workforce that lacked morale. If a business ensures that all the hygiene factors are met it will not necessarily motivate the workforce but will avoid conflict between employer and employee. In order to motivate the workforce the business has to acknowledge that all employees are able to achieve the motivators.

Woodward, Burns and Stalker

Joan Woodward, Burns and Stalker developed the contingency approach in the late 1950s and early 1960s. This theory is based on the belief that there is no one best method to motivate people applicable to all situations.

Good working relationships between employees and employers are achieved when each side values the opinions and decisions of the other. The employer will treat the employee fairly and try to meet employees' needs as far as is possible. The employee will work hard and give their best to the business at all time.

If an employer ensures that employees have good working conditions, job security and maintains good working relationships between colleagues then the likelihood will be that employees will be fully motivated.

CASE STUDY

Manjit's motivation

Manjit and Simon had been working for the same manufacturing firm ever since they left school ten years ago. Unfortunately, due to the economic climate the business was suffering a major loss in sales. Management decided that Simon would have to be made redundant. They offered him an excellent redundancy package and he left the business with no hard feelings. Manjit remained with the business, but was required to undertake some of Simon's work as well as his own. He was finding his workload increasingly difficult to cope with and when he tried to discuss this with the management he was told that he would have to cope or leave.

1 **How do you think Manjit felt when Simon was offered redundancy?**

2 **How would this decision have affected Manjit's motivation?**

3 **With reference to the motivational theorists, how could the business ensure that Manjit remains motivated?**

A motivated workforce benefits the business

As you can see from the last section, if an employee is treated well and all their needs are met by the employer they will work hard and be totally committed to the organisation they work for. This, in turn has many benefits for the business.

A business which meets the needs of its workforce and can keep them committed and motivated will have much higher levels of productivity, which will increase the profits of the business. It could also reduce the costs of manufacturing the product due to the workforce working more efficiently, which again increases the profitability of the business. Some businesses choose to share this increased profit with their employees by way of a bonus or increase in pay. This is a way of recognising and valuing employees' hard work and giving a reward. This will act as a further motivator to the staff.

ACTIVITY

Write down the things that motivate you to come to college. Compare your list with two other group members. Are you all motivated by the same things?

Increase in production

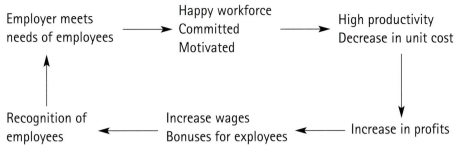

Figure 5.2 *Increase in production*

Increase in sales

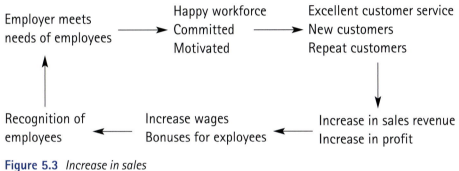

Figure 5.3 *Increase in sales*

Possible consequences of poor working relationships

It is not always the case that a business is able to maintain good working relationships. How relationships are developed and maintained is down to the role the employer or managers decide to take within the business. The possible consequences of a business not having good employee/employer co-operation are outlined below:

- the business gains a poor reputation and cannot recruit staff
- lack of co-operation between staff and management can lead to poor quality work
- high staff turnover
- high absenteeism rate
- difficult to recruit new members of staff
- employees work to rule or strike.

The business gains a poor reputation

When a business has gained a poor reputation for staff relations they may find it increasingly difficult to recruit new members of staff. If the area where the business is located has high levels of employment, people will not want to work for a business that is known to treat its employees unfairly. If the area has high unemployment, people may only want to work for the business as an absolute last resort. Customers may also not buy the businesses products/services if they are concerned about the way it treats its staff.

Lack of co-operation

As workers become increasingly dissatisfied with their job they may well reduce their co-operation with management. This could result in employees working slowly, an unwillingness to accept change and only meeting the minimum requirements of their job. The end result of this action could be that employees produce work of very poor quality. This would result in products being returned to the business and a lot of dissatisfied customers.

High turnover of staff

Staff will not stay in a business that continually has poor working relationships.

High staff turnover is expensive. New staff will need training and during their training they will not be as efficient as existing staff. If there is a time delay between one member of staff leaving and the new employee starting there is pressure put on existing staff to cover extra duties. This may cause new conflict between existing workers and employers.

High absenteeism rate

Staff that are not happy at work are more likely to take time off sick. When a member of staff is away, productivity will fall and other members of staff may be required to cover some of their duties. The cost to companies in sick pay is large and in 2000-2002 an estimated 40 million working days were lost – over 33 million due to work-related ill health and 7 million due to workplace injury.

Employees work to rule or strike

The ultimate weapon of an employee is to withdraw their labour and go on strike. This is a way of clearly stating to the employer that conditions must improve. The legislation concerning strikes has been tightened over the last decade. A strike is now only legal if over 50 per cent of the workforce has agreed to this as a necessary form of action to get their voice heard by the employer and changes made.

A work to rule is where employees decide that they will not undertake any extra duties or overtime as laid out in their contract of employment. If the business was very busy and needed the workforce to work extra hours to meet a deadline it would not have the manpower to do so. This course of action is often the final one for employees who work in organisations such as the health service and education. It would appear unethical to withdraw their labour completely and could reduce public sympathy to their cause.

ACTIVITY

If you have a part-time job, describe the relationship between you and your employer.

Links between the moral and ethical treatment of employees and business performance

There is legislation which clearly outlines the rights of employers and employees within the workplace as outlined below:

- Employment Rights Act
- Health and Safety at Work Act
- The Sex Discrimination Act
- The Race Relations Act
- The Equal Pay Act
- The Disabled Persons Act.

This legislation has been put into place to ensure that employees and employers have a framework in which to work together and achieve good working relationships. It clearly outlines the rights of not only the employee but also the employer. Each piece of legislation ensures that everybody is treated fairly and equally regardless of their gender, colour, disability or race and can work within a safe environment. A breaching of these Acts by either the employee or employer will result in prosecution.

We will be looking at this legislation in more depth in the coverage of assessment objective 5.

As we have seen, if employees are treated fairly and have a good working environment they will give their best performance to the business. They will remain loyal and enthusiastic about their job. These factors alone will help the business achieve maximum performance. The more time employers and management spend consulting the workforce and trying to find compromises between the needs of the individual business and employees' needs, the greater the chance the business has of remaining competitive and obtaining maximum performance and still maintaining good working relationships.

ACTIVITY

As a group discuss the different types of working environment you would like to work in.

Portfolio tip

In order to enhance the depth of your evidence you need to relate your theoretical evidence to a selected business or businesses. The use of examples will demonstrate a thorough understanding of the topics covered.

AO2 Investigate and explain job roles in business

Every employee will have a set job role. This role will include all the duties and tasks that they will be expected to fulfil throughout their normal working week. For example, the job role of a receptionist working in a doctors' surgery could include the following tasks:

- answer the telephone
- deal with the general public
- maintain the appointment system
- organise patient lists.

How organisational charts and job descriptions assist in defining job roles

Before any organisation can start recruitment and selection of employees it will need to define clearly the job the person will be required to undertake. This is known as a job description. A **job description** will explain to an employee what their tasks and responsibilities are, who their line manager is and, if appropriate, staff they will have responsibility for.

How the job role fits within the organisation is illustrated through the use of an organisation chart. The purpose of an organisation chart is to show how employees fit into an organisation and their levels of responsibility. It will also illustrate who their line manager is and how decisions and communication flow within the business.

An organisation structure will help a business draw up job descriptions as it clearly illustrates how each job fits into the overall structure of the business.

In your Unit 1 work you looked at the different ways a business could structure itself. These different structures are illustrated through organisation charts.

Hierarchical charts

A hierarchical chart is an organisation chart that has lots of layers. The people with the most power are at the top of the chart making all the decisions. The decisions are passed down through the layers to the employers at the bottom of the chart. The management style of this kind of organisation chart is often **autocratic**.

Autocratic management is where decisions are made without consultation with the other employees. Decisions are passed down the chain of command and employees have very little say in how they manage their own work.

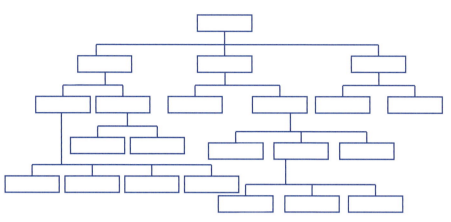

Figure 5.4 *A hierarchical organisation structure*

Flat organisation charts

A flat organisation chart has fewer layers and the management style is often **consultative**.

Consultative management is where employees are consulted about decisions before they are made. Employees are allowed to put forward their own suggestions and take some control over their own work.

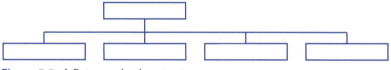

Figure 5.5 *A flat organisation structure*

Matrix charts

A matrix structure will take employees from different departments to work together as a team. This type of structure is often used when a group of people are required to work on a specific project.

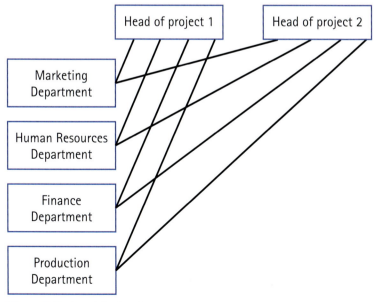

Figure 5.6 *A matrix structure*

The importance of employees knowing what they are responsible for

In order for a business to remain efficient and competitive it must run like clockwork. This can only happen if employees are clear about what they are responsible for and the tasks they are expected to undertake as part of their normal working day. In a large supermarket it would not look very good if all the staff were stationed at the tills and no one was re-stocking the shelves, or even worse, if all the staff had decided they wanted to stack the shelves and nobody wanted to work on the tills.

Clearly defined job roles give employees a feeling of security. They are fully aware of the tasks they are responsible for and will often take great pride in undertaking them to a high standard.

An organisation chart will give an employee status within the company. An employee will know who they take instructions from and, if they have any problems, with whom they are to discuss these. If an employee has responsibility for other members of staff this will also be clearly illustrated.

Key job roles

Within any business there are a number of key job roles. Each different level of job will carry different authority, responsibility and will require different qualifications and skills.

The diagram illustrates how the hierarchy of job roles fits into an average large business.

Figure 5.7 *Hierarchy of job roles*

Chairman

The chairman sits at the top of the business and is elected by the other directors. In some businesses the chairman may also be the managing director. The chairman's role is to chair board meetings and he/she will work in conjunction with the other members of the **board of directors**.

A board of directors is voted to run the business of behalf of its shareholders. They make the decisions concerning the businesses future.

The board of directors makes strategic decisions for the business

Managing director/Chief executive

In the private sector, the chief executive would normally be known as the managing director. The role of the managing director is to co-ordinate the work of, and advise the other directors and managers. They will oversee the running of the business. The managing director will be assisted by other executives or directors who make up the board of directors. The role of the board of directors is to make the **strategic decisions** which will take the business forward.

A board of directors can be made up of two types of directors, executive and non executive. An executive director works for the business on a full-time basis. A non-executive director does not work for the business but is invited to sit on the board because of their personal skills and knowledge. They are able to offer an unbiased view because they are not concerned with the overall success of the business.

Key responsibilities and routine duties of the board of directors:

- To decide the strategic plan for the business.
- To establish targets for the business to enable it to meet its strategic plan.
- To set policies and strategies to enable the business to achieve its targets.
- To make financial decisions.
- To ensure the business remains within the law, for example health and safety legislation.
- To oversee the activities of the business.
- To participate in policy making decisions e.g. recruitment and selection, grievance procedures.

You can see from the bullet points above that the main role of the board of directors is to plan the future of the business. They are the group of people who make the **decisions** concerning the direction of the business. They will set the overall strategic **aims, objectives** and **targets** for the business. The board of directors will also make the ultimate decision if there is a problem within the business.

Problem solving is often a group activity

Directors

All directors will have two responsibilities. They will be part of the group which decides the long-term plans of the business as well as being responsible for the work of their own allocated area. For example a director could be allocated responsibility for health and safety, human resources, production or finance.

Key responsibilities and routine duties of directors

- To establish the strategic plans for their department which will be directly linked to the overall strategic plan of the business.
- To establish targets for their department to enable them to meet the strategic plan for the department.
- Informing departmental managers of any decisions that have been made by the board of directors.
- To ensure the department remains within the law, for example health and safety legislation.
- Monitoring the department's achievement of targets set and reporting these back to the board of directors
- Working in close liaison with their managers and informing them of any decisions made by the board of directors.
- Receiving feedback from their managers concerning progress and developments taking place within the department.
- Delegation of duties to employees within the department.

Directors also play a major role in the decision making of a business. They are required to implement the decisions of the board of directors within their own department. Some decisions may not be easy to implement within a department and therefore one of the skills they will need is problem solving. A director will set the objectives and targets for their own department.

Managers

There are often many different kinds of managers within a large organisation. Some managers are responsible for people whilst others are responsible for tasks.

Key responsibilities and routine duties of managers

- To carry out the instructions of the director of the department.
- To organise the work of members of staff within the department. This could involve staff rotas or simply the allocation of different tasks on a weekly or daily basis.
- To implement relevant legislation with the department, for example health and safety legislation.
- Monitoring the work of staff to ensure that the business is running effectively.
- Checking that departmental targets are being met.
- Making decisions which directly relate to the work of the department.
- To encourage and practise good working relationships within a department. This could include carrying out appraisals to identify staff training needs, personal problems or the identification of staff suitable for promotion with the business.
- To receive feedback from employees and to give feedback to employees concerning the strategic decisions of the business.
- To give feedback to directors of progress and developments with the department.

A manager will undertake less decision making as their main responsibility is to implement decisions. They will require problem-solving skills as they are often working closer to the customer. A manager is unlikely to **set targets** but will be responsible for their implementation within the department.

Supervisors

Supervisors are responsible for a small number of people. They are required to support and train employees at work. They have to ensure that a set job is completed on time and they will report directly to a designated manager. They will often be responsible for the quality assurance of the product/service.

Key responsibilities and routine duties of supervisors

- To carry out the instructions of the manager.
- To assist the manager in the allocation of the work to other staff members.
- To ensure that all relevant legislation, for example health and safety, is complied with.
- Monitoring the work of staff to ensure that the business is running effectively.
- Working in conjunction with the manager to ensure that departmental targets are being met.
- To encourage and practise good working relationships within a department. To support staff within the workplace offering advice and guidance as required.
- To receive feedback from employees, and to pass this on to the manager.
- To pass on information concerning the department received from the manager to employees.

A supervisor's role is to monitor and support staff. They may make simple decisions and have to overcome simple problems. However, they will often have to refer to their line manager prior to taking any action. They are unlikely to be responsible for setting targets.

Operatives

Starting at the bottom means you have only one way to go ... up

When you start work you may be at the bottom of the organisational structure. You will be required to follow the tasks as outlined in your job description. You will usually be a member of a team and therefore working with the support of other employees. Initially you may be closely supervised to ensure that you understand your role within the business.

Key responsibilities of operatives

- To carry out your allocated tasks as outlined in your job description.
- To follow instructions given by your supervisor or manager.
- To comply with legislation, for example health and safety.
- To build effective and efficient working relationships with other members of staff.

An operative is unlikely to be involved in the decision-making process. They are unlikely to set targets, but may be involved in discussions concerning current and future targets for their department.

Pay and benefits

The more qualifications that a job needs, and the greater responsibility it carries, the greater the likelihood that it will secure a higher rate of pay. If we refer to the structure of jobs above you would expect the chairman to receive a higher salary than a supervisor. Below are examples of three jobs each with different salary levels.

Accountant

In a private practice, trainees' average starting salaries vary between £8,000 and £23,000 a year depending on qualifications. In London a trainee can expect to earn around £28,000.

From this example above you can see that pay increases according to the level of qualifications and where the employee lives. A higher rate of pay is usually paid for London jobs due to the high cost of living in the city.

Human Resources Officer

Salaries in this area start around £12,000. However, the average salary is £17,712 and employees can earn up to £25,000.

From this example again you can see that the graduation in salary is probably due to the level of qualifications and experience that an employee has.

Office Worker

A junior secretary in London can get a salary of between £10,000 and £18,000, However, a senior secretary/personal assistant or an executive assistant can take home up to £30,000. Salaries for administrative work are similar, ranging from £12,000 to £30,000. Outside London the top rate for a personal assistant is lower at between £18,000 and £25,000. The salaries for office work are graded on levels of responsibility. A personal assistant will have a lot more responsibility than a junior secretary and can therefore demand a higher salary.

Qualifications, skills and personal qualities required

It is very difficult to clearly illustrate the qualifications, skills and personal qualities required for different levels of jobs. Higher-paid jobs require a much more confident, highly articulate individual than that required for the position of operative, but qualifications may not be as clearly defined as personal qualities. It is clear from the descriptions in the advertisements shown below that for the higher jobs the applicant must be able to set targets and be self-motivated. The potential employee must also have the skills necessary to manage a team of people. These skills are not requested for the lower-skilled jobs.

ACTIVITY

1 As a group collect advertisements for different types of jobs. Identify the skills and qualifications that each job requests balanced against the pay and benefits offered. Compare them with the four advertisements shown below.

2 Working in small groups design a job advertisement for a part-time shop assistant for your local supermarket. Consider suitable working hours, pay and conditions. What qualifications and experience do you think the potential applicant will need?

Job 1: Customer Services and Group Consumer Director

Salary – £75,000

Benefits – pension scheme and generous holiday allowance

This is a senior management position. The position will report to the Chief Executive. The person appointed will have a hands-on, operational role running the organisation's call centre, and the Business Development Directorate, which converts all strategic initiatives into practical delivery and the agency's new Innovation Centre, a state-of-the-art facility intended to promote change. The appointee will regularly attend the board and executive team meetings.

Personal skills required include:
- ability to contribute to the strategic development of complex organisations
- articulate the needs of all customers, contributing actively across all our services to ensure they are rooted in customer needs.

No qualifications were requested.

Job 2: Business Account Manager

Salary: £50,000

Benefits – attractive bonus, quality car and full range of executive benefits

This is a broad ranging Business Development role within a leading company supplying the major grocery multiples. The company is looking for a high-potential individual with real commercial ability and the headroom to grow in the role and the company.

Responsible for:

- managing a business account with a multi-million-pound sales value
- ensuring account objectives are met
- leading and influencing multi-disciplinary teams including trading, operations, finance and IT
- developing strategic growth opportunities
- adding significant value and progressive profit growth.

Personal qualities:
An impressive individual with a solid demonstrable track record in category management and key account development into grocery and key account development into grocery multiples is required. Probably aged from early 30s. You will have excellent relationship and management skills with commercial flair.

Qualifications:
Graduate qualified

Job 3: Information Communications and Telecommunications Equipment Co-ordinator

Salary: £17,409–£23,313 – 37 hours per week

The role remit extends to the planning and co-ordination of departmental and inter-agency projects, regular monitoring of IT security and standards of supplier performance, problem escalation and product evaluation.

Qualifications:
You will be educated to A level or equivalent, with detailed knowledge of Windows for Workgroups, Windows NT4/2000, MS Office 2000, Ethernet networking and TCP/IIP. You will need at least 2 years' experience working in a similar role and have good knowledge of current computer/security legislation.

Job 4: Income Assistant

Salary: £15,056–£17,978 – 37 hours per week

This position will form part of a busy team dealing with an increased workload around the student term time. The post will assist in all aspects of the University's income collection and receipting procedures.

Experience:
You must have experience of working with modern income collection techniques, be conversant with legal requirements of income recording and must have a customer care philosophy when dealing with the public. You should have proven experience of using main frame computer systems in a large organisation and Microsoft PC procedures especially Excel and Word.

AO3 Stages of the recruitment process

For the applicant, replying to an advertisement is the first stage of the recruitment process. For a business, there have been many stages leading up to placing the advertisement. Below is a flow diagram of the different stages involved in recruitment and selection of new employees.

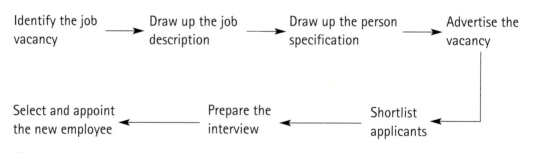

Figure 5.8 *The recruitment process*

Identifying the vacancy

Businesses may require new employees for a number of different reasons:

- an employee moves on to another business
- an employee retires
- an employee leaves due to ill health
- the business has expanded.

When a business is faced with the first three of these situations it must decide if it wants to replace the member of staff who is leaving. Sometimes employees are not replaced as the business decides to re-organise its workforce and the tasks of the exiting employee are shared out between current members of staff.

If the business has expanded the new position will have been advertised because current staff members cannot cope with the workload.

Drawing up a job description

Once a business has decided that it does require a new employee it must then decide exactly what the job will entail and the responsibilities to be undertaken by the new employee. It is an opportunity for a business to change the tasks and responsibilities allocated to a particular job. The business will discuss the duties and responsibilities currently being undertaken by the existing employee and a **skills audit** will be conducted. All of this information will help the business to draw up a job description for the new position.

A job description is a document that is sent out to potential employees which gives a summary of the job and the main responsibilities. It allows a potential applicant to see exactly what the position entails.

ACTIVITY

Draw up a job description for the position of a part-time shop assistant in your local supermarket. Base this on your advertisement created in the previous task on page 192.

GLOSSARY

Skills audit: identification of the skills necessary to carry out the job.

FAMILY HEALTH SERVICES
Job Description

Post: Database Data Input Clerk

Grade: A & C Grade 2

Accountable to: Team Leader – Grade 4

Job Summary: General clerical duties associated with inputting data via VDU relating to patient registrations.

Principal Responsibilities:

1) Assists with maintenance of computerised database by inputting data via a VDU and verifying information received from surgeries via an electronic link including:
   - patient registrations and cancellation of registrations on doctors' lists
   - amendments of information e.g. changes of name and address including postcodes.

2) Issues medical cards and deals with transmission of medical records.

3) Processes data relating to items of service claims and payment of general practitioners.

4) Undertakes general clerical duties associated with the above, including checking computer printouts, despatch of routine correspondence and filing.

5) On a rotational basis answers telephone queries and deals with related general correspondence.

6) Undertakes any other duties which may be allocated from time to time.

Figure 5.8 *An example of a job description*

Drawing up a person specification

The person specification outlines the educational qualifications, experience and knowledge/skills a potential applicant is required to have in order to complete a job. These qualities are often divided up into essential and desirable. A potential applicant is then able to match their own skills to those required to see if they would be suitable for the job being advertised.

FAMILY HEALTH SERVICES

Person Specification

Post: Database Data Input Clerk

Education/Qualifications

Essential: GCSE English
IT qualification
Ability to communicate effectively both verbally and in writing

Desirable: GCSE Mathematics

Experience

Essential: Proven experience in clerical work including data processing

Desirable: Previous experience of reception duties

Skills/Ability/Knowledge

Essential: Keyboarding and communication skills

Desirable: Ability to maintain computerised database systems

Other Requirements

Ability to deal with general practitioners, and the general public on the telephone and in person.

Must have a pleasant personality and be prepared to work flexible hours.

Figure 5.9 *An example of a person specification*

This specification will be used to assess a candidate's suitability for the post. Applicants should be able to meet all the essential requirements of the job and it will be to their advantage if they are able to offer some or all of the desirable elements.

ACTIVITY

Draw up a person specification for the position of part-time shop assistant in your local supermarket. This links with the advertisement and job description already created on pages 192 and 195.

Advertising the vacancy

Once the business has completed the above stages it must then decide where to advertise the new position. There are many different methods a business could use to advertise a position and often this is governed by the type of job being advertised. Some are outlined below:

- national newspapers
- local newspapers
- specialist newspapers and magazines
- local radio
- Job centres
- recruitment agencies
- adverts in shop windows.

A business must decide if the potential employee could come from the local area or if the person required may need to be recruited from a different area of the country due to **skill shortages**.

Often higher management positions are advertised nationally and lower position jobs are advertised locally.

The advertisement must contain sufficient information to attract potential employees and briefly outline the job and how applicants can apply for the position.

> **GLOSSARY**
>
> **Skill shortage:**
> Where the skills required for the job are in short supply in the local area.

Shortlisting applicants

Once a job has been advertised the business will hopefully have received lots of applications. If a business were to receive 20 applicants for a position it would be too costly for them to interview every candidate. The business will match the candidate's applications to the person specification and interview those candidates whose skills most closely match those on the person specification. It is usual for a business to interview only six candidates.

Preparing for an interview

An interview should be a two-way process. The employer will wish to find out about the candidate and discuss their previous experiences, personal qualities and ideas concerning the position they have applied for. The candidate will want to find out about the business and whether they would like to work for them.

In order for this process to run efficiently and smoothly the business must take some time to carefully plan the process. The following list outlines the aspects a business should consider prior to the interview day.

- Has the room been booked?
- Who will be conducting the interviews? Are they available and aware of the time and place where the interviews will take place?
- Is the room free from distractions and possible interruptions?
- Has the room been arranged correctly – table, chairs, refreshments?
- Has reception been informed of the names of interviewees and the procedure to deal with them?
- Does the waiting-room look comfortable and relaxing, and is there some company literature available for the candidate to read?
- Have all members of the interview panel studied the candidates' application forms thoroughly?
- Are all the members of the interview panel aware of the part they will play in the interview and the questions they will be asking?

ACTIVITY

Working in groups plan the interview for the part-time shop assistant for which you drew up a person specification on page 196. Think about how many people would be on the panel and what kind of questions would be asked.

Selecting and appointing a new employee

Once the interview process is over the interview panel has to decide which applicant they want to appoint. They will base their decisions on how the interviewees presented themselves at the interview, answered their questions and interest shown in the job being interviewed for.

When the decision has been made the successful applicant will be notified either by telephone or by letter. Once the successful candidate has accepted the position in writing the business will notify the other candidates that they have not been successful. Unsuccessful candidates are entitled to feedback from the interview panel concerning their interview performance. This will help them with future interviews.

Legal and ethical obligations

The recruitment and selection process is governed by equal opportunity legislation. This is to ensure that all candidates – regardless of their gender, sexual orientation, race or disability – are treated fairly within the recruitment process. We will be looking in more detail at this legislation in assessment objective 5. Briefly, the following equal opportunity legislation must be adhered to.

The Sex Discrimination Act 1975 is in place to ensure that a business does not discriminate against a potential candidate because they are either female or male. If both applicants have the same level of qualifications, skills and knowledge they must both be interviewed and judged on criteria other than their gender.

The Race Relations Act 1976 is in place to ensure that a business does not discriminate against a potential candidate because they are not English. The candidate must be judged on their qualifications, skills and knowledge as outlined in their application.

The Equal Pay Act 1970 ensures that both male and female employees are offered the same rate of pay for the same level of work.

The Disabled Persons (Employment) Act 1995 states that a business must make a reasonable effort to accommodate a disabled person if they have the qualifications, skills and knowledge necessary to undertake the job.

During the interview process the panel members must be very careful not to allow their own prejudices and personal opinions to cloud their judgement of a candidate. For example, if a panel member did not like face piercing and one of the candidates had a nose stud but was the most suitable person for the job, this should not affect their decision.

ACTIVITY

Look at the scenarios below and consider whether they breach any of the legislation briefly outlined above. State which Act you think they breach, giving your reasons why.

Advert in newsagent's window. Newspaper boys required for early morning paper rounds.

Question – A female applicant was asked if she was considering starting a family within the next two years.

Interview – A disabled applicant scored the best on the shortlist form but was not invited to interview as the business was worried about coping with his disability.

Discussion – A business had just recruited a new female employee. She was doing exactly the same job as her male counterparts. During a discussion in the canteen she found out that she was being paid 75p less per hour than her male colleague.

Role play
In small groups, design four short role plays that demonstrate two of the above Acts being breached and two being complied with fully. Perform the role plays to your class and see if the rest of the class can guess which Acts are being covered and if they were breached or complied with.

Portfolio tip

In order to achieve the higher grades for this assessment objective you need to ensure that you include examples of the recruitment process used by a selected business or businesses. Legal and ethical obligations that affect the recruitment and selection process could be evidence within the coverage of the other bullet points outlined in the specification.

AO4 Staff development programmes

Performance management is about a business looking after its employees. It involves discussing with them what they particularly enjoy about their job, what they find less enjoyable and if any training needs have been identified which would enable the employee to perform their job better. From these discussions a business can begin to plan its training and development programme.

Reasons for and benefits of training

Businesses train their employees in order for them to become more efficient at the work that they are required to do. A well-trained workforce will be able to mke products of the highest quality and offer the best possible customer service, through detailed product knowledge. A well-trained employee is much more efficient than one who has to continually distract other members of staff asking how to do something. Being well trained will also give an employee the confidence to do their job well. Having the right skills to complete a task will also reduce the pressure and stress on an employee.

Training programmes are carried out for a number of different reasons.

- To provide staff with the knowledge and skills that they require in order to perform their job efficiently.
- To meet skills shortages within the business. If a business cannot recruit the people required they may train internal members of staff.
- To give the employee a higher skills base in order to extend or expand their job role within the company. This could lead to promotion.
- To update employees' skills on new equipment, machinery or new legislation.
- To improve employees' performance in order to achieve targets.
- Customer service training in order to meet higher levels of customer satisfaction.

Benefits of training to the employer include:

- efficient staff
- motivated workforce
- highly skilled employees
- happy employees due to reduction in pressure and stress
- staff who feel valued
- lower **labour turnover**.

GLOSSARY

Labour turnover:
The number of employees who leave a business every year. It is measured by:

$$\frac{\text{number of leavers in one year}}{\text{Total number of employees}} \times 100 = \text{per cent}$$

The lower the percentage the better.

Benefits of training to the employee include:

- higher skills base – could help achieve promotion or new job
- motivation
- less stress and pressure
- feel valued by management
- happier as they have the knowledge and skills necessary to complete tasks efficiently
- better working environment.

ACTIVITY

As a group discuss the training that you have participated in recently. How effective did you think this training was? Did it enable you to do your job more efficiently?

Methods of training

There are two types of training: on the job and off the job. On-the-job training is undertaken within the business. The training will be directly related to the job that the person is performing. For example, a new employee may be shown how to use a piece of equipment by an existing employee. The major advantage of this type of training is that it is 'hands on' and relatively cheap. The disadvantages are that the trainer may not be very experienced and there may be interruptions.

On-the-job training

ACTIVITY

Have you received any 'on-the-job training'? If so, write down how it was conducted, how long it lasted and whether you think it was the best way to be trained.

There are different methods for on-the-job training and some are outlined below.

- Observing or learning by watching others – the new employee shadows and watches an experienced employee perform their job. The disadvantage is they may pick up not only good but bad habits as well.

- Mentoring – a new employee is paired up with an existing employee. If they have any problems or concerns they are able to approach their mentor to seek help and guidance. Mentoring does not offer job-specific training but personal support for the new member of staff.

- Coaching – an existing member of staff demonstrates the skills necessary to perform a job. The new member of staff then completes the task under the supervision of the coach.

Off-the-job training involves being trained away from the actual place of work. It can be conducted in-house or outside of the workplace such as a local college. If the training takes place within the organisation a room will be set aside for this purpose. The main advantage of off-the-job training is that the trainers will be specialist, there will few distractions and employees will be able to fully concentrate on the training being delivered. The major disadvantage is the cost of such events. Employees will be required to be released from their normal work for the duration of the training and external training agencies are often expensive. Off-the-job training could be delivered through the following agencies:

- the business's own training centre
- local colleges
- distance learning courses
- adventure courses – to build team leader skills.

Types of training

It has now become widely accepted within businesses that training is not only beneficial to the employees but also to the business. It should not just be seen as relevant only to those starting a new job. Training is the process that helps to improve the performance of an employee and creates an employee who is able to adapt to change. This is vital if a business is to survive in today's highly competitive and fast-moving world.

A good training programme which will meet the needs of the business and the workforce can be achieved by firstly assessing the needs of the workforce. It is vital that feedback is received from employees concerning the training they have received in order to assess whether it has met the needs of the employee and business.

A business that is committed to developing a training programme for its employees can apply to be accredited with the Investors in People award.

Induction

Induction training

Induction training is the initial training an employee receives when they join a business. It will usually include the following points:

- welcome and introduction to the business
- terms and conditions of employment
- future plans and targets of the business
- tour of the buildings
- health and safety
- use of IT facilities
- transfer to department.

The purpose of induction training is to welcome the new employee to the business and to give them an understanding of how the business operates. Health and safety training in the first few days is vitally important to ensure that the new employee is aware of specific evacuation and safety procedures related to the job they are about to start. Often new employees will be required to watch a health and safety video which will clearly explain the procedures they are expected to follow. Induction is also an opportunity for new members of staff to meet other new and existing staff members and friendships can be formed. This gives new employees confidence and allows them to become effective within their new position as quickly as possible.

ACTIVITY

As a group discuss the induction process that you underwent at school or college. Did you find it useful? Plan an induction programme for next year's students. Justify your suggestions.

Upgrading skills

We live in a rapidly changing world. Modern technology moves at a very fast pace. In order for employees to keep up with new developments they may need to have their current skills updated. For example, computer programs are being developed all the time. If a company decides to install a new accounts package, the accounts staff will need training in order to be able to use the more complex package. When Curriculum 2000 was first introduced into colleges, teachers attended training courses in order to become familiar with the new syllabuses. Legislation is often updated and employers may need to send employees on courses to become familiar with the new developments being introduced.

Multi-skilling

One of the developments in the workplace has been the idea of having a multi-skilled workforce. This means that each employee will be able to perform more than one task. The advantage of this is that should one member of staff be absent, another member of staff will have the skills necessary to cover the absent employee. The employee will also be able to undertake different jobs and will not become bored just performing one job at a time. Being able to complete different jobs on different days or weeks may also increase an employee's motivation as they are not doing the same job day in day out. For example, in a supermarket an employee may be trained to operate the tills, work on the customer service desk and serve on the delicatessen.

In order for a business to multi-skill their workforce they must decide which jobs each employee will be undertaking. The employee must then be trained in each chosen area.

CASE STUDY

Suitable training

Zaynap and James run their own business manufacturing plastic containers for the food industry. They purchased the business two years ago with the intention of updating the business in order to improve productivity. Within the next six months they are going to install two new machines on the production line and a computer system. They are aware that the Disability Discrimination Act changed things on 1 October 2004 and they are not sure if their business will be compliant with the new legislation. As the business is expanding rapidly they are also about to recruit two new employees to work on the production line and a new member of staff to help with administration.

Zaynap and James are aware that their staff will need training but are not sure what would be the best methods to suit all the different needs of their employees. They have asked you for the following help:

1 Outline the different types of training they could use in order to meet the needs of their employees.

2 Suggest a suitable induction programme for the three new employees.

PORTFOLIO GUIDANCE

In order to achieve this assessment objective you will need to investigate two businesses to find out how they undertake appraisals and the training they offer their staff. You could work in pairs, with each of you investigating a different business. Don't forget you can share information but you must write it up independently.

Assessment objective 4 is the only one which has to be directly linked to two selected businesses. However, the more examples you are able to use throughout your work the higher your final grade will be. This is because you will be able to apply the knowledge you learnt throughout this unit.

Appraisals

Appraisals and their benefits

The appraisal process is critical in identifying the training and development needs of individuals. They usually take place annually. Appraisals become an ongoing scheme to review how work is carried out and plan future actions. It is an opportunity for employees and employers to:

- look back at goals reached and standards met
- assess of areas of strength and weakness
- look forward, with a focus on improving performance.

Appraisals are also an opportunity to:

- recognise accomplishments and celebrate successes
- strengthen relationships and improve teamwork
- know what is expected in the future – and how to accomplish it.

A typical **appraisal process** is outlined below:

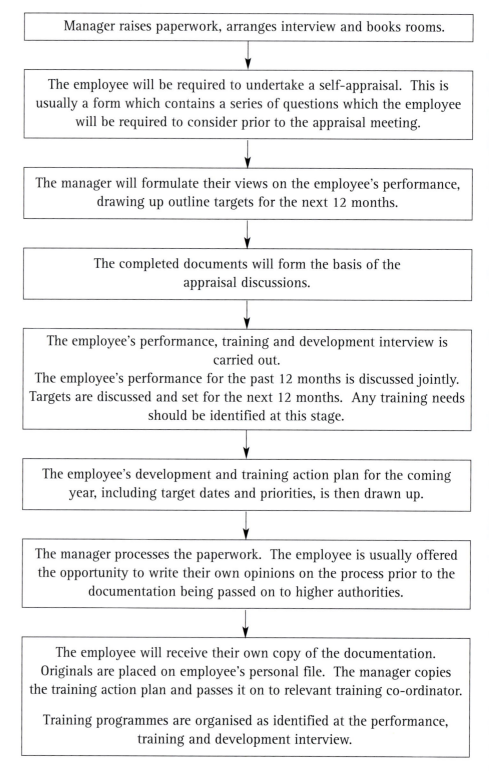

| Manager raises paperwork, arranges interview and books rooms. |

The employee will be required to undertake a self-appraisal. This is usually a form which contains a series of questions which the employee will be required to consider prior to the appraisal meeting.

The manager will formulate their views on the employee's performance, drawing up outline targets for the next 12 months.

The completed documents will form the basis of the appraisal discussions.

The employee's performance, training and development interview is carried out.
The employee's performance for the past 12 months is discussed jointly. Targets are discussed and set for the next 12 months. Any training needs should be identified at this stage.

The employee's development and training action plan for the coming year, including target dates and priorities, is then drawn up.

The manager processes the paperwork. The employee is usually offered the opportunity to write their own opinions on the process prior to the documentation being passed on to higher authorities.

The employee will receive their own copy of the documentation. Originals are placed on employee's personal file. The manager copies the training action plan and passes it on to relevant training co-ordinator.

Training programmes are organised as identified at the performance, training and development interview.

Appraisals give the employee an opportunity to discuss how they feel they are getting on within the business. It enables the employee to discuss in private concerns they may have about their job role and also offer ideas and suggestions on how to improve their working environment. It is an opportunity for a manager to listen carefully to their staff and come to agreements on how they can improve their performance. Being interested in staff is a very important part of motivation and the maintenance of good working relationships. A good appraisal is where the employee does most of the talking and should be encouraged to suggest how they could improve their own performance and any career developments they would like to pursue.

QUESTIONS

Have you ever participated in an appraisal?

Did it follow the same process as outlined above?

If not, how did it differ?

Did you find it helpful?

AO5 Employment protection, health, safety and equal opportunity

Employees are protected from dishonest employers through employment protection legislation. Employers also have rights under this legislation in order for them to be able to deal with 'difficult' employees.

Legal reasons for issuing a contract of employment

Under the **Employment Rights Act 1996** all employees are entitled to receive a contract of employment, provided their work lasts for more than one month. This must be received no later than two months after commencement of employment. The contract of employment must contain the following information:

- the name of the employer and employee
- the date when the employment began
- remuneration (pay) and the intervals at which it is to be paid
- hours of work
- holiday entitlement

- sick leave and sick pay entitlement
- pensions and pension schemes
- notice of termination required by employer and employee
- job title or a brief job description
- where the job is not permanent, the period for which the employment is expected to continue, or if it is for a fixed term, the date when it is to end
- the place of work
- details of any relevant collective agreements with trade unions or staff associations which directly affect the terms and conditions of the employee's employment.

Contents of a contract of employment

Job title

This is the title of the position an employee is being appointed to do. For example:

Clerical Assistant Grade 2

Hours of work

The Working Time Regulations state that no employee can be made to work more than 48 hours per week unless they choose to do so. This section will outline the hours the employee is required to work. The hours could be described as outlined below.

Monday – Friday 9.00 am–5.30 pm with one hour for lunch.
Or simply 37.5 hours per week

Shift patterns could be described. For example:

6 am–2 pm, 2 pm–10 pm and 10 pm–6 am.

Flexitime may be in operation and the contract will explain how this works within the business. Flexitime is where the employee is required to work a set number of hours per week but can choose when to do these hours between set core times. For example, the employee is required to work 37.5 hours per week. The business is open from 7 am to 7 pm, but the core hours the employee must be in work are 10 am to 12 pm and 2 pm to 4 pm. The remainder of the hours can be fitted in around the opening times of the business.

Hours of work could also include arrangements for overtime.

Rate and method of payment

As from October 2004 the National Minimum Wage is:

- main (adult) rate for workers aged 22 and over – £4.85 per hour
- development rate for workers aged 18-21 inclusive – £4.10 per hour
- new young workers' rate for 16- and 17-year-olds – £3.00 per hour
- 16- to 17-year-old apprentices will be exempt from the new young workers' rate.

This section outlines how much the employee will be paid. This could be an hourly rate or an annual salary. If an employee is paid hourly it may include overtime rates as applicable. Salaried employees are not often paid overtime. Their salary reflects the hours they are required to work in order to complete their workload.

The method of payment will state how and when the employee will receive payment for the work undertaken. Employees can be paid weekly or monthly.

Employees will also need to know how they will receive their wages. This could be by cheque in a pay packet, or payment via their bank account.

Holiday arrangements

Under the Working Time Directive every worker, whether full-time or part-time, is entitled to four weeks' paid holiday a year. The leave entitlement is not additional to bank holidays. There is no statutory right to take bank holidays off.

A week's leave should allow workers to be away from work for one week. It should be the same amount of time as the normal working week. For example, if an employee works a five-day week, he or she is entitled to 20 days' paid holiday. If an employee works a three-day week he or she is entitled to 12 days' paid leave.

The employee will be informed in this section the leave they are entitled to. It may also state when leave can be taken and how much notice the employer requires before leave can be taken.

Notice period

This section will inform the employee how much notice is required by either party in order to terminate employment with the business.

If an employee is paid weekly the notice period required is usually one week. If an employee is paid monthly then often a month's notice is required on either side.

Pension arrangements

A lot of businesses offer their employees a company pension. This section will outline what percentage of the employees' pay will be deduced each week/month to go towards their pension fund. It will also state the amount the business will contribute to the employee's pension.

Trade union rights

This will outline any collective agreements that the company has with trade unions. The employee will have the choice whether to join a trade union or not.

Disciplinary procedures

From October 2004 **all** businesses must have a written disciplinary and grievance procedure in place. This must cover:

- the disciplinary rules which apply to the employee
- the job title or name of the person to whom the employee can apply and the way in which the application can be made if the employee is dissatisfied with any disciplinary decision
- any further steps which follow from the making of such an application.

ACTIVITY

As a small group, think of a job that you could do upon leaving college. Draw up a suitable contract of employment for the position chosen.

Responsibilities of employers and employees

As soon as you start work you will be required to comply with legislation that has been developed in order to keep you safe in the workplace. There are many Acts in place to ensure that employers do not abuse their workforce and put their lives at risk.

Factories Act 1961

Factories have been defined as premises where persons are employed in manual labour. The Factories Act states how the employer must ensure the health and safety of the workforce. There are two provisions. One focuses on health and the second focuses on general safety provisions.

The health provisions are outlined below:

- cleanliness
- overcrowding
- temperature - not less than 60°F after the first hour of work
- ventilation
- lighting
- drainage of floors
- toilets
- medical supervision.

The general safety provisions of the Act are complex and focus on the protection needed on dangerous machinery to avoid employees injuring themselves. The Act also covers other safety aspects which would be specific to a factory, for example the use of ladders.

COSHH

COSHH stands for Control of Substances Hazardous to Health Regulations 2002. Using hazardous substances can put employees' health at risk. Therefore, this Act was brought into force to ensure that employers control employees' exposure to hazardous substances.

Hazardous substances are anything that can harm an employee's health if they are not properly controlled by adequate ventilation. These substances can be found in nearly all workplaces, for example factories, shops, mines, farms and offices. They can include:

- substances used directly in work activities – glues, paints, cleaning agents
- substances generated during work activities – fumes from soldering and welding
- naturally occurring substances – grain dust, blood, bacteria.

Most commercial chemicals will bear a WARNING label to indicate if COSHH is relevant.

> **Did you know?**
>
> *Washing-up liquid does not have a warning label but bleach does – COSHH applies to bleach but not washing-up liquid.*

COSHH safety sign

RIDDOR

RIDDOR stands for Reporting of Injuries, Diseases and Dangerous Occurrences Regulations 1995. The Act requires employers to report work-related accidents, diseases and dangerous occurrences. The Act applies to all employers but some minor incidents may not need to be recorded. An employer needs to report:

- deaths
- major injuries
- accidents resulting in over three days' injury
- diseases
- dangerous occurrences
- gas incidents.

An example of a major injury would include fracture of a limb. Fingers, thumbs or toes are excluded.

An example of a reportable disease would be some skin diseases such as occupational dermatitis, skin cancer, chrone ulcer, oil folliculitis/acne.

A dangerous occurrence is defined as where an incident does not result in a reportable injury, but which clearly could have done – for example a dangerous substance travelling by road is involved in a fire or the contents released.

Lockhill Industrial Plant
Accident report form

Name of casualty ....

Exact location of incident ....

Date of incident ....

What was the injured person doing? ....

How did the accident happen? ....

What injuries occurred? ....

Treatment given ....

Medical aid sought ....

Name of person dealing with incident ....

Name of witness ....

If casualty was a child, what time were parents informed? ....

Was hospital attended? ....

Was the accident investigated? .... By whom? ....

Signed .... Position ....

Figure 5.7 *An accident report form*

The reporting of accidents and ill health at work is a legal requirement and allows enforcing agencies to identify where and how risks arise in the workplace. The **enforcing agencies** can help and advise employers on preventive action to reduce injury, ill health and accidents.

Health and safety at work regulations

The basis of the British health and safety law is the Health and Safety at Work Act 1974. This Act sets out the general duties which employers have towards employees and members of the public, and employees have to themselves and to each other.

The Health and Safety at Work Act requires all employers as far as is practicable to ensure the health and safety of their employees.

'Reasonably practical' means that the degree of risk in a particular job or workplace needs to be balanced against the time, trouble, cost and physical difficulty of taking measures to avoid or reduce the risk.

The Health and Safety at Work Act 1974 applies to all work premises. Anyone on the premises has responsibilities under the Act. The Act requires employers to:

- provide safe access to the premises
- maintain safe machinery, equipment and systems of work
- provide safe and healthy premises e.g. adequate toilets, heating, lighting and ventilation
- provide safety training for employees
- produce a Safety Policy Statement of which all employees must be aware (if there are more than five employees)
- provide a safe environment for visitors to the premises
- keep an accident book in which details of any incidents are recorded.

The Act requires employees to be responsible for:

- taking reasonable care at all times for the health and safety of themselves and others in the workplace
- using safety devices when required
- co-operating with employers on all safety matters including training.

The Management of Health and Safety at Work Regulations 1992 generally make more specific what employers are required to do to manage health and safety under the Health and Safety at Work Act. The Act includes the following sections.

- Management of Health and Safety at Work Regulations 1992: require employers to carry out risk assessments; make arrangements to put into place measures to limit risks; appoint competent people and arrange information and training for all staff.
- Workplace (Health & Safety & Welfare) Regulations 1992: cover a wide range of basic health, safety and welfare issues such as ventilation, heating, lighting, workstations, seating and welfare facilities.
- Health and Safety (Display Screen Equipment) Regulations 1992: set out requirements for work with Visual Display Units (VDUs).
- Personal Protective Equipment at Work Regulations 1992: require employers to provide appropriate protective clothing and equipment for their employees.

> ### GLOSSARY
>
> **Enforcing agencies:** These include the Health and Safety Executive or local council.

- Provision & Use of Work Equipment Regulations 1998 require that equipment provided for use at work, including machinery, is safe.
- Manual Handling Operations 1992: cover the moving of objects by hand or bodily force.
- Health and Safety (First Aid) Regulations 1981: cover requirements for first aid.
- The Health and Safety Information for Employees Regulations 1989: require employers to display a poster telling employees what they need to know about health and safety.
- Employers' Liability (Compulsory Insurance) Regulations 1969: require employers to take out insurance against accidents and ill health to their employees.

The main requirement on employers of this Act is to carry out **risk assessment.**

Risk assessment should eliminate hazards

Risk assessment is usually straightforward in an office situation but can become a lot more complicated when identifying possible risks to health and safety within a chemical plant, building site or oil rig. Having carried out risk assessment an employer also needs to:

- ensure that any potential hazards identified in the risk assessment are either eliminated or the necessary heath and safety measures are put in place
- appoint competent people to help set up and monitor heath and safety arrangements
- set up emergency procedures such as fire drills etc.
- provide clear information and training to employees.

The UK Health and Safety Commission (HSC) and the Health and Safety Executive (HSE) are responsible for the regulation of almost all the risks to health and safety arising from work activity in Britain. Their mission is to ensure that risks to people's health and safety from work activities are properly controlled.

ACTIVITY

Working in small groups, walk around your school or college making a note of any health and safety risks that you find. Return to your classroom and discuss your findings. What action do you think the school/college should take to overcome these problems?

Noise at Work Regulations 1989

Ear protection must be worn in certain situations

Did you know?

A workplace has a noise problem if people have to shout or have difficulty being heard by someone about 2 metres away.

This Act requires workers to be protected from loud noise. Exposure to loud noise can cause permanent hearing problems. These problems can include loss of hearing ability, or some people may suffer from a permanent sensation of noises or ringing in the ears known as 'tinnitus'.

Recent research estimates that 170,000 people in the UK suffer deafness, tinnitus or other ear conditions as a result of exposure to excessive noise at work.

This Act requires employers to ensure the following:

- reduce noise exposure as far as is reasonably practicable
- if employees' daily exposure to noise is 85 dB(A) or more employers must provide them with information and training on the risk to their health. Ear protectors must be provided if requested
- if the noise exposure is more than 90dB(A) or more then ear protectors must be supplied, checks must be in place to ensure they are being worn properly and the areas marked in which they should be worn.

Below is a guide to the noise levels:

- a normal conversation 50–60 dB(A)
- a loud radio 65–75 dB(A)
- a busy street 78–85 dB(A)
- a heavy lorry about 7 metres away 95–100 dB(A)
- a pighouse at feeding time 110 dB(A)
- a chainsaw 115–120 dB(A)
- a jet aircraft taking off 25 metres away 140dB(A)

The Offices, Shops and Railway Premises Act 1963

This Act introduced the first occupational safety controls in offices, shops and railway premises. If a business intends to employee someone to work in a shop or office premises they are required by section 49 of the Offices, Shops and Railways Act 1963 to complete the relevant documentation and submit it to their local authority. The Act defines the requirements for safety, health and welfare of employees. The main parts of the act are outlined below:

- premises must be kept clean with a minimum of 40 square feet of space per person working in the office
- offices must be adequately heated with a temperature of 16 degrees centigrade by the first hour of working
- there must be sufficient lighting in offices, corridors and stairs
- there must be an adequate supply of fresh or purified air, supply of drinking water and arrangements for hanging and drying of clothing
- employees who mainly do work sitting down must be provided with adequate seating and in some cases foot-rests
- employees must be provided with a suitable facility where they can take their meals
- floors, passages, and stairs must be kept in good order, with suitable handrails for stairs
- dangerous parts of machinery must be guarded and under 18s are not allowed to clean potentially dangerous machinery.

Equal opportunity legislation

So far we have looked at the legislation the government has put in place to ensure that an employee's health and safety are protected. The next section of legislation looks at how employees are protected through equal opportunity legislation. These Acts were brought into force to ensure that everybody is treated fairly in the workplace regardless of their gender, religion, race or possible disability.

The Sex Discrimination Act 1975

This Act makes it illegal to discriminate against anybody on grounds of their gender or marital status. Discrimination can be direct or indirect. Direct is where a position could be advertised as 'salesmen' or it could be indirect such as a job advertisement requesting an employee who can lift 25kg. This could exclude a woman from applying.

There are some instances where a job is allowed to be advertised for a specific sex. This could be due to the nature of the job, for example, a housemaster to be responsible for the care of young men, or a housemistress to care for young women.

The Equal Opportunities Commission was established to investigate complaints of discrimination.

The Race Relations Act 1976

It is illegal to discriminate against anybody due to their race. The Act is enforced by the Commission for Racial Equality which can give employers advice about how to ensure that they are not inadvertently discriminating against different ethnic minorities in their recruitment and selection processes.

The Equal Pay Act 1970

The Equal Pay Act gives an individual the right to the same rate of pay/salary and benefits as a person of the opposite sex in the same employment, where the man and woman are doing:

- like work or
- work related as the same under an analytical job evaluation or study
- work that is proved to be of equal value.

The employer will not be required to provide the same pay and benefits if it can prove that the difference in pay or benefits is genuinely due to a reason other than one related to sex.

The Disabled Persons (Employment) Act 1994

This Act states that employers with more than 20 employees should have a quota of approximately 30 per cent who are considered to be disabled. Under the **Disability Discrimination Act 1995 section 4** makes it unlawful for an employer with more than 15 employees to discriminate against a disabled person. However, from 1 October 2004, the Disability Discrimination Act includes employers with fewer than 15 employees.

The Act means that employers must not discriminate against disabled employees or job applicants because of their disability. The employer may have to make reasonable adjustments to the workplace if they already have a disabled employee or a disabled person applies for a job.

Reasonable adjustments to the workplace could include:

- rearranging furniture to provide better access
- reallocating some duties of a job to another member of staff
- allowing someone to work more flexible hours
- allowing someone time off for rehabilitation or treatment
- providing information in an accessible format such as large print, Braille or on audio tape so that they can do their job
- providing a piece of specialist equipment such as a textphone for a hearing impaired person or a screen reader for a visually impaired person
- moving a disabled person to another available vacancy or to a more accessible site.

Facilitating access for disabled workers is a 'reasonable adjustment'

Reasonable adjustments to the way an employer recruits staff could include:

- making application forms available in large print or Braille
- allowing applications to be made in formats other than in writing, for example on audio tape
- providing a sign language interpreter for interviews
- moving the interviews to an accessible venue.

Portfolio tip

In order to achieve this assessment objective you could design a staff handbook that describes employment protection, health and safety and equal opportunity legislation.

ACTIVITY

Taking each item of legislation covered within this section, outline one consequence if a business failed to follow the law.

For example, if a leisure centre failed to follow COSHH by not supplying an employee with gloves when using chemicals for the swimming pool, the employee could receive serious burns to their hands.

AO6 How disagreements at work arise and are resolved

As we have seen throughout this unit, businesses will want to avoid disagreements between themselves and their employees. Disputes are costly and damaging to businesses and employees alike.

Grievance and disciplinary procedures

A grievance procedure outlines what the employee must do if they have any concerns or complaints about their work, employment terms, working conditions or relationships with colleagues.

There is no set list as to what should be included in a business's grievance procedure. Its aim is to resolve problems as fairly and quickly as possible. The Acas code of practice sets out that a disciplinary and grievance procedure should:

- be straightforward and in writing
- allow for the rapid resolution of problems
- be made known to all workers.

The stages within the procedure will vary according to the size and structure of individual businesses. The procedure should specify:

- how and to whom a worker should raise an issue
- where to go next if the issue cannot be resolved at this level
- what the time limits are for each stage of the procedure
- the right to be accompanied by a colleague or trade union official at any hearing.

Businesses will have a formal procedure that they are required to follow by law before they are able to 'sack' an employee. There are usually three stages to the procedure.

Stage one – a verbal warning. The employee has a meeting with their line manager to discuss the problem. This could be that the employee has been ten minutes late three times in the last week. The employee will be warned that they must improve their time keeping or the next stage of the procedure will be a written warning.

During the course of the meeting the line manager may discover that there is not a bus that the employee can catch to get them to work on time. The employer may decide to change the employee's hours and therefore the matter will have been resolved amicably.

Although stage one is known as a verbal warning, it will be recorded on the employee's staff record.

Stage two – this is a formal written warning. The second stage is used when the behaviour or standard of work of the employee has failed to improve after the verbal warning. The employee will be asked to attend a meeting with the management of the business to discuss the problem. The employee will be issued with a formal written warning which will clearly identify the improvements that are required and the timescale that these must be achieved in.

If an employee is struggling to do their job the employer may suggest they move to a lower grade or may offer the employee further training.

Stage three – this is the last stage of the procedure. The employee has again failed to meet the targets set. Another formal meeting with management will take place and new targets with a time limit will be set. Failure to meet these targets will result in the employee being asked to leave the business.

Fair and unfair dismissal situations

The disciplinary procedures outlined above are there to ensure that employees are only asked to leave their employment due to their failure to meet realistic performance targets. An employer has a right to expect his/her employees to turn up to work on time and to produce work of a high standard. By the same token an employee has the right to be protected from unscrupulous employers.

An employee is considered to have been dismissed from employment fairly if the employer has followed the procedures outlined above. An employer does not have to follow the three-stage procedure if the employee does something that would be considered gross misconduct of behaviour. This could include coming into work drunk or under the influence of drugs, assaulting a customer or another member of staff, stealing from the business or behaving in such a way that could cause harm to themselves, another member of staff or a customer.

An unfair dismissal is where the employee has been dismissed from their employment for reasons which are not considered to be reasonable.

If an employee feels they have been dismissed unfairly they can take their case to an industrial tribunal. This is a board of independent people who will listen to both sides of the argument and decide whether the employee was dismissed unfairly or not. If the case is found in favour of the employee the employer may be required to re-instate the employee or offer them compensation for loss of earnings.

Aims of trade unions

A trade union logo

Trade unions are voluntary organisations which represent the interests of employees. Employees are free to join a union if they wish to do so. Unions will charge their members an annual subscription, and offer a range of benefits which include legal advice and representation during disciplinary or grievance procedures and negotiations on the employee's behalf for increases in wages and working conditions. They will also lobby government in order to influence changes in legislation which will make employees' working lives easier. Their aims are to:

- improve the pay of workers
- improve working conditions and secure longer holidays
- protect members' jobs
- provide local, social and welfare facilities
- influence government policy by sponsoring Members of Parliament and contributing money to political parties.

Trade unions are able to represent the views of many employees and therefore their bargaining power to ensure improved conditions of employment are enhanced. It is much easier for one organised body to negotiate on behalf of the whole workforce for a pay rise, rather than one individual undertaking their own negotiations with management.

Different types of trade unions

Craft unions represent skilled workers from one occupation, for example AUEW, the Amalgamated Union of Engineering Workers, represents employees working in engineering.

   General unions represent mainly unskilled workers from many different occupations, for example, the TGWU (The Transport and General Workers' Union).

   Industrial unions represent mainly workers in one industry. For example, the NUM (National Union of Miners) represents miners.

   Professional or **white-collar unions** represent skilled workers mainly in the service industries, for example the NUT (National Union of Teachers).

CASE STUDY

Holiday agreements

In August 2004, the threat of bank holiday chaos at airports was lifted as British Airways and unions came to an agreement. After two days of talks the unions representing the 11,000 check-in staff and baggage handlers were understood to be ready to accept the 8.5 per cent pay rise over three years. As part of the deal, BA was ready to pay an extra £1,000 sum to workers as a series of lump sums, making the deal worth 14.5 per cent overall. The money was no longer thought to be connected to set targets for cutting absenteeism which was one of the major sticking points earlier in negotiations. BA only wanted the money paid if the staff took less than 16 days sick leave a year which is twice the national average. The unions and BA agreed to set up a plan to tackle absenteeism which is not linked to pay. The leaders of the Transport and General Workers Union and the GMB recommended the deal in fresh ballots to BA workers.

The GMB is known as the Britain's General Union as it represents many different types of employees.

1 Outline the agreement that was reached between British Airways and the unions.
2 Identify the two unions involved in the negotiations.
3 Why do you think the unions did not want the pay deal to be linked to reduced absenteeism?
4 Suggest and justify ways you think BA and the unions could reduce the number of sick days taken by employees.

Employment tribunal

If an employee feels they have been unfairly treated and are not happy with the result of consultations with their employer they can decide to take their case to an **employment tribunal**. Employment tribunals are judicial bodies established to resolve disputes over employment rights.

Judicial bodies are a group of people who make decisions which will be accepted by the general public.

They hear applications and appeals about matters to do with work. These matters can include unfair dismissal, redundancy payments, sex, race and disability discrimination, together with some issues relating to wages and terms and conditions of employment.

An employment tribunal is like a court but not so formal. However, like a court it acts independently and cannot give legal advice. Almost all hearings are open to the public.

The tribunal generally has three members. The 'chairman' is legally qualified and is appointed by the Lord Chancellor. The other two members are **lay members** and are appointed by the Secretary of State for Trade and Industry. These people are chosen because they have a wide experience of dealing with work-related matters.

GLOSSARY

Lay members:
People who do not have a legal background.

Each party and their witnesses give evidence on oath. Witnesses can be asked questions by the other side, the lay members and the chairman. When all the evidence has been presented both sides will sum up their case. The tribunal comes to their decision in private and sends the decision and reasons to both parties. Appeals can be made but are limited to points of law.

Acas – Advisory, Conciliation and Arbitration Service

Acas is a publicly funded organisation which works independently with impartiality and maintains confidentiality in all its dealings. It was founded in 1974 and now employs approximately 900 staff based in 11 main regional centres throughout England, Scotland and Wales, with the head office in London.

Acas is best known for its role in helping employers and employees resolve disputes known as 'conciliation'. Acas gets involved if both sides feel they can help them make some progress. It is entirely voluntary and therefore both sides must agree that this is the best way forward.

When Acas is called in to a business to act in a conciliation role their aim is to:

- sort out the issues
- find common ground between the two sides
- give people the space to calm down and see the problems from the other side too (sometimes this involves taking the dispute out of the media spotlight)
- have meetings with each side separately and together to discuss and explore the issues, then start negotiating a solution
- repair relationships and build up trust.

The overall aim of the process is to get the two sides to reach their own agreement that will work.

European Court of Justice

The European Court of Justice deals with disputes and is responsible for upholding the laws of the European Union. Its job is to ensure that all the laws are interpreted and applied in the same way right across the European Union.

It sits in Luxembourg and comprises 15 judges, one judge from each member state.

The court was established in 1952 when the European Union was first started. It sits and hears cases all year round.

ACTIVITY

As a group discuss why you think it is important that we have employment tribunals, Acas and the European Court of Justice. Research any recent cases that the last two organisations have been involved in recently.

Portfolio tip

In order to enhance your evidence for this assessment objective try and relate your theory to a selected business. Investigate recent industrial action and how these disputes were resolved.

SKILLS CHECK

1 Describe Frederick Herzberg's theory of motivation.

2 Describe how good employer and employee relations help to increase motivation.

3 What are the possible consequences of a business not having good employee/employer co-operation?

4 What are the main responsibilities of a manager?

5 What kind of tasks would a general clerical assistant have to undertake?

6 Design a job description for a clerical assistant – make up a suitable organisation.

7 Draw a flow diagram which outlines the different stages of the recruitment and selection process.

8 What are the benefits to an employer and employee of participating in regular appraisals?

9 What are the advantages of observing or shadowing a member of staff in order to gain the skills necessary to work on a production line?

10 Give an example when you would use the following types of training. Give reasons for your choice.
   – On the job
   – Off the job.

11 What information should be found in a contract of employment?

12 What are the main requirements of COSHH?

13 Describe the responsibilities of employers and employees under the Health and Safety at Work Act 1974.

14 Describe the damage excessive noise can have on employees. What can a business do to avoid injury to their employees?

15 What is a disciplinary and grievance procedure?

16 What constitutes unfair dismissal?

17 What role do trade unions play in today's workplace?

Promotion in business

Getting Started

To survive and be successful, businesses must provide products and services that customers wish to buy. However, all products need to be promoted to customers. Promotion involves telling customers about products and persuading them to buy through advertising and other techniques. Even excellent products can fail in the market if potential customers simply don't know about them or the business is not able to persuade customers to buy them.

The aim of this unit is to give you knowledge and understanding of promotional techniques that are used by businesses. To complete this unit successfully you will need to address the eight assessment objectives in the specification and to achieve assessment objectives 3 to 8 you must produce evidence based upon a real life promotional campaign in a business organisation that you have investigated.

This unit will cover

- A01 Describe the purpose of promotion and factors that lead to effective promotion.
- A02 Describe the barriers to effective promotion.
- A03 Define the market position of a chosen business and identify its current promotional objectives.
- A04 Describe the types of promotional techniques available to the chosen business.
- A05 Identify the main controls on promotional techniques available to the chosen business.
- A06 Explain how the business decides on the most suitable media for promotional campaigns.
- A07 Recommend and justify a promotional campaign for the chosen business.
- A08 Explain how the recommended promotional campaign's effectiveness may be evaluated.

AO1 The purpose of promotion and effective promotion

Promotion is the way in which businesses make customers and potential customers aware of their products and services and persuade them to buy them rather than rival products or brands. Promotion is usually carried out by the marketing function of a business.

The purpose of promotion

The purpose of promotion is to:

- raise awareness of the product or service
- generate sales
- compete with other businesses operating in the market.

Promotional material may be informational or persuasive. Informational material gives customers information about the product to help them make up their minds about whether to buy, for example, price lists, catalogues and menus. **Persuasive** material has little information about the product but relies heavily on other factors such as style or image to sell the product. Television advertising on the whole tends to be persuasive rather than informational.

People who work in marketing often use the acronym **AIDA** to summarise the main stages of successful promotional activity. There are four stages in promotion.

A is for Attention. A successful piece of promotional material such as an advertisement will aim to get the customer's attention. Promotional material may contain interesting graphics, music or snappy slogans to get the customer's attention. Words and phrases such as 'new', 'sale' and 'special offer' are often used to grab attention. Consumers are bombarded with all sorts of promotional material so a promotional message will need to stand out from the rest. If the promotional message does not gain the customer's attention it has failed.

I is for Interest. Promotional material should make the customer interested in finding out more about the product or service. Potential customers should be provided with enough information to create interest in the product. This may lead to them phoning a supplier or visiting a company website, store or showroom for more details.

D is for Desire. The next stage is to make customers want to have the product. It may offer some obvious benefits to them, for example a new washing-up liquid may claim to clean dishes faster. In some cases promotional material may suggest that a product such as a body spray may make the wearer more attractive to the opposite sex or that an energy drink will make them better at their job.

A is for Action. The final stage in the process is getting the customer to go out to buy the product or service. This may involve telling consumers where they can obtain the product and providing telephone numbers if it is a mail order business or a web address if it is an Internet business.

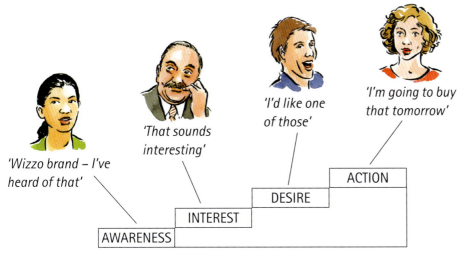

'Wizzo brand – I've heard of that'

'That sounds interesting'

'I'd like one of those'

'I'm going to buy that tomorrow'

ACTION

DESIRE

INTEREST

AWARENESS

Figure 7.1 *The four stages of AIDA*

To raise awareness

The first stage of any promotional campaign, particularly for a new product, is to make customers and potential customers aware of the product or service. In a competitive market a new product may be 'invisible' unless the business uses promotional techniques to attract attention to the product that is being marketed. Even a high-quality and reasonably priced product can fail if too few of the potential customers know that it is available. The market for magazines is highly competitive and any new magazine that is launched will have to be supported with a range of promotional techniques if it is to stand any chance of establishing itself in the market. In spring 2004, two new men's magazines *Nuts* and *Zoo* were launched. Both were aimed at a similar market and both were supported by big advertising campaigns on television and elsewhere.

To generate sales

Every promotional method involves some sort of cost to the business, such as the cost of printing material, placing advertisements in the media or staff time. Therefore, most promotional campaigns are expected to increase sales of the product. Increased sales will bring more cash into the business known as **sales revenue**. A promotional campaign accompanying the launch of a brand-new product will aim to generate sales and gain market share. However, a promotional campaign may also aim to raise the profile of a business over a longer time period or change its image and may not necessarily lead to an immediate increase in sales of the product.

Sales revenue is calculated by multiplying the number of items sold by the price charged for each item:

Number of items sold × selling price = sales revenue.

This is the cash coming into the business from sales.

To compete in the market

Most products and services are sold in competitive markets which means that customers have a choice about which brand they buy. Businesses will spend money trying to persuade customers to buy their brand. Many well-established products are still supported by extensive promotional activity. Persil and Kit Kat have been on the market for decades but the owners of these brands, Unilever and Nestlé, still spend millions of pounds annually promoting these products despite the fact that customers have a good understanding and awareness of the brands.

Spending huge amounts of money on advertising and other promotional material also makes it difficult for new firms to enter the market and compete. Walkers is the market leader in the UK crisp market and the company spends heavily on advertising. A new brand of crisp would find it very difficult to compete with Walkers as the business would have to match Walkers' promotional spending to establish itself.

ACTIVITY

Look at the following commonly bought household products and services:

cornflakes   mobile phone service   toilet rolls   shampoo   car insurance
non-alcoholic drinks   hand-held game console   gas or electricity supplier
newspaper

- Which brands do you or your family buy?
- Does the advertising and promotion of these brands play any part in your decision to buy?

Branded products

Factors influencing the effectiveness of promotion

Promotional material is like any other piece of communication. Businesses are sending out a message to a target audience. A simple model of communication is shown below.

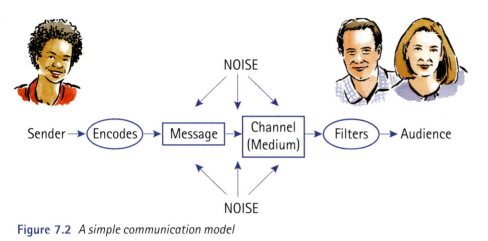

NOISE

Sender → Encodes → Message → Channel (Medium) → Filters → Audience

NOISE

Figure 7.2 *A simple communication model*

A simple example of a promotion may help to illustrate this. Softsilk are running a television advertisement to promote their new shampoo. In this case the sender is the company and the message is that they have a new shampoo on the market. The chosen medium is television and they believe that their receivers or audience are mainly women in the 16–50 age group.

Factors which will influence how effective the promotion is include:

- **How messages are encoded.** Code refers to the format that is used for the message. Messages may be wording such as 'special offer – 50 per cent off' or images, logos or music may be used. Advertisements for Guinness and Stella Artois lager are complex and stylish pieces of promotion which offer little or no information about the products but are all about developing a distinctive image.

- **Receiving messages.** The message may not always have the desired effect on the receiver. The message may not be clearly understood by the receiver for a number of reasons to do with their age, culture, level of education or because the message itself is not clear. The message needs to be targeted at the correct audience to stand more chance of success.

- **Reactions to the message.** Generally, the purpose of promotion is increased sales or encouraging a more positive image of the product. The use of a celebrity such as David Beckham to promote a product is based on the view that the receivers of the message will have a positive view of the footballer. However, if the receiver dislikes footballers and David Beckham in particular, then the promotion may not be successful with that individual.

● **Clarity**. The promotion is unlikely to be successful if the language or images used are complex or unclear. It may be that too much jargon is used or the level language is too high or too low for the audience. Many people are put off by computers and financial products because of the jargon they encounter.

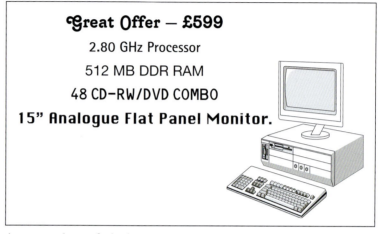

Jargon can be confusing!

● **The attention span of the watcher or listener**. A promotional poster is a permanent format that the reader can look at for as long as they wish to. However, if they are driving their car at the time, they may have only a few seconds to take in the message. Similarly, a 15-second radio advertisement can be effective, but the majority of the audience will not be listening closely and they will not recall information such as a phone number unless the advertisement is repeated regularly.

ACTIVITY

In pairs or small groups consider the following:
● Identify four advertisements that make use of a celebrity. Why do you think the particular celebrity was chosen?
● Identify two advertisements that you feel are not effective and give your reasons.

Portfolio tip

In your portfolio you should describe what the purpose of promotion is and what factors lead to effective promotion of the product or service supplied by your chosen business.

AO2 Describe the barriers to effective promotion

There are things that can prevent the promotional message achieving its purpose, these are known as **interference** and these are listed below:

- competing messages
- attention span
- existing perceptions
- filtering
- distortion.

Competing messages

Every day most of us receive thousands of sounds and images. Many of these are very familiar, some are new and interesting, while others seem irrelevant. A promotional message will have to compete with many others and if it cannot get our attention it is not effective. An advertisement for a new car will be competing with many other promotional messages from rival car manufacturers.

Attention span

A customer who has gone to a car showroom with the aim of buying a new car is likely to want to spend quite some time with a sales representative. However, a 15-second television advertisement during the commercial break in a film may be missed by viewers who have gone to fetch a drink or largely ignored by those who are chatting.

Filtering

Most of us have ideas and prejudices about what we like and don't like. Sometimes the audience may interpret a message in a way that the advertiser did not expect. This could be because the message is unclear or ambiguous or the audience received it at an unexpected time or through an unexpected medium. The advertisement may be supported by a piece of music that the listener does not like or show images that the viewer finds patronising or annoying.

Distortion

The message may not be communicated effectively because of some sort of interference. The message may be delivered too quickly or the language used may be unsuitable for the audience. There may also be a technical problem with the chosen medium e.g. a website crashes or the reception of a radio signal is poor.

> **QUESTION**
>
> What are some of the barriers to getting a promotional message across to potential customers effectively?

AO3 The market position of a business and its promotional objectives

Market positioning refers to where a business positions its products or brands in the market. Some businesses are large and dominate their market while other smaller businesses may struggle to survive. Market positioning also includes how the company sees itself and the type of products and customers that it supplies. Some brands are seen as being 'up-market' e.g. Rolex, Rolls Royce, Armani. These products have an image of exclusivity and are aimed at higher income groups whereas others have a more 'down-market' image.

Market growth and market share

When analysing its market position, a business will need to assess the current state of the market and its place in the market. A firm is more likely to enjoy success in a growing market rather than a declining one. The market for a product or service may be growing because of fashion or social trends leading to rising sales figures for most of the businesses in that market. Life will be much more difficult if the market for a firm's products is in sharp decline.

Calculating percentage change

In the year 2003 total market sales of a product came to £184m. In 2004 market sales totalled £208m. Use the following method to calculate the percentage change in market size:

1. Subtract the smaller figure from the larger one to find the actual change: £208m − £184m = £24m
2. Divide the actual change by the amount *before* the change: £24m/£184m = 0.13
3. Multiply by 100 to arrive at the percentage change: 0.13 × 100 = 13%
4. The market grew by 13 per cent.

Calculating market share

Market share is the proportion of the total market sales that are made by one company or brand or product. In Unit 1 we learned that the firm or brand that has the biggest market share is known as the **market leader** and if a firm is able to increase its market share it shows that it is winning customers from its competitors. A declining market share is likely to be a serious cause for concern for a business as it means that it is losing out to the competition.

Sales of Brand X
Total market sales $\times$ 100 = Percentage market share

Business profile

Some products and brands are much more recognisable in the market than others. Brands such as Coca-Cola, Sony, Nike and McDonald's are high-profile brands which are recognised across the world. Businesses such as these can afford to sponsor big international events, such as the Olympics and Champions League football, and gain from the worldwide publicity that this brings. Other products and brands may not be known outside of their own specialised markets. There may well be a business such as a nightclub or chip shop which is well known locally but unknown to the public outside your area.

Image

While business profile refers to how well known or recognised a business is, image refers to how customers or members of the general public see the business. Some businesses or brands promote an image of quality and exclusivity e.g. Rolls Royce cars and Gucci clothing and accessories. Other businesses promote themselves as being cheap and their promotional material emphasises this e.g. Iceland the food retailer and easyJet the budget airline both have a 'cheap and cheerful' image. Once a firm has an image in the customer's mind it can be very difficult to change. Skoda cars used to be regarded as being cheap, but not necessarily good quality. The company is now owned by Volkswagen and the cars are built to a higher quality standard, but the company still faces some customer resistance because of its previous image.

> ## Did you know?
>
> *Persil is the market leader for washing detergents. 30 per cent of the UK's 17 million households use Persil for their washing which is more than any other single brand.*

easyJet's 'cheap and cheerful' image

ACTIVITY

How would you describe the image of the following businesses or brands?
(a) Ferrari
(b) Body Shop
(c) RyanAir
(d) French Connection
(e) Poundstretcher Stores
(f) the *Sun* newspaper
(g) Estée Lauder cosmetics

SWOT analysis

SWOT analysis is quite often used as a way in which marketing managers can assess how well a product, brand or company is performing in its market. SWOT stands for:

Strengths

Weakneses

Opportunities

Threats

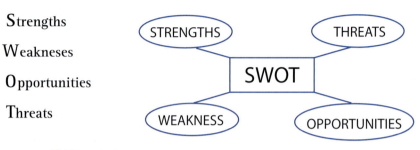

Figure 7.3 *SWOT analysis*

Strengths are the advantages that the business believes it has over its rivals in the market. These may include things such as having a high-quality product, excellent distribution network or an original design. Marks and Spencer is seen as offering high-quality customer service while RyanAir offers very low prices on its airline tickets. It is important that managers are honest when assessing what they think are the strengths of the business or product.

Weaknesses are those areas in which the product or brand is not performing as well as its rivals. For example, the business may have higher prices or a smaller range of products than its rivals. Complaints from customers about products will often be a way of highlighting some areas of weakness within the business. Some of Marks and Spencer clothing suffers from having a dull image among younger shoppers while RyanAir tends to operate from airports located well away from main destination cities.

Opportunities are circumstances that the business is able to take advantage of and exploit such as the collapse of a major competitor in the market or a change in fashions or tastes. A relaxation of licensing laws would create opportunities for pubs and bars to open longer hours. If a celebrity is spotted wearing a brand of clothing or an accessory such as sunglasses, then this can become a great promotional opportunity for the business.

Threats are circumstances which threaten the success of a business such as more competition in the market or changes in the law. For example, if the government decides to open up postal delivery services in the UK to create competition it would threaten the profitability of the Post Office and the jobs of some Post Office workers. However, it would be an opportunity for private courier and delivery services.

Strengths and weaknesses are **internal factors** that the business has some control and influence over. Opportunities and threats come from outside the business, the **external environment,** and cannot be controlled in the same way. Once the managers of a business have carried out an assessment of these issues, then SWOT analysis can provide the basis of a future plan or strategy. The business will need to look hard at any weaknesses and try to put them right and consider how opportunities can be exploited.

CASE STUDY

Fitness Village

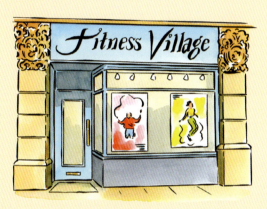

Fitness Village is a health club offering a gym, sauna, steam room and tanning room. It is owned by a husband and wife team who used all their savings to set up the business and it is currently the only fitness club in the area. Membership has grown in the two years since the club opened as more and more people are becoming concerned about health and weight issues. The club has built up a friendly image and produces fitness programmes to meet the individual abilities and needs of its members and even offers advice on diet. The tanning room opened only a year ago and has been hugely popular.

The success of the business has surprised the owners and at times the gym and other facilities are fully booked and they are not currently taking on any new members. However, it is rumoured that the national chain Fitness Warehouse is considering opening up one of its clubs in the area. Another concern is that two reports have appeared in the press recently highlighting the potential skin damage that can be caused by sunbeds.

1 **Carry out a SWOT analysis for Fitness Village.**
2 **Suggest how the owners could deal with any problems or issues raised by the SWOT analysis.**

PEST analysis

Businesses need to be aware of changing market trends and the political and economic climate. PEST stands for political, economic, social and technological factors. **PEST analysis** is a management tool for analysing some of the external forces that act upon a business. The business does not have any control over these forces but it will have to be aware of them and respond to them if it is to remain competitive.

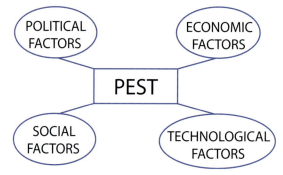

Figure 7.4 *PEST analysis*

Political factors

Changes in government and changes in the laws passed by the government may have a big impact on the business. For example, when the Labour government was elected in 1997 it introduced a minimum wage for the first time in the UK. This increased costs for a number of businesses in low-pay industries such as catering, cleaning and textiles. Similarly, when all forms of tobacco advertising were banned in the UK this had a big impact on the promotional activities of tobacco companies.

Economic factors

Businesses are inevitably affected by economic forces. The economy may move through periods of boom and recession, the Bank of England may raise or lower interest rates and the value of the pound may rise and fall against other currencies. All of these economic changes may influence the amount of money that consumers in the UK are willing to spend on products and they may change business costs which can affect the performance of a business.

QUESTIONS

During 2004 the world price of oil reached an all-time high. What effect might this have had on the following businesses?

(a) a transport business   (b) a bicycle shop   (c) a food manufacturer.

How might a rise in interest rates affect the following businesses?

- a retailer of computers, televisions and other electrical equipment.
- a new car dealership
- an estate agent.

Social factors

Over periods of time consumer tastes, fashion and habits change. These trends may have important effects upon UK businesses. It is obvious that in industries such as fashion and music, styles change and businesses need to adapt if they are to remain competitive. More women now work outside the home and far less time is spent preparing meals at home. There has been a massive growth in the convenience food industry over the last twenty years which reflects this.

Technological influences

Changes in technology will threaten some existing businesses while creating opportunities for others. The mobile phone industry has had huge growth over the last decade and Vodafone has become one of the UK's largest businesses. The Internet has created great opportunities for firms such as EasyJet and Amazon. Over the same time period, certain products and businesses have become virtually obsolete.

QUESTIONS

1 Identify one recent change in the law or a proposal to change the law that would have an effect on business in the UK.

2 Identify an economic issue that may currently be affecting UK business.

3 Identify a product, fashion or music trend that is currently enjoying increasing popularity.

4 Describe a new piece of technology that is gaining popularity.

CASE STUDY

'No smoke...'

The government and health groups in the UK are becoming increasingly concerned about the dangers of passive smoking. The British Medical Association (BMA) has estimated that at least 1,000 people every year die as a result of breathing other people's smoke. Workers in pubs, bars and restaurants are particularly at risk from passive smoking. In the United States, the city of New York has banned smoking in all public places. In August 2000, Pizza Hut banned smoking in all its eating places. The UK government is coming under pressure to take a tougher line on smoking and many health groups believe that there should be a ban on smoking in public places.

In pairs or small groups consider the following.

1 **Analyse some of the possible effects on businesses in the UK of a ban on smoking in public.**

2 **Do you think smoking should be banned in all public places?**

Did you know?

Dry cleaning businesses in New York complained that their takings dropped when smoking was banned in public places in the city. Apparently, people's clothes no longer became smoky after a night out in the city so they didn't need to use the dry cleaners so often!

Portfolio tip

You should assess the current market position of your chosen business and identify its marketing objectives. Are there any market trends or external factors such as the state of the economy which may have an effect on the business?

Marketing objectives

Marketing objectives are those aims or targets that a business is trying to achieve with its marketing strategy. Some typical marketing objectives are:

- to increase market share
- to become established in a new market
- to diversify the product range
- to change the public image of the product or business.

ACTIVITY

Wotznew plc, a clothing retailer, operates 37 shops in the UK. It has recently received adverse publicity over the low wages paid by one of its suppliers in Morocco. The company also has plans to develop a new range of cosmetics and to open six stores in Holland.

List three possible marketing objectives for this business

AO4 Different types of promotional techniques

There is a wide range of promotional techniques that a business can use. These can be divided into **above the line** and **below the line** techniques.

Above the line promotion

Above the line promotion involves using **independent media** to promote a firm's products or services. Popular examples of this type of promotion include television, national and local press and radio advertisements. Outlined below are some of the most important and popular forms of advertising products and services in the UK.

Newspapers

Newspapers may be national, covering the whole country, regional or local. Some are published daily, such as the *Daily Mirror,* while others are available weekly, such as the *News of the World.* A popular tabloid newspaper such as the *Sun* may sell over 3 million copies per day and be read by double that number of people across the whole of Britain. On the other hand, a free weekly newspaper may be read by only a few thousand people in a particular area. Newspaper advertising is useful for businesses of all sizes.

The cost of advertising in a newspaper or magazine is related to the numbers of readers, known as the **circulation.** A full-page colour advertisement in a popular daily paper such as the *Sun* will cost tens of thousands of pounds just for one day. Obviously only large businesses with big advertising budgets can afford to place advertisements such as this. Small and medium-sized businesses are much more likely to use regional and local newspapers. Advertising costs will be lower as these papers will have a smaller circulation. However, a smaller business may want to only attract customers from the local area and the local press may be the ideal way to attract customers. Businesses such as restaurants, second-hand car dealers and small building firms are likely to make use of local and regional newspapers.

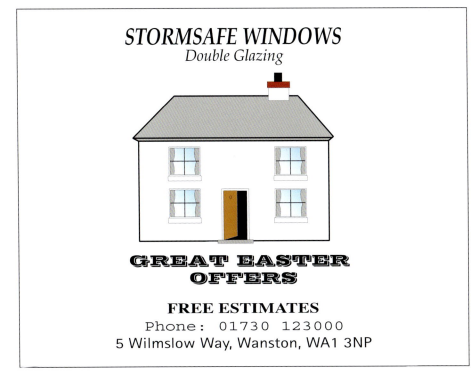

An example of an advertisement in a local newspaper

One of the advantages of newspaper and magazine advertising is that the information is in a permanent format. Customers can be given details about the product or service, prices, contact numbers and addresses and they can keep this information and refer to it later. Newspapers and magazines are provided in public libraries and are left in places such as in-house canteens and doctor's waiting rooms and so will be read by far more people than those who actually buy them.

QUESTIONS

Explain why are you likely to see an advert for the Ford Ka in the *Daily Mail* but not an advertisement for a local motorcycle repair business.

Magazines

Magazines are another popular means of advertising. These advertisements also have the advantage of being in a permanent form but, whereas daily newspapers have a short lifespan, magazines are often still being looked at several months after they were published. Magazines can be used to target a particular audience. For example, the *Investor's Chronicle* is read by significant numbers of high-income earners, while *Marie Claire* is bought mainly by women. Some magazines are aimed at a particular hobby or interest while others are aimed at people who work in a certain type of job or industry.

QUESTIONS

In which type of magazine are you likely to find an advertisement for?

(a) a new four-blade razor

(b) disposable nappies

(c) a new DVD release

(d) a new nail polish with Lycra

(e) specialist yacht insurance

(f) body boards

(g) pedigree kittens

(h) tap dancing shoes

(i) a new release from Eminem

(j) a new satellite channel.

Television

Television has transformed advertising in Britain over the last 50 years. The first point to make is that advertising of products is not permitted on the BBC but only on television channels such as ITV, Channel 4, Sky etc. These channels rely on charging businesses to advertise their products and services. Television advertising generates hundreds of millions of pounds in revenue every year which enables television companies to produce and buy programmes.

The ITV network is made up of a number of regional companies. For example, Meridian is broadcast in the south of England while Granada covers the north-west. A business with a regional customer base might decide to advertise on its local ITV channel. A national company may choose to advertise its products on all of the ITV networks. This is a way of reaching millions of households all over the country, but it is very expensive. The cost of placing an advertisement will vary depending upon the number of likely viewers.

Television advertising is able to use strong visual images and music to send out messages about the product. Most television advertising is **persuasive** rather than informative and it can be a very effective way of reaching millions of potential customers and developing a brand image. However, the cost of making a good-quality advertisement is high, particularly if it involves using a well-known celebrity. The advertiser will then have to pay thousands of pounds just for a slot at peak viewing time. This means that television advertising is not an option for small and medium-sized businesses. It is also not suitable for communicating a lot of technical information about products.

Ratings war

Ratings refers to the number of viewers watching a programme. The more viewers that a programme has, the more the television company can charge for advertising in breaks during that programme.

Viewing figures for week ending 19 September 2004
Top 5 programmes
EastEnders (Mon/Sunday BBC1) 13.1m
Coronation Street (Mon/Sat ITV1) 12.4m
Emmerdale (Mon ITV1) 8.7m
Doc Martin (Thurs ITV1) 8.3m
Heartbeat (Sun ITV1) 8.0m
(Based on BARB data)

> ### Did you know?
> In 2004 it cost almost £83,000 for a single 30-second advertising slot in the centre break of Coronation Street networked across all of the ITV regions.

QUESTIONS

1 What type of products and services tend to be advertised on television at the following times:

  (i) weekday mornings

  (ii) during half time of Champions League football

  (iii) Saturday mornings?

2 In pairs or small groups, identify four television advertisements that you currently like and explain what you find appealing about them. How much information do they provide about the product that is being advertised?

Outdoor advertising

Outdoor covers a range of different approaches to advertising including posters, advertisements on the side of buses and taxis, balloons and at football and other sports grounds. You will even find advertisements on the back of train and car park tickets. The various types of outdoor advertising have some of the advantages of newspaper and magazine advertising in that they are in a permanent format and they can target potential customers in a certain area or who have a particular interest.

Billboards at prime sites, such as near traffic lights at a busy road junction, can be relatively expensive to advertise on and they may be vandalised. Some companies have their own hot air balloons in amusing or interesting shapes to help promote their products at outdoor events during the summer months e.g. Bristol balloon fiesta. This is unlikely to be an option for small and medium-sized businesses.

Outdoor advertising

Cinema

Cinema attendances declined during the 1980s with the growth in videos but they recovered strongly during the 1990s. Films can be categorised by age and type e.g. action, comedy, romance etc. so the audience can be targeted quite effectively by advertisers. A new Disney animation will have a large number of children and their parents in the audience, whereas an Italian film with English sub-titles will have a very different type of audience. There are limited opportunities for advertising in the cinema – usually before the feature film. However, like television advertising, cinema advertising can make use of music and strong visual images to capture people's attention and create a brand image.

QUESTIONS

What type of products and services tend to be advertised at the cinema?

Radio

There has been huge growth in commercial radio over the last 20 years. Like the independent television companies, commercial radio stations earn income by charging businesses to advertise their products and services on the radio. Independent radio stations in the UK target many different types of audience and different parts of the country. Stations may specialise in playing particular types of music e.g. classical music, Asian music, jazz or hip hop while some rely heavily on listener phone-ins and chat shows. Some stations are national, such as Virgin, but the majority are regional or local, e.g. Capital covers London while BRMB covers much of the West Midlands.

Independent radio stations generally have a good knowledge of who their typical listeners are in terms of age, gender and lifestyle at different times of the day. This is known as the **listener profile**. This enables businesses to target particular audiences with their advertising. Like television advertising, the cost of advertising tends to vary according to how many listeners the advertisement is likely to reach and the quality of the advertisement itself. Radio advertising can be a relatively cheap and effective way for local and regional businesses to advertise their products. People are able to listen to the radio while doing other things such as driving or working. This can be an advantage but the drawback is that listeners are often not really concentrating and they are unlikely to remember phone numbers and contact details unless they are frequently repeated.

QUESTIONS

1 Which radio stations do you listen to?
2 List some of the products and companies that you hear advertised on the radio.
3 Why do you think they have chosen to use local radio?

E-marketing

E-marketing refers to electronic marketing, that is the Internet. The Internet has provided businesses of all sizes with new promotional opportunities over the last few years. A business may set up its own website which gives basic information about the business and its products or it may decide to have something more sophisticated with interactive graphics and on-line ordering systems. Customers of all of the large supermarket chains such as Tesco and Sainsbury's are able to order their weekly shopping over the Internet and have it delivered to their home. The number of E-businesses and amount of E-marketing is likely to continue to increase.

The Internet also enables businesses to contact customers and potential customers directly by email. If a company has a database of its customers then they can be contacted with information about new products that are being launched or special offers. Supermarket loyalty cards give the supermarkets a huge amount of information about their customers and those who use on-line services can be easily contacted.

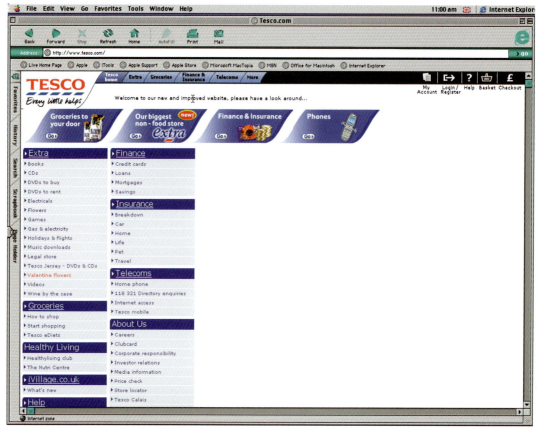

Tesco homepage

ACTIVITY

Copy out and complete this table showing the advantages and drawbacks of the various types of above the line advertising.

ADVERTISING	Advantages	Disadvantages
National Press		
Local Press		
TV Advertising		
Local Radio		

Table 7.1 *Different types of advertising*

Below the line promotion

We have seen that television and press advertising is known as 'above the line promotion'.

Below the line promotion involves all the other promotional activities that businesses use, such as trade promotions, sponsorships, discounts, prize draws, money-off coupons etc.

Sales promotions

Sales promotions aim to encourage customers to buy more of a firm's products. We are all familiar with money-off coupons, free gifts with magazines, prize draws and the acronym 'BOGOF' – buy one get one free. Food stores such as Iceland offer link purchases such as giving away a bag of oven chips if the customer buys a certain brand of beefburger. A firm may also try to appeal to its customers by promising to donate a sum of money to charity for every item sold.

In-store promotions can be very effective

Public relations

Public relations (PR) involves trying to present the business and its products to the general public in a more favourable light. PR activities are not always about selling more products in the short term. Assessment objective 3, earlier on in this unit, referred to the **profile** and **image** of the business. PR activities are often aimed at creating a particular image for the business e.g. that a business cares about the environment or supports its local community. A local car hire company may spend a few hundred pounds sponsoring a local school football team. This is unlikely to increase its sales but it may improve its image locally and if the team is successful it may gain some extra publicity.

If a company such as Coca-Cola or Sony are to release a new product or set up a big new sponsorship deal they may well decide to issue a **press release** or hold a **press conference** to inform the media of their plans. The company presents its news to an audience of press, television and radio journalists and it may allow questions. This will generate considerable publicity for the business. Small and medium-sized businesses may try to get articles about them into the local press or be interviewed on the local radio station.

Sponsorship

We are all very familiar with sponsorship of sports teams and major sporting events. Vodafone currently spend £9 million per year sponsoring Manchester United. Sports stars and celebrities are often used to endorse products – meaning that a celebrity is linked with a particular product. Companies obviously believe that there are benefits in being associated with high-profile events or celebrities. The football Premiership is sponsored by Barclays Bank and even many television programmes are now sponsored e.g. *Coronation Street* is sponsored by Cadbury's chocolate.

Sponsorship advertising is now an integral part of sport

Not only are some television programmes sponsored by companies but **product placement** deals mean that a company can pay a producer of a film or programme to have its products shown prominently in a programme or film. In recent years, James Bond films have often clearly shown Sony, BMW, Philips and other well-known branded products being used by the hero. The company knows that films such as this will be seen by large audiences internationally and that their brand will benefit from being associated with a character such as James Bond.

ACTIVITY

1. In pairs or small groups identify the sponsor(s) of the following:
   (a) *Hollyoaks* (b) *Emmerdale* (c) the London Marathon
   (d) Arsenal Football Club (d) your local football team (e) *The X Factor*

2. Why do you think that the brands/companies that you identified above have chosen these particular sponsorships?

3. Which famous people are associated with the following products or brands?
   (a) Sainsbury's foods (b) Renault Clio (c) Walkers crisps (d) L'Oréal hair products (e) John Smith beer (f) Virgin Mobile (g) Pilot sunglasses.

Point of sale promotions

Point of sale promotions are used to support the product at the point where it is actually sold to the customer. This may include attractive displays in the store, leaflets and posters giving information about the product or a video or other demonstrations of the product in use, e.g. kitchen gadgets or cleaning products are sometimes promoted this way in department stores. Some products are shown through interactive displays on a computer screen.

Supermarkets often run promotional offers on particular drinks or food products and give away free samples for customers to try in store. This is then often backed up with money-off coupons or other special offers to encourage customers to buy the product once they have tried it. Certain parts of supermarkets such as the end of aisles are known as 'hot spots' because they tend to generate higher levels of sales. Items which are being heavily promoted that week may be prominently displayed in one of these hot-spot areas to catch the customer's eye and increase sales. A great deal of thought is given by the big supermarkets to the location and display of products in the store.

Retailers may use more subtle ways to encourage customers to buy particular products. In-store bakeries not only provide customers with fresh bread but the aroma of freshly baked bread may appeal to customers' sense of smell and lead to them buying more products. In-store coffee shops similarly produce delicious coffee smells which may subtly lead to increased sales.

Supermarket in-store promotion

Branding

Branding is very important for promotion of products. Brands such as Ford, McDonald's, Sony, Heinz and Nike are recognised across the world and these companies spend huge amounts of money promoting their brand name. Branding helps customers to recognise products and it gives them reassurance about the quality of products. Branding is often linked in with a particular logo, design features or distinctive packaging. Nike is the Greek goddess of victory which is an appropriate choice for a sports wear company and the Nike 'swoosh' is a very recognisable logo.

Real business

Kit Kat has been on sale for over 70 years and is the UK's best-selling chocolate snack bar. Even the company are not sure where the brand name originally came from!

The distinctive Nike flash

QUESTIONS

1 When buying the following household products, which brand does your family usually buy?

   (i) Instant coffee (ii) toilet rolls (iii) washing powder or liquid (iv) cereal (v) oven chips (vi) shampoo (vii) washing-up liquid (viii) toothpaste

2 Briefly describe the brand logos or distinctive design features of the following products:

   (i) Adidas (ii) Jif lemons (iii) French Connection clothing (iv) Heinz foods (v) Parker pens (vi) Dyson vacuum cleaners (vii) Legal & General Insurance (viii) Apple Mac computers (ix) Marmite (x) Lloyds TSB Bank.

Apart from obvious logos, businesses may also use particular colour schemes for their stores and vehicles and use distinctive lettering or layout on their business stationery and signs. The aim is to make the particular brand or business stand out from its competitors and perhaps to develop a **corporate identity**. The use of colour and lettering can be used to create a stylish, fun, modern or traditional feel. A diner catering for families will take a different approach to its colour scheme and style than an expensive bistro restaurant. Likewise, you may have tried using different fonts on your computer to give different effects to your work.

Corporate identity is the particular image that a business presents to the world.

Exhibitions and trade fairs

Some businesses, particularly those which sell commercial and industrial products rather than consumer products, may decide to promote their products and services heavily at exhibitions and trade fairs. Almost every industry will have its own specialist trade fairs. The Motor Show is of great importance for car manufacturers and for businesses selling products and services linked to cars and motoring. Similarly, the annual Boat Show at Southampton is an important promotional opportunity for yacht builders, sail makers and a host of other businesses providing marine products and services.

Direct marketing

Direct marketing involves directly approaching customers. This may include sending mail shots or emails, telephone selling or selling on the Internet. We are all familiar with receiving telephone calls at home from double glazing, power and finance companies during the evening.

The Internet has created new opportunities for direct selling. Budget airline companies such as easyJet and Ryanair sell all of their flight tickets directly to customers over the Internet. Similarly, Tower Records sells large numbers of CDs from its website and regularly contacts customers with details of special offers and new releases. The clothing retailer Cotton Traders has a small number of stores but sells mainly by mail order.

Computers and word processing software have meant that a business can send an apparently personalised letter to thousands of households across the country. The company simply purchases a mailing list giving names and addresses of potential customers, sends out a letter addressed to them by name and it can vary the contents of a fairly standard letter to take account of local or other differences. However, sending paper mailshots and catalogues can be a rather wasteful and inefficient approach to marketing. Mailshots incur postal costs as well as the cost of the promotional material, and colour catalogues in particular are expensive to produce and deliver. Many households are irritated by what they see as 'junk mail' and simply throw it away without even looking at it. It would also be a waste of resources sending a mail order catalogue of gardening products to an address which is in fact a tower block in an inner city area.

Carefully targeted mailshots can be effective

The Internet enables even small firms to email large numbers of potential customers at minimal cost. Once again, a business simply buys a list of email addresses of potential customers and then contacts them with details of products and special offers. As with 'junk mail' some people are irritated by this 'spam' but it can be a cheap promotional tool. This form of direct marketing tends to be at its most effective when it is used to target people who have already purchased the product before. An individual who has purchased a book or DVD over the Internet is likely to make repeat purchases in the future. The big supermarkets who operate loyalty cards have a huge database of customers and they know which type of products they prefer to buy. This means that they are able to target particular customers with special offers and new products and services. So, for example, if the supermarket is bringing out a new range of cat food it can target customers who already purchase cat food.

ACTIVITY

Despite the popularity of the Internet with home users, only a comparatively small number of businesses have been successful in selling their products to consumers over the Internet.

(a) What type of products are commonly purchased over the Internet?

(b) Why are customers happy to buy these products over the Internet?

(c) What type of products are customers less willing to buy over the Internet and why?

CASE STUDY

JayCee motors

Jason runs a second-hand car business. He buys quality used cars, has them serviced and cleaned and then sells them on to the public. Jason's girlfriend, Cindy, helps out part-time with paperwork and the accounts.

Jason has been disappointed with the low level of sales over the last few weeks and is planning to run a special bank holiday promotion. He intends to offer special price discounts on the next bank holiday Monday and has decided to place extra advertisements in the local paper and for the first time spend money on some local radio advertising. Cindy has suggested that Jason

hires a bouncy castle for the day at the showroom and enters customers who take a test drive into a prize draw. She has also suggested asking Martin Le Tizer, a retired footballer who lives locally, to come along on the day to open the bank holiday promotion.

1 Consider each of the promotional activities suggested and state whether you think it is an example of above the line or below the line promotion.

2 Explain the possible advantages and outline any drawbacks of these promotional activities.

AO5 Identify the main controls on promotional techniques

Businesses in the UK are able to choose how much they spend on promotional activities and they can decide upon the methods they will use to promote their products and services. Assessment objective 4 explained the wide variety of promotional techniques that a firm can use. However, it is important that the material in advertisements or promotional activity does not break the law or damage the image of the business. Promotional material is aimed at encouraging or persuading customers to buy products and services so there is a danger that businesses may make exaggerated or misleading claims to increase their sales. There are a number of legal and other constraints on advertising material that aim to protect consumers and these are looked at below.

Advertising Standards Authority

The Advertising Standards Authority (ASA) is an independent body that monitors advertisements, sales promotions and direct marketing in the UK. This means that it covers newspapers, magazines and billboard advertising and from November 2004 also takes responsibility for TV and radio advertising. The ASA runs the British Code of Advertising, Sales Promotion and Direct Marketing (known as the CAP code) to ensure that advertisements are legal, decent, honest and truthful. Advertisements should also not cause grave or widespread offence. If a complaint made by the public about an advertisement is upheld then the advertising industry will not handle the advertisement.

In the past, the ASA received hundreds of complaints about a Club 18–30 poster campaign which appeared to encourage drunkenness and promiscuity among young people and had slogans such as 'Beaver España'. Benetton has frequently been criticised for using shocking images in its advertising and the RSPCA withdrew a newspaper advertisement showing a pile of dead dogs which was part of a shock campaign to deter people from buying dogs as Christmas presents.

QUESTIONS

What might have been the objections to the image used by the RSPCA mentioned above?

The Independent Television Commission (ITC)

The ITC monitors broadcast advertising on television and radio and a number of rules exist to control this form of advertising. Rules cover issues such as nudity in television advertising and the use of actors and TV personalities. Newsreaders are prevented from advertising products and actors are not allowed to appear in advertisements during programmes they appear in. For example, a *Hollyoaks* actor could not appear in an advertisement for a product in a commercial break during an episode of *Hollyoaks*. There are also controls on products appearing in television programmes. For example, the Newton and Ridley beer served in the Rovers Return on *Coronation Street* is a brand made up purely for this programme. Television companies must be careful in showing recognisable brands in its programmes although recently a number of product placement deals have been agreed.

Codes of Practice

A code of practice is not a law but a guideline for the industry. Reputable companies which care about their public image will want to follow these codes which lay out best practice and non-acceptable behaviour within their industries. As we have seen above, a code of practice constrains the advertising industry and similar codes of practice exist in many other industries such as the travel industry and motor retailing. Not all businesses will follow these codes but reputable businesses will do so and customers will generally prefer to deal with these businesses.

Legal constraints on advertising

So far all of the controls that have been discussed are operated by the industries themselves. However, there are a number of laws in Britain which aim to protect the consumer from inaccurate and misleading advertisements.

The Trade Descriptions Act 1968

The Trade Descriptions Act 1968 is probably the most important legal protection for the public when considering advertising and promotional material. The Act states that claims made about products must be true and it also covers 'sales' and 'price reductions'. For example, it is an offence to claim that shoes are leather if they are not and sale items must have been on sale at the higher price for at least 28 days in the previous six months.

The Sale of Goods Act 1994

This Act was first introduced in the nineteenth century and was one of the first laws aimed at protecting consumers. To comply with the law, goods should be **as described**. So any claims about the content of the goods or where they are made must be true. The Trade Descriptions Act now deals more fully with this issue. Goods must also be of **merchantable quality** which means that there must not be any serious flaws or defects within them and they should be **fit for the purpose** they were bought for. For example, a pair of football boots should be reasonably hard wearing and not fall apart after one game. However, a pair of fashionable women's sandals would not be expected to stand up to heavy use. If products are defective or not fit for the purpose the buyer is entitled to a full refund. It is illegal to display notices in shops such as 'No refunds given'.

The Consumer Protection Act 1987

This law was introduced to bring the UK into line with other European Union countries in 1987. The Act makes businesses liable for any damage or injuries to customers caused by a defective product that they have supplied. So, for example, a business supplying a defective electric hairdryer would be liable for any injuries caused to a customer. However, more relevant to promotional material is the fact that the Act makes it illegal to state that the goods are being sold at below the manufacturer's recommended price unless this is true. It is also an offence to suggest a false price reduction.

Trading Standards

The main job of the local **Trading Standards Office** is to enforce consumer protection laws and give advice to consumers about their legal rights. Trading standards officers are employed by local County Councils or Unitary Authorities and part of their job is to visit shops and other business premises to check that laws are not being broken.

   If customers feel that descriptions about products have been false or inaccurate or that products have not lived up to claims made about them then they can approach their local Trading Standards Office. They will then investigate customer complaints and take cases to court if they feel that the business is at fault. This means that customers themselves do not have the expense of taking the business to court. Firms that are found to have broken the law may be fined but more importantly they will receive bad publicity which can have a damaging effect on their business.

The Monopolies Commission

The Monopolies Commission was set up after the Second World War to monitor the behaviour of large companies in the UK. The Monopolies and Mergers Commission (MMC) was scrapped in 1999 and replaced with the Competition Commission. The job of the Competition Commission is to remove anti-competitive practices and encourage fair competition between businesses in the UK.

The Office of Fair Trading

The Office of Fair Trading (OFT) is a government body which has the job of ensuring that companies are following the Fair Trading Act 1973. This Act aims to try to encourage fair competition between firms and prevent them following anti-competitive practices.

CASE STUDY

Alf's Bargain Wonderland

'Bargain Wonderland' is a retail store selling a wide range of relatively cheap, low-quality products. In an effort to boost sales, Alf has splashed a number of promotional posters across his store. A number of customers have complained to the local Trading Standards Office about some of Alf's claims.

Consider the following material and state whether the posters may be in breach of the law.

'Fantastic micro music system – was £29.99 now £19.99!'

'British made pure wool jumpers only £9.99.'

'Probably the best value in town – leather trainers £10.99!'

'Branded perfumes – £5.00 less than recommended selling price.'

'Quality bath towels only £2.99.'

'Take away a bargain – but no refunds given.'

'Stay dry – showerproof jackets £6.99.'

Portfolio tip

You should consider what are the main controls on the promotional material used by your chosen business.

AO6 Choosing media for promotional campaigns

All forms of promotional activity that are open to businesses will have a cost and all businesses large or small will have a certain budget available to them. Multinational businesses like Microsoft, Coca-Cola and Ford will be able to spend millions of dollars per year on their promotional material. A small second-hand music and games shop may be able to spend a few hundred pounds per year. However, no matter how small or large the budget that is available, the business will want their promotional material to be **cost effective**. This means that they feel that it represents good value for money. We have already looked at the wide range of media that are available to businesses in assessment objective 4.

Some of the main factors that a business will consider when deciding which media to use are outlined below.

Does it reach its target audience?

No matter how eye catching or entertaining an advertisement may be, it will not achieve its purpose of increasing sales of a product if it does not reach potential customers. Television is watched by different groups of viewers at different times of the day or week. With television advertising it is important to consider when potential customers are likely to be watching television and which programmes they are likely to be watching.

Newspapers, magazines and radio programmes all have their own reader or listener profiles. Potential customers can be targeted by factors such as their age, gender, income and where they live. For example, a typical reader of the *Daily Telegraph* may be characterised as male, aged between 35 and 65, working in a non-manual job with above national average earnings. With this typical reader profile, the *Daily Telegraph* may therefore be a poor choice to advertise a new range of organic baby foods. Newspapers, magazines, radio and television stations all have a very good knowledge of the typical audiences that they reach and are able to give advice to advertisers about the size of the potential audience and other important characteristics about the audience.

Below is the possible readership profile of a fictitious celebrity gossip magazine *Hey Look!*, showing the percentage of readers by age and gender.

Age range	Female	Male
16–25	28	6
26–49	40	8
50 +	16	2

ACTIVITY

In pairs or groups contrast the typical reader/listener/viewer profiles for each of the following:
- *Heat* magazine and *Motor Cycle News*
- The *Financial Times* and the *Daily Star*
- The *Chart Show* on Sunday afternoon and *Woman's Hour* on Radio 4.
- *Hollyoaks* and *Panorama*.

The cost of advertising

The cost of advertising is likely to be a major influence on the type of advertising that the business is likely to use. Producing simple fliers and posters, or paying a person to walk around a busy shopping precinct with posters displayed on sandwich boards, are all relatively cheap ways in which a local business could advertise its products or services. However, if a chocolate manufacturer such as Cadbury is to launch a brand-new product it will need to use media which are capable of reaching a mass audience and this will inevitably cost a lot more.

It has already been mentioned that the cost varies according to the size of the audience. Granada reaches far more viewers than West Country television so it is more expensive to advertise on Granada. In a similar way, more people will watch *The X Factor* than *Watercolour Challenge* and so advertising during a commercial break in *The X Factor* will cost more than during a less popular programme.

Below are some examples of the approximate costs of different types of advertising:

- a full-page colour advertisement in a popular tabloid newspaper may cost as much as £35,000 for one day
- a pitch-side advertising hoarding at a League Two football club might cost £700 for the season
- 1,000 black and white A5 leaflets may cost about £25, the equivalent of 2.5p each.

ACTIVITY

Find out the cost of a colour, quarter-page advertisement in your local newspaper.

The nature of the product or service

We are very familiar with television and national press advertising because we are consumers and these forms of advertising are ideal for promoting **mass market consumer goods** such as toothpaste, shampoo and crisps. However, many businesses do not supply consumers such as ourselves. Some businesses produce products or provide services which are used by other businesses. For example, a company which manufactures train engines, or a firm which makes packaging for the fast food industry, would use other methods of promoting its products. Television advertising would be an expensive and not a very effective way of promoting their products to customers.

Some products are not aimed at a mass market but are aimed at a smaller, specialist niche market. An example might be a business that makes specialist shoes for rock climbers. This is a relatively small market in the UK and the business will need to consider how best to reach the target market. Advertisements in climbing and extreme sports magazines are likely to be more cost effective than local radio or press advertisements.

ACTIVITY

Suggest a suitable means of advertising the following:
(a) a new pre-school in your area
(b) a bodyspray (c) a racing kayak
(d) a new accountancy software package.

The marketing mix

The marketing mix is the blend of 4 key elements used when marketing a product or service, often referred to as 'the 4 Ps': **product, price, promotion and place** (see page 54)

Figure 7.6 *The marketing mix*

We have seen that some products are considered 'up-market' or exclusive while others have more of a cheap and cheerful image.

A business has to get all four ingredients right. The image of a high-quality product may be damaged if the price charged appears to be too low or the company decides to run a promotional campaign offering 'Krazy price kuts!' or other similar down-market techniques. A business will need to consider where the product is sold (place) to ensure that customers are able to get hold of the product easily and manufacturers of expensive perfumes prefer their products to be sold in department stores rather than supermarkets.

The business must co-ordinate its activities to try to anticipate the impact of its promotional activity. McDonald's once ran a 'Buy one Big Mac and get one free' promotion. There was a huge increase in demand and restaurants quickly ran out of stock, leaving many customers disappointed and the image of the business suffered.

Ethics and the law

We have already seen that advertisements must stay within the law, particularly the Trade Descriptions Act. However, most businesses will wish to be seen as ethical. Ethics is a set of beliefs and values or a sense of right and wrong. An advertisement may not break the law but it may be seen by some people as insensitive, exploitative or promoting values or lifestyles that they disapprove of. This may lead to members of the public complaining to the Advertising Standards Authority. For example, an advertisement for an anti-perspirant showing people escaping from a burning office block was criticised as being insensitive to the families of victims and the survivors of New York's 9/11 tragedy. However, some businesses like to use shock tactics in their advertising and enjoy the publicity that this can generate. RyanAir, for example, spent a relatively modest amount of money on a newspaper advertisement showing the Pope with a humorous speech bubble referring to RyanAir. There were many complaints but the company felt that the benefits from the publicity outweighed any criticism.

AO7 Recommend and justify a promotional campaign for the chosen business

To achieve this assessment objective you will need to develop a promotional campaign for your chosen business and justify your ideas. The first issue that you will need to consider is the aim of the promotional campaign. What is the campaign hoping to achieve? You will need to decide on the overall aim of your campaign and set targets that progress can be measured against. Typical promotional objectives might be:

- to increase market share
- to successfully launch a new product or service
- to become market leader
- to develop a strong brand image
- to improve customer perception of the product or company.

Once the main objective of the campaign has been set, the areas that need to be considered when planning the campaign are:

- methods of promotion
- timing
- target audience
- key messages.

Methods of promotion

It is essential that you have a good understanding of your chosen business and what it is trying to achieve. If you are looking at a large business selling its product to a mass market, supported by a multi-million pound promotional budget, then you will have more promotional options available than a local takeaway restaurant.

The size of the budget that is available will obviously influence the amount and type of promotional activity that the business undertakes. We have seen that television advertising can have great influence on customers and can be particularly effective with mass-market consumer products such as cereals, cosmetics, beer etc. However, it is expensive and therefore not an option for small businesses serving a local market.

Timing

Many businesses undertake regular advertising using local or national media. For example, a local cleaning company may spend £80 per month advertising its services in a local free newspaper. However, there are times when a firm may undertake promotional campaigns to support the launch of a new product or a special event such as an Easter price promotion.

Target audience

The recommended campaign will need to clearly identify the group of potential customers that is being targeted. If a promotional campaign is to be cost-effective it must be aimed at the appropriate target audience, be it young people or industrial customers.

Key messages

The promotional campaign must be communicating clear and unambiguous messages. The aim of the campaign may be to make potential customers aware of a new product launch or it may aim to try to create a more socially responsible image for the business. If the business is attempting to create an up-market and stylish image it will need to produce an appropriate advertisement and give thought to the media that are to be used.

ACTIVITY

This activity is based on the following case study which will help you to prepare for your own promotional campaign that will be part of your portfolio evidence.

CASE STUDY

'Pants'

Naomi and Emma are planning to open a women's lingerie shop in West London. While they are aware that over half the underwear in the UK is bought at Marks and Spencer, they still believe that a market exists for quality women's underwear which offers something different from chain store garments. They believe that their target market is women aged 16 to 35. They plan to open their shop in two months' time and feel that they can spend up to £2,000 on promoting their business.

In pairs or small groups, suggest a promotional campaign for 'Pants', giving reasons for your choice of promotional techniques.

Portfolio tip

It is very important that your campaign is realistic in terms of the budget that the business has available. For example, television is not a realistic option for most small and medium-sized businesses. It is important that you justify and give reasons to support your chosen campaign.

AO8 Evaluating the effectiveness of a promotional campaign

No matter how large or small the promotional budget that a business has, it is important that the campaign is cost-effective. In other words, the benefits gained from the campaign should be greater than the costs of the campaign. You will have to explain how you will judge whether the campaign is successful. Ultimately the campaign will have to be measured against the objectives that were set. If the objectives were achieved then the campaign can be considered a success.

Some of the most obvious criteria that the campaign can be measured against are changes in:

- sales levels
- market share
- brand loyalty.

Sales levels

We have seen that most but not all promotional campaigns have the aim of increasing sales. A business must decide whether it is aiming to increase the **volume** of sales, that is the number of items sold, or whether it is hoping to increase **sales revenue,** which is found by multiplying the number of items sold by the selling price.

CASE STUDY

Laser Computers Ltd

Laser Computers is a retailer based in Sheffield selling computer and peripherals. In March they sold 50 printers at a typical selling price of £100. In April, Laser Computers ran a special price promotion offering a 25 per cent discount on all printers and they sold 60 that month.

1 Calculate (a) Sales revenue in March
             (b) Sales revenue in April
2 Would you describe the April price promotion as a success?

Repeat sales

A consumer buying a computer printer or a washing machine would probably not expect to buy another one for several years. However, a restaurant or dry cleaning business will rely upon customers returning on a regular basis. This is known as repeat sales. A promotional campaign may have the aim of encouraging repeat sales by, for example, offering discounts off their next purchase. A business will need to consider how it intends to measure repeat sales.

Market share

Market share is a useful way of measuring how a product or brand is competing in its market. If a product is gaining market share it means that it is performing better than its competitors. Big name brands such as Kelloggs, Cadbury's and Heinz will wish to maintain or increase their market share and it will be a key measure of success for them.

Brand loyalty

Some promotional campaigns are aimed at encouraging customers to stick with their existing brand and not to switch to rival products. This is particularly true for market leaders such as Nescafé and Persil. Market research can reveal customers' attitudes towards brands and how loyal they are to the company's brand.

ACTIVITY

Last year a company achieved sales of £20m in a market estimated to be worth £200m. What was the firm's market share?

ACTIVITY

Coca-Cola has been the UK's best-selling carbonated soft drink for many years. Why does the company continue to spend millions of pounds on promotional activity in the UK?

Portfolio tip

Evaluation involves making a judgement. In this case you will need to decide how you will assess whether or not the campaign is successful. You will obviously need to consider what the aims of the campaign were and judge the performance of the campaign against these aims.

SKILLS CHECK

1. List 3 purposes of promotion.

2. Explain 3 factors that may influence the effectiveness of promotion.

3. Outline some of the barriers to effective promotion.

4. Briefly explain the following terms:
   (a) market share
   (b) brand image
   (c) SWOT
   (d) PEST.

5. What is the difference between **above the line** and **below the line** promotion?

6. Give one advantage and one drawback of each of the promotional techniques below:
   (a) a television advertisement
   (b) an advertisement in a local paper
   (c) sponsoring a local football team.

7. Briefly explain the role of the Advertising Standards Authority (ASA).

8. What is the purpose of the Trade Descriptions Act?

9. What factors will a business take into account when deciding which promotional methods to use?

10. How can a business assess whether its promotional campaign is a success?

Keeping customers happy

Getting Started

This unit is all about customers and how to keep them happy. Most of us have gone into a shop and been met by rude staff who make it clear that they don't want to be there and have no interest in offering us any kind of service. They may even be talking to a colleague about last night's events and paying no attention to us at all. On the other hand, occasionally we experience good customer service that makes a real impression on us.

You may be working, perhaps part-time, in a job that requires you to have contact with customers, and this will give you the opportunity to provide the evidence needed for your portfolio for this unit.

For those of you who are not currently working, or who may not be in the type of employment that enables you to provide evidence for this unit, it will be possible for you to carry out the practical tasks required by role play (simulation) exercises (or a mixture of real situations and simulation).

By working through this unit, you will have the opportunity to investigate good customer service – what keeps customers happy.

For the first two assessment objectives in this unit, you will select a business on which to base your studies and will look at the different types of customers who use that business. You will then investigate what customer service is and why it is important to your selected business.

Successful achievement of this unit will give you a good understanding of customer service. It will also give you confidence in dealing with people in different situations, as well as enabling you to finalise a sale in a face-to-face situation.

This unit will cover

- AO1 Identify and describe the different types of customers of the selected business.
- AO2 Show how good customer service may help the performance of the selected business.
- AO3 Describe ways in which customers are protected by consumer law and the ways in which they can obtain advice and support.
- AO4 Deal with customers to meet a range of their requirements (five situations), review own performance and identify areas for development.
- AO5 Demonstrate sales skills (one situation), review performance and propose further development.

AO1 Different types of customers

For the first two assessment objectives in this unit, you will need to select a business on which to base your studies. This may be where you work, or where you are on work placement. If this is not possible, you may be able to obtain the evidence needed based on a group visit or your tutor may be able to arrange for a speaker to come to your school or college. You will then have opportunities to question the speaker. However, it is important that the business you select is one that will enable you to obtain all the evidence you will need to successfully complete both AO1 and AO2.

Once you have selected your business, you will then need to identify and clearly describe all the people that use the business. The types of customers you will describe are:

- individuals
- groups
- people of different ages
- people from different cultures
- non-English speakers
- people with specific needs, e.g. wheelchair access
- young children
- business men and women.

Types of customers

Of course, the nature of the business will often influence the type of customers who use it. For example, the customers of a designer fashion boutique are likely to be quite different to those who use a local department store.

Individuals

Dealing with individual customers in a business may mean one-to-one communication over the telephone or in a face-to-face situation.

When talking to a customer on the telephone, it is important to listen carefully to what is being said. It is a disadvantage not to be able to see the customer, because you cannot see any non-verbal signs (body language). However, the tone of the customer's voice will usually make it obvious how they are feeling and you will then be able to respond appropriately.

Customers making telephone calls may be angry or distressed because they have a problem or a complaint. You must use tact and kindness in dealing with them. If you can't deal with their problem promptly, promise that you will find out for them. Give them a time limit but remember that it is very important that you phone the customer within that time limit, even if you haven't yet resolved the problem. Not knowing what is happening is one of the most frequent complaints customers make when dealing with staff.

When dealing with customers face-to-face, ensure you are polite and friendly and keep eye contact at all times. If a customer is angry, you must always keep calm and ensure your voice is at medium tone – never shout. For example, if you are working on the customer services desk of a store and a customer is complaining that some clothing doesn't fit because the label is wrong, take action immediately. Ensure that the customer can see that you are taking the problem seriously and find out what action he or she would like you to take, such as replacing the garment or giving a refund.

Groups

Many businesses deal with groups of customers. For example a coachload of holidaymakers on a day trip may arrive for lunch at a cafe where you work. You would need to ensure that they feel welcome, even though you might not be too pleased to see them without advance notice, as you are already very busy.

When dealing with groups of people, it is important to make sure that they can all hear what you are saying. Position yourself so that they can all hear you. Speak slowly and use questions to check whether they have all heard. Try to ensure that members of the group have the opportunity to speak to you alone – they may wish to ask for information or advice that they do not wish the other members of their group to hear.

People of different ages

Different approaches and skills are required when dealing with different age groups. For example, the way you communicate with young children would be very different to the way you talk to senior citizens. For example, some older people may have difficulty with their hearing or sight. With practice and experience, you will learn how to assess a situation and you will be able to adjust the tone and volume of your voice and the speed at which you speak.

Young people, such as young teenagers, also need to be considered in this category. This age group can be very independent and you can often assume that if they have come to you for help, it is probably a genuine problem. Be careful not to be patronising. Put them at their ease – and smile!

Care must be taken to ensure that the needs of all age groups are catered for and this may take considerable patience.

People from different cultures

People coming into your business who are from different cultures may feel that their needs are not being met in full. For example, in a restaurant they may not be able to find food on the menu suitable for their needs or in a store they may not be able to find clothing of the style they require. It is also possible that they may not have good English speaking ability. Great care and patience will be needed to ensure people in this category feel appreciated.

Non-English speakers

Communication with people who speak little or no English can be very difficult. However, if there is no one available who can speak their language fluently, communication is often possible using hand signals, drawings or pointing at words in a customer's phrase book.

Try to speak more slowly than usual, but don't be tempted to shout – raising your voice will not help someone who doesn't understand what you are saying and it could result in causing the customer distress.

People with specific needs

People with specific needs include those who are hard of hearing, have problems with their sight or with their mobility. Part III of the Disability Discrimination Act came into force in 2004 which states that businesses providing services to customers make permanent physical adjustments to their premises to ensure that disabled people have full access at all times.

For those who have difficulty in hearing, loop systems have been installed in many premises, such as cinemas and banks. Loop systems help someone with hearing difficulties to use a hearing aid or a loop listener to help them hear sounds more clearly, by reducing or cutting out background noise. For example, in a cinema, a deaf person can use a loop system to hear the film more clearly. Loop systems, however, cannot produce stereo sound, but this may be possible with the use of infrared systems, which consist of a transmitter and a listening recorder. With infrared systems, sound is fed to the transmitter in the same way as with the loop system, either by a direct electrical connection or via a microphone and it is then transmitted as an invisible infrared light to where the person is sitting.

As a result of the Disability Discrimination Act, wheelchair access has been improved and extended in businesses that require people to have access to them. Ramps and pathways have been constructed and handrails installed to ensure access to all parts of the premises. However, wheelchair users in a supermarket may need help to reach the goods that are stacked high up on a shelf or may need help in a petrol station to fill up their cars and make payment.

People with specific needs are often self-sufficient and independent. For example, a person who has sight problems may be accompanied by a guide dog at all times, even in a supermarket or restaurant. A person who is deaf may have some difficulty in communicating but many are able to lip read and some businesses train their staff in sign language. Be sure you speak clearly, not too quickly and face the person at all times to facilitate lip reading. Sometimes, it may be helpful to write down what you wish to say.

Young children

Young children can be particularly difficult to deal with, especially if they are noisy or boisterous. Care must be taken to ensure they understand what you say to them. Questioning is a good way to find out whether or not they have understood what you have said to them. Very young children, who may have strayed from their parents' side, may not be able to tell you their name or they may be frightened, especially if the store is one they haven't visited before. A great deal of patience is necessary to deal with young children.

Sensitivity must be shown when dealing with small children

Business men and women

Business men and women can be quite demanding. They will want quick and efficient service and can protest loudly if they feel they are not getting it. Business customers may be particularly favoured by your organisation if they bring in a lot of revenue, although some business customers may take advantage of being favoured customers by demanding reduced prices or extra services without increased prices. Treat them with tact and refer them to someone more senior if appropriate.

CASE STUDY

China Blue

- -

China Blue is the retail outlet of Devon Ceramics and is situated on a major road in Totnes in the county of Devon. The core business is ceramics design and manufacture and the company supplies many supermarkets and other stores throughout the UK with a range of homeware and other gifts. China Blue is much more than a shop, however, and has developed into a thriving visitor centre, which offers customers a well-stocked shop as well as a ceramics studio and a coffee shop where people can meet, eat and relax.

The studio offers visitors the opportunity to paint a piece of pottery to their own design. There is a huge range from tiny ornaments to large vases and dishes. Everything is provided including brushes, paint, sponges and stamps. There are experienced staff on hand to provide ideas and help throughout the process. Once the design is complete, customers can leave it for staff to glaze, ready for collection later or it can be posted. They are also able to try out the potter's wheel.

China Blue is situated in a large tourist area, on the outskirts of Dartmoor and close to the beaches of Torbay. It attracts locals all the year round and holidaymakers during the tourist season, especially when the weather is not so good and people are not able to take advantage of the facilities of the local beaches.

The majority of China Blue's customers are families with young children, couples and organised groups of all ages and cultures, some of whom speak little or no English. Customers who are on their own mostly browse in the shop or enjoy a snack in the coffee shop and occasionally meet up with friends. China Blue has ensured good and easy access to all parts of the visitor centre for everyone.

Fully describe the types of customers who use China Blue. Please bear in mind that a bulleted list of customer types is not sufficient.

Portfolio tip

In order to provide the evidence required in your portfolio for this assessment objective, you will need to choose a business and fully describe each type of customer who uses that business. You should bear in mind that a bulleted list of the types of customers is not sufficient.

AO2 Good customer service may help business performance

In this section, you will investigate what makes good customer service and how this may help the performance of the business you have selected.

There has been a great deal of research carried out on customers and the service they receive from companies they do business with. This research has shown that customers will probably tell more than twice as many people about a bad experience than when they receive good customer service.

Excellent customer service brings benefits for the business

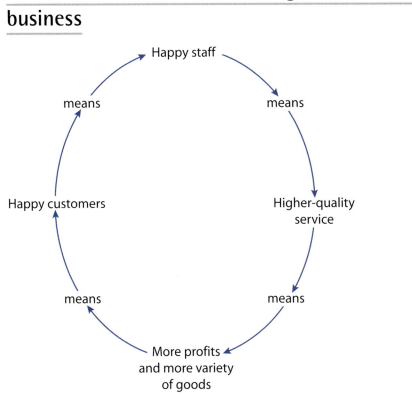

Figure 11.1 *The cycle of good customer service*

Customer service can be described as all the activities that affect a customer's experience of dealing with a particular business. These activities may include how their needs are satisfied and the way they are treated by staff. Businesses that offer a high level of customer service will often offer higher-quality products and will ensure customer loyalty.

Benefits for the business which result from excellent customer service include:

- increased sales
- satisfied customers
- more customers through repeat business and recommendations
- better public image
- an edge over the competition.

Increased sales

Good customer service provided by staff who are attentive and caring leads to happy customers who tell everyone about the wonderful service they have received. For example, a garage offering car repairs ensures that customers are informed of the repairs required and the approximate cost before the repairs are carried out. On picking up their cars, customers are given the invoice as well as the empty boxes to show the spare parts that have been used. This procedure helps to assure the customer that the work has been carried out to a high standard and that the repairs required were genuine.

Customers who are happy with what a firm provides will give more business to that company. More business means more money coming into the business. This enables the company to offer a greater range of products, which also leads to increased sales.

Satisfied customers

Businesses operate in a world where competition for customers increases every year. Word-of-mouth recommendations from existing customers are free – they don't cost the businesses anything. Satisfied customers who are happy with the products (or services) will tell family and friends which will result in more sales and even more happy customers. It is more cost-effective to keep a loyal customer than it is to try to find new ones. It is also cheaper to try out new products on existing customers than spending money trialling them on new customers.

More customers

Customers who are happy with the service they receive will tell everyone about the company. Recommendations from happy customers will lead to more customers who will be encouraged to come and try for themselves. It will also lead to increased trade through **repeat business** – customers who are happy will come again and again.

Better public image

A company which tries very hard to provide good-quality products and an excellent customer service will benefit from an increased reputation and a better public image. This means that people will hear about the company's efforts to offer good products and excellent service and the company will benefit from increased income.

An edge over the competition

Any business that does not care about its customers can probably get away with this as long as there is no other business providing a similar service or product. If customers cannot buy their goods or get their services from anywhere else, they will probably feel they have no choice but to use that company, even though they are very unhappy with the quality of the products and the customer service. However, that could change. It only needs a new business to open up in the locality which does offer high-quality goods or service and an excellent customer service for the other business to soon see its custom disappearing. The new business will achieve an edge over the competition which will probably result in the existing business reviewing its policies and procedures in an effort to win back customers.

Portfolio tip

Many businesses have their own customer service policy and procedures, including your own organisation. Therefore, you may be governed by these to some extent when demonstrating practical skills during this unit.

CASE STUDY

Customer Service in China Blue

China Blue has worked hard to create an image and reputation as one of the leading theme destinations in the tourist region of South Devon. Considerable resources have been, and are still being, invested in promoting China Blue as a fun place to visit. All staff are trained in customer service to ensure that they offer a friendly service, promoting a varied range of quality products that offer value for money and a pleasant, stress-free environment. The company is keen to ensure that customers leave feeling good and wanting to return.

Sandra Robbins is the Manager of China Blue and part of her job is to monitor customer satisfaction, oversee customer complaints and to advise the directors on any improvements that need to be made. The company's policy on customer service has attracted new business, reduced the number of customer complaints and encouraged repeat business. Another aspect of Sandra's job is to regularly check all aspects of customer safety and to ensure easy access to all sections of the visitor centre.

Each member of staff is responsible for ensuring that the company's policy on customer service is carried out at all times:

- customers are the most important people and should be treated as such at all times
- courtesy and politeness cost nothing and can make the difference between a satisfied and disgruntled customer
- customers are to be made to feel welcome – they will hopefully then recommend the business to others and return in future.

The company has recognised that employees working in the visitor centre should reflect the high quality of the goods on sale. To this end, staff undertake training in customer service and both the business and staff have benefited from this training. Staff have a greater sense of motivation, purpose and pride in their work, and this had led to opportunities for promotion for some staff.

Sandra is convinced that the reason sales have increased over the past year is partly due to business expansion and partly due to the new training programme in customer service that has been introduced for staff.

Describe what makes good customer service and how this has helped the sales performance of China Blue.

AO3 How customers are protected by consumer law and ways to obtain advice and support

In this section, you will look at some of the many laws of England and Wales that protect consumers (another word for customers) and the ways in which they can seek help, advice and support.

Consumer laws

The major laws you need to be able to describe are:

- Sale of Goods Act
- Trade Descriptions Act
- Weights and Measures Act
- Food and Drugs Act
- Food Safety Act.

Sale of Goods Act

The main purpose of this Act is to ensure that quality is maintained in the goods that are sold to the public. The Act has since been amended by the Sale and Supply of Goods Act 1994. Together, the Acts state that people buying goods should expect those goods to:

- be of 'satisfactory quality', which means that the goods must be of reasonable quality when sold; there should be nothing wrong with them – no defects or faults. Aspects of quality include:
  - appearance and finish
  - freedom from minor defects
  - safety
  - durability
  - be fit for the purpose for which they are sold; for example, when you buy a television and then switch it on, there must be a picture, not just sound

- match any description of them, including a verbal or written description, as well as a picture or drawing, whether the description appears on an advertisement, on the packaging or on a sign or poster. For example, you may buy a pair of trousers and the label on the outside packaging states that they are made from polyester and cotton. When you get them home, you discover a label on the trousers that states 100 per cent nylon. The shop which sold the trousers may have committed an offence under the Sale of Goods Act

- match the sizes or weights shown on the packaging.

If a business sells something to a customer, even an item sold as a special offer in a sale, that fails to meet the above conditions, then the customer is entitled to a refund.

Trade Descriptions Act

This is a very important piece of consumer legislation. The main reason the Act was introduced was to ensure that people who advertise goods and/or services do so accurately. Anyone who sells something (or provides a service) to someone else must ensure that the description in the advertisement is accurate and in no way misleading or false. The Act includes the contents, price, packaging, advertising and promotional materials of a product or service.

Under the Act it is illegal to sell something as being 'reduced price' unless that article was sold at the original higher price for a period of 28 days prior to being reduced. If the goods were not sold at the higher price, then the business must display a sign stating they have never sold the article at the higher price.

The Trade Descriptions Act gives trading standards officers the power to go into any business premises and to remove any products that are not what they appear. For example, a shop selling videos that are advertised and priced as originals, but the videos are fakes, could be prosecuted.

Weights and Measures Acts

Under the Weights and Measures Acts 1963 and 1979, it is illegal for a business to sell goods that are not to the specific weight or measure, as described on the packaging. Manufacturers must ensure that their goods weigh or measure exactly what is displayed on the packaging or label. For example, a business that sold you half a litre of coke that was in fact less than half a litre, could be prosecuted for selling coke that was not to the specific measure.

Recent European Community directives have meant that amendments to the Act have been necessary because the UK has now adopted metric weights and measure systems.

Food and Drugs Act

Under this Act, all food products must be accurately labelled with the ingredients contained in the food. It is also illegal to sell any food which is unfit for consumption or contains harmful additives, for example some colouring preservatives in sweets and chocolates. The Act allows environmental health officers to close down any premises that sell unfit food products.

The Act has been amended by various hygiene laws that maintain how food products should be prepared in restaurants and pubs, but the Food and Drugs Act 1955 is still in force.

Food Safety Act

This Act ensures that businesses do not:

- sell food that is unfit for people to eat
- sell food that is not what the customer is entitled to expect, in terms of content or quality
- describe or present food in a way that is false or misleading.

ACTIVITY

Work in groups to discuss the situations that follow. Decide what action should be taken, if any, and include the legislation that covers each situation.

1 You buy a pair of shoes and the next day the heel comes off. The shop manager refuses to give a refund because he says they are dancing shoes and not intended for day-to-day wear.

2 You bought a T-shirt last week and now you've decided you don't like the colour and style. You have taken it back but the sales assistant in the shop won't give you a refund.

3 You and a friend have bought some CDs in a sale. When you tried them, neither of them would work properly. When you took them back to the shop, the salesman said he didn't need to give you a refund because they were bought in the sale.

4 You have bought an oven-ready chicken in a supermarket – the label said it weighed 1.66 kg but when your mum weighed it before cooking, it weighed only 1.42 kg. You take it back to the shop but the staff refuse to do anything as they feel it must be your fault as their systems are totally accurate.

Help and advice for consumers

There are many ways in which consumers can obtain help, advice and support. The major sources are listed below:

- Trading Standards
- Environmental Health
- Citizens Advice Bureau
- Trade Associations
- Consumers' Association
- utilities watchdogs.

Trading Standards

Trading Standards departments are a function of local government and are funded by local taxes, such as council tax. Each local authority is responsible for the Trading Standards service and decides the priorities and resources.

Trading Standards protect consumers by ensuring that trade is carried out lawfully, fairly and safely. Some examples of the work of Trading Standards Officers are:

- to advise people on their legal rights under civil law and to work out a way to resolve complaints
- to advise businesses on their legal obligations under consumer protection legislation
- to take legal action against businesses who disregard the law, especially in cases of fraud or negligence.

There are various ways in which Trading Standards Officers can help. They can:

- advise you on the law and your rights
- advise you on the best way to pursue your rights
- help you through the small claims court procedure
- investigate if the criminal law has been contravened.

People who wish to complain about the way a product has been sold or about the quality of the product itself can contact their nearest Trading Standards Office. The telephone number can be found in the directory under 'Local Services' or 'Trading Standards'. A complaint can be dealt with by a Trading Standards Officer who will be able to advise the person making the complaint on the best action to take.

Environmental Health

Environmental Health Officers are employed by local authorities to ensure that places where people live are safe and hygienic. Another part of their work is to inspect premises to see that health standards are being maintained. Their work is concerned with the maintenance of a healthy and safe environment in the home, at work and during recreation.

A major part of their work is in food hygiene. They inspect places where food is prepared or sold and they work with local health authorities with regard to infectious diseases. However, Environmental Health Officers also inspect and advise on housing conditions, atmospheric pollution and smoke control areas.

One of the major reasons people have contact with Environmental Health Officers is to do with noise levels. If a neighbour is having a noisy party which is still going in the early hours of the morning, it is the Environmental Health Officers who will deal with complaints from neighbours.

Citizens Advice Bureau

Most towns now have a CAB

The Citizens Advice Bureau (CAB) offers free, confidential advice to anyone. There are many individual offices, each is a registered charity and relies on volunteers to run it as well as grants from local authorities and sponsorship from local businesses and individual donations. Volunteers act as advisors and help solve millions of problems every year, ranging from solving housing problems to writing letters and representing people in court.

Citizens Advice was set up in about 1939 and, therefore, has a long history of helping people in many situations. It sets standards for advice, training, equal opportunities and accessibility.

Most towns and cities in England and Wales have a Citizens Advice Bureau – the nearest one can be found in the local phone book or Yellow Pages or by searching the Internet.

Trade Associations

There are many reputable Trade Associations through the United Kingdom. Traders, such as construction workers, stonemasons, farriers and craftsmen such as jewellers and carpenters sign up with an appropriate Trade Association, entitling them to use the Guild of Master Craftsmen badge. Many consumers feel safer using someone who is a member of a Trade Association because the majority of these protect consumers from poor-quality workmanship.

However, just because a person is a member of a trade association is no guarantee of that person's competence. Some trade associations publish a Code of Fair Trading with which their members must comply. In a recent meeting of over 30 different trade associations, it was stated that anyone who wished to use a person's skills because he or she is a member of a trade association should check directly with the association involved to ensure that person is a current member.

The Consumers' Association

The familiar face of Which? magazine

The Consumers' Association has been researching and campaigning on behalf of consumers since 1957 and has approximately 700,000 members. The Association also publishes *Which?* magazine and this contains many articles on products and services, helping consumers to make choices. For example, if someone wishes to buy a computer and is confused by the choice available, they can look at a back issue of the magazine – available from all libraries. They will find detailed information on models, sizes, prices and guidance on value for money and this will help them to make an informed choice.

Utilities watchdogs

Utilities are companies that provide water, sewage, electricity, gas, telephone, post etc. to the public. There are watchdogs for each utility who are regulators responsible for overseeing each of the utilities.

Ofwat is the regulator of the water industry – companies who provide water supplies to our homes and businesses as well as those who deal with sewage disposal and treatment.

Energywatch is the independent watchdog for gas and electricity consumers. They provide free, impartial advice on a range of energy issues and investigate complaints on behalf of consumers. For example, if you have a problem with the gas supplied to your home, Energywatch will investigate for you.

Ofcom is the regulator for the UK communications industry, with responsibility for television, radio, telecommunications and wireless communications services (mobile phones). Ofcom exists to help people who use either of these services. For example, if you receive a text message on your mobile phone that asks you to ring an expensive telephone number to claim a prize holiday and you have not requested this, you could complain to Ofcom who would investigate on your behalf.

Postwatch is the Consumer Council for Postal Services. It looks after the interests of consumers and will take up complaints on behalf of customers of Royal Mail, Parcelforce Worldwide and Post Office Limited as well as licensed providers of postal services.

ACTIVITY

Work in groups of four. Each group should discuss the following situations. Decide which of the above organisations would be the best to contact for help, advice and guidance. After the discussions, the class should meet together to discuss each group's findings.

1   You have noticed a leak in the water pipe in the pavement near your home. You have contacted your local water board but no action has been taken.

2   Your mum works as a self-employed word processor operator. Five months ago, she did 10 hours of work for a businessman who operates a small business selling specialist postage stamps from his home in a nearby town. The man has refused to pay the £60 outstanding. Your mum has decided to make a claim through the small claims court but doesn't know how to do this.

3   You keep receiving a gas bill from a major gas supplier. You have telephoned and written several times to explain you don't have gas connected to your flat.

4   You notice that the changing rooms at your local swimming pool are very dirty. The showers and toilets do not appear to have been cleaned for quite a while. The swimming pool is owned by a private sports company, but you have not been able to find out any contact details.

5   Your employer runs a cleaning business and has private and business customers, many of whom send orders and pay bills by post. The firm moved into a unit on a new industrial estate four months ago and since then the service has been very intermittent – sometimes there are no deliveries for days on end. Your employer has made many enquiries at the local sorting office and complained in writing and by telephone but the service has not improved. He is most concerned that his customers' cheques are not reaching him promptly.

6   Your uncle is keen to buy a new hi-fi system but is bewildered by the variety of equipment and different prices. He has visited several shops but still can't make a decision as to which one would suit him best and one that he can afford.

Portfolio tip

In order to provide the evidence required in your portfolio for this assessment objective, you will need to describe in depth the ways in which consumer law protects customers and also a broad range of sources of advice and guidance in relation to consumer issues.

AO4 Deal with customers to meet their requirements and identify areas for development

In this section, you will have opportunities to practise dealing with customers in a range of situations and review your own performance in these practical tasks. You will then be able to identify areas for development.

To help you in the practical tasks in this unit – dealing with customers in five different situations – we will look at the areas which you should consider before tackling these tasks:

- appropriate presentation (dress, personal hygiene, attitude)

- operate using a range of communication methods (face-to-face, over the telephone, in writing)

- use appropriate personal communication techniques (effective listening, appropriate body language, appropriate pitch and tone of voice, appropriate language).

Appropriate presentation

You should always dress appropriately – ensure the clothes you wear are appropriate for the job you are doing. However, this does not mean you should turn up for work wearing clothes which are dirty and untidy. Casual but smart is a term often used these days and some companies may have a strict policy concerning shoes; many do not allow staff to wear trainers.

Some companies provide a uniform and will expect their employees to wear this at all times. Usually the uniform will be designed to suit the job. For example, if you are working in a refrigerated area, you will be provided with a special protective suit, gloves and headgear. If you are working at a till in a supermarket, you will be provided with a smart blouse or shirt, skirt or trousers.

Think about it

Look at yourself in a mirror before you go to work. Do you like what you see? What will customers' opinions be of your appearance? You will find it will help if you keep these questions in mind.

As well as your clothes, think about your hair. Many companies have strict policies concerning hair, especially for those people who work with

Did you know?

First impressions really DO matter!

food. Long hair should be tied back and jewellery kept to a minimum. Staff handling food are usually asked to remove bodypiercing or to cover up piercing with tape.

Personal hygiene

Personal hygiene is also important, not just for the customers, but for people who work with you. Ensure you make every effort to avoid body odour by showering or bathing regularly and using a deodorant. Remember that changing to a different brand of deodorant may be necessary from time to time. Washing clothes regularly (or having them dry cleaned) will kill odour-causing bacteria. Avoid regularly eating highly flavoured food, such as garlic, as its odour can come through the pores of your skin.

Many of us suffer from bad breath from time to time, usually because of something we have eaten, or because we smoke or possibly due to gum disease. Some simple measures such as brushing and flossing your teeth regularly, regularly drinking water, using mints or a mouthwash can help.

Attitude

One of the major things that influence customers' feelings about a business is the way the staff deal with them – the staff's attitude. Having a friendly, positive attitude can be difficult but is so important – first impressions do count and the way the customer is greeted and treated is a vital part of those first impressions.

When dealing with customers, employees should be polite, tactful and show empathy (understand how someone is feeling) and smile! Keep in mind how you prefer to be dealt with when you are a customer. Ensure body language is appropriate and try to be punctual at all times. If you arrange to meet a customer at a particular time, make sure you are there, ready to deal with the customer and his or her particular requirements.

Operate using a range of communication methods

There are different ways to communicate with customers. You may be dealing with customers face to face, by telephone or by writing to them. The most important point to bear in mind is that you must be polite and attentive at all times, never angry, too weary to bother or patronising. Remember you must always remain in control.

Face-to-face communication

The best way to judge how a customer is feeling is to use your eyes and ears. When dealing with a customer face to face, listen carefully to what they have to say and at the same time, take note of any body language they may be showing. For example, a customer who is red in the face and very agitated, perhaps tapping his fingers on the counter, will probably be an angry or frustrated customer. The way you speak to a customer will be determined by the actions and manner of that customer.

Over the telephone

If you are speaking on the telephone to a customer, listen carefully and you will be able to judge how the customer is feeling. You will soon be able to tell if the customer is angry because of the way he or she speaks, as much as by what is said.

When answering the telephone:

- answer the phone within five rings if at all possible

- try to ensure you are in a good mood before you pick up the phone – a smile may help; a customer will be able to tell immediately if you are grumpy and this will not help if he or she has telephoned with a complaint

- greet the customer with a 'hello', immediately followed by your name and section

- concentrate completely on what the customer is saying; effective listening means that you don't allow yourself to be distracted

- find out as soon as you can what the customer is telephoning about – don't interrupt; use questioning to help clarify the customer's needs

- while the customer is talking to you, write down the important points

- tell the customer what you intend to do; if you need to put the phone down, tell the customer – don't leave him or her on hold without saying what you're intending to do

- if you can't find out immediately what the customer needs to know (or to resolve a problem or complaint) promise to ring back and give a specific time (e.g. within the next half an hour or between 11.00 and 11.30) and always ring back on time – even if you haven't managed to find out all the information needed

- finish the call by ensuring the customer knows that you care and that you will help; make sure the customer finishes the call – don't put the phone down until the customer has done so.

In writing

When writing to a customer, often in response to a letter, you will need to ensure that the letter is correctly displayed, that the appropriate manner and tone is used and that it contains the right information. The manner will differ if you are responding to a customer enquiry, which would include the facts required in a businesslike way or responding to a customer complaint where you would be tactful and apologetic. An example of a letter responding to a customer's letter of complaint is shown below.

LIME STREET FURNITURE WAREHOUSE

312 LIME STREET
BRISTOL
BS4 5YH
Tel: 01117 313 218

[Today's date – day, month, year]

Miss A J Loeb
Old Bakehouse Cottage
Market Square
Bath
BA6 9AU

Dear Miss Loeb

OUR INVOICE NO 1001B/221

Thank you for your letter, which I received this morning.

I was very sorry indeed to hear of the problems you experienced when your new bed was delivered last Monday, especially as you have been a loyal customer of our company for many years.

I have spoken to the delivery staff. They have said that they were in a hurry to finish their deliveries and were under the impression that you had someone who could help you put the bed together. They have assured me that they will make more thorough enquiries of customers in future.

We apologise very sincerely for the problems you have experienced and enclose a voucher giving you 10% off your next purchase. We will do our very best to ensure that we offer you a better service and hope that this unfortunate event will not affect our future business dealings.

Yours sincerely

Tan Si Moi

Tan Si Moi
Sales Assistant

Enc

Figure 11.2 *A letter to a customer in response to a complaint*

Appropriate personal communication techniques

When you speak to customers, your first priority should be to find out exactly what their needs are. When you know what it is they want to do or what they need, you can then decide what action to take.

Effective listening

Effective listening is achieved when you are able to repeat what the customer has said to you! This is not as easy as it sounds. It means that you are able to listen carefully and at the same time be attentive to customers' needs. Customers appreciate being treated by attentive staff – it helps them feel important. To be an effective listener, you need to listen carefully and not to interrupt. In this way, you will find out exactly what the customer wants or needs. You may find it helpful to make notes while you are listening.

To help in your efforts to discover the customer's needs, you may need to give the customer some help, by prompting or asking questions. It is usually best to start by asking questions that will be answered with 'Yes' or 'No'. These are called **closed questions**. For example, you might like to start with a simple, 'May I help you?'. Then move on and ask questions that will give you more clues as to their needs; questions that don't require a simple 'yes' or 'no'. These are called **open questions**. For example, if a customer has brought back a product under complaint, you might ask when they bought the product and whether they have the receipt, as this will tell you who served them, at what till (if appropriate) and when etc.

You might find it useful to summarise what the customer has said to you and to use questions to clarify anything.

Appropriate body language

Appropriate body language is vital. Research has shown that people receive the largest part of a message that someone is trying to communicate to them by the body language being used. Body language shows people how we feel by the way we use our facial expressions, eyes, gestures and body posture etc.

When dealing with customers, try to ensure that your body language gives the correct signals:

- maintain eye contact – avoiding looking at the customer directly can give the impression that you may have something to hide or that you may not be telling the truth

- keep still – constant movement can be disturbing, or even threatening; however, if you lean slightly towards the customer, this can indicate that you are interested in what he or she has to say

- smile and give a positive sign, such as nodding your head while they are talking – this can show the customer that you care and can be trusted.

Body language can be used very effectivly to show that you empathise with the customer – that you are listening to what the customer is saying – and that you care!

Eye contact and a smile make all the difference

Appropriate pitch and tone of voice

Whether you are speaking to a customer face to face or by telephone, the pitch and tone of your voice should be your normal speaking voice. However angry the customer may be, keep your voice and tone at a reasonable level. It is much more difficult for someone to remain angry with another person if that person is reasonable, calm and polite.

When listening to your customer, try to identify the tone of voice that is being used. For example, you will be able to detect whether or not the customer is angry, frustrated or annoyed.

Don't interrupt, and don't be too quick to reply. Give the customer a moment, just in case they want to say something else.

ACTIVITY

Work in pairs to practise effective listening. Write down three short sentences such as:

1 'I'm 17 next Tuesday and will have my first driving lesson.'
2 'The Forest Driving School has a special offer.'
3 'I'd love to drive a Ferrari (or substitute another preferred make, model).'

Don't discuss what you've written down. Sit facing your colleague and, speaking in your normal voice, say the words you've written. Ask your colleague to repeat back what you have said and check that they remembered all the relevant facts. Change over and listen to what your partner has written down and repeat back what has been said, as near word perfect as possible. Try this again using more information and more difficult facts. By practising, you can learn effective listening.

Appropriate language

Ensure your language is appropriate at all times and that you can be understood. Do not swear or use slang as customers may be from another country or even another area in England where slang may mean something else.

Meet customer requirements by:

- giving advice

- providing information

- providing assistance

- resolving problems, complaints

- offering extra services.

In this section, you need to demonstrate the practical skills of customer service. You may do this through your part-time job or work placement or if this isn't possible, through role play but the situations should be as realistic as possible.

   You should consider, first of all, the situations you could use for these tasks. Talk to your section manager, team leader, employer or tutor to discuss how you could carry out these tasks. You need to use a mixture of face-to-face, telephone and written responses, but you must use face to face to deal with a dissatisfied customer in resolving the problem or complaint situation. You should take into account any procedures your company has for dealing with these situations as you will need to follow these. Speak to your tutor if you are in any doubt.

   You will also need to consider how you will provide the evidence required for your portfolio. For example, your section manager, team leader or employer (or your tutor if he or she is visiting you at the time) can complete a witness statement or you may be able to provide a candidate assessment sheet.

   If you use role play, you should write or word process the situation and include this as part of your evidence in your portfolio.

Giving advice

Think about the situation you could arrange for this. You can use any response – face to face, telephone or written. For example, if you are working in a shop, your team leader or section manager may be able to arrange for you to be on the customer service desk so that you can carry out the practical skills involved when giving advice. You could consider a situation where you give advice over the telephone – look back at page 284 for information regarding communicating with the customer by telephone.

ACTIVITY

Use this activity to role play giving advice to a customer by telephone. Ask your tutor to help you organise this. You will need to ask someone to play the part of the customer and for someone to act as observer. Before you start, prepare for the activity by thinking about the details you will need in order to give advice to the customer in the situation outlined below.

Working at a computer games shop

You work as a part-time assistant on Saturdays for Gordon's Computer Games, a shop selling computer games. You receive a phone call from a customer who has just bought a computer game from your shop but cannot get it to work. You have a good knowledge of the products your shop sells and have played most of them yourself, both at work and on your PC and PlayStation at home. The customer needs advice on how to load the game in order to enable her son to play it.

Role play this situation, ensuring you give the customer the advice required by telephone. Ask for feedback from the 'customer' and observer. Make notes as to what went well and what you could have done differently, partly based on their feedback and partly on your own experience.

Change round so that you get a chance to role play as the customer, the person giving advice and the observer.

Providing information

You can use any response for this situation (face to face, telephone or written). Think about the situation you could use for this; for example, if you are working in an office, your team leader or section manager may be able to arrange for you to reply to a customer's letter asking for information. Customers often telephone for information but if the information they require is complex, they will write letters – in which case, a letter would be sent in reply.

ACTIVITY

Use this activity to practise writing a letter to a customer. Ask your tutor to help you with this – look back at page 281 for information regarding writing to customers. Ensure you prepare for the activity by thinking about the details you will need in order to provide the information required in the situation outlined below.

You are on work placement for Moores Motorcycles, a shop that sells motorbikes in your town centre. You receive a letter from Mrs Jayne Major, 15 Babbacombe Road, Edgbart, TY1 4NQ. She wants to buy a motor scooter for her daughter for her 16th birthday and would like to know which one would be the most suitable; she tells you how much she can afford. She also wants to know about the tests that her daughter will have to pass before she can take the scooter out on the road. You will need to have a good knowledge of the motor scooters your company sells and about the rules and regulations regarding 16-year-olds riding them on the road, including the tests they need to take, to ensure the information you give the customer is accurate. You may find it helpful to go back to page 143 – where you researched this topic.

Ensure your letter is well displayed and that the language and tone you use is appropriate. Check you have not made any errors and that you have provided the customer with all the information that was required.

Providing assistance

This usually requires you *doing* something, rather than just speaking to the customer. You can use any response for this situation (face to face, telephone or written). Think about the situation you could arrange for this. For example, you are working in a shop and a disabled customer asks you to reach some goods that are too high for him or her to reach. Consider giving advice face to face – look back at page 283 for information regarding communicating with the customer in this way.

ACTIVITY

Use this activity to role play providing assistance to a customer face to face. Ask someone to play the part of the customer and someone else to be the observer.

You work part time as a sales assistant, stacking shelves at Jojo's Mini Supermarket. While you are stacking shelves, a customer comes up to you and asks you where he can find frozen pizzas. You respond by taking him to the correct aisle, showing him the pizzas, ask him if these are the correct ones and, before you leave him, ask if you can do anything else to help him.

Role play the situation, ensuring you provide the assistance the customer requires. Ask for feedback from the 'customer' and observer. Ensure you make some notes on what went well and what you could have done differently, partly based on the feedback you have received and partly on your own experience.

Change round to give everyone the opportunity to experience role playing as the customer, the person providing assistance and the observer.

Resolving a problem or complaint

You must use a face-to-face response to deal with a dissatisfied customer. Your firm may have a procedure for dealing with customers who have a complaint and this may be similar to the one shown below.

Greet the customer

↓

Find out what the complaint actually is

↓

Listen carefully and sympathetically to the customer – to find out all the details

↓

Ask questions to clarify

↓

Empathise with customer

↓

Record the details – look at the goods being returned (if appropriate) and the receipt

↓

Check all relevant details, including records such as an order book if appropriate

↓

Apologise and take action by offering a replacement or a refund – whichever is appropriate in the individual situation

↓

Resolve customer's problem or complaint

↓

Consider follow-up action such as a voucher or a letter signed by the manager, whichever is appropriate

↓

Ensure you report the complaint to your team leader, supervisor or manager so that appropriate action can be taken

Figure 11.3 *A typical complaints procedure*

ACTIVITY

Use this activity to role play dealing with a customer's complaint in a face-to-face situation. You will need to ask someone to play the part of the customer and someone to be the observer.

You work Wednesday afternoons and Saturdays in Flora's Florists. Flora is very busy doing some last minute alterations to a bride's flowers for a wedding today – the flowers are to be collected in less than 10 minutes' time. A customer comes into the shop and you can see immediately that she is very upset. She tells you that she ordered some flowers last week to be delivered for her mother's birthday yesterday. Another sales assistant had served her. Unfortunately, the wrong flowers had been delivered – she had ordered her mother's favourite flowers, red carnations, but spring flowers had been delivered by mistake. Although she had written a card to go with the flowers, the card was missing.

You need to deal with the 'customer'. Use the information given above to resolve the customer's complaint, by using role play. Ask someone to be the customer and another person to be the observer.

Use the feedback from the 'customer' and observer with your own notes to review what went well and what you would do differently next time.

Change round to give everyone a chance to role play as the person dealing with the complaint, the customer and the observer.

Offering extra services

This is where you offer that extra something to a customer! There are many opportunities for offering extra services to customers, depending on the type of job you are doing. For example, you may offer to help with packing shopping or perhaps take the customer's shopping to his or her car.

ACTIVITY

Use this activity to role play offering extra services to a customer face to face. You will need to ask someone to play the part of the customer and for another person to act as observer.

You work as a part-time waiter in a restaurant on Friday, Saturday and Sunday evenings. You have served two people with their meal and it's now late on Saturday evening. You have enjoyed a good relationship with them during the evening – they are very friendly and it has been easy to please them. During the evening, they have told you they live in a village four miles away and, because they have been drinking, they don't want to drive home. You are tired and want to close but decide to offer to call a taxi for them.

Role play the above situation and on completion, make notes as to what went well and what could have been done differently, using feedback from those taking part in the role play as well as your own experience.

Change round to ensure everyone has an opportunity to role play the person offering extra services, the customer and the observer.

Review performance and propose training or other changes leading to improvement

Immediately you finish each situation, you should make notes (as advised in the activities above) so that you can review your performance. Think about what went well and consider any areas that could be improved. What could you have done to make the situation better for the customer – to offer an improved service.

Another consideration is that there may be a training programme that might help you. For example, if your product knowledge needs updating or you were not sure of your company's procedure for dealing with a particular situation.

You may be able to recommend changes to the procedures your company has put in place for dealing with situations such as those described above. Most businesses use information from staff, especially where a customer has complained, in order to put things right and to try to ensure it does not happen again.

Portfolio tip

In order to provide the evidence required in your portfolio for this assessment objective, you need to demonstrate competence in dealing effectively with customers in the five situations outlined above. On completion of the tasks, you will identify scope for development by writing or word processing your recommendations for changes to procedures or for a training programme.

You should ensure that you submit a completed Witness Statement for each of the five situations. You should sign each one and your assessor (who may be your tutor) should also sign and date each one also. Video and/or tape recordings should also be submitted as part of your evidence, if appropriate.

AO5 Demonstrate sales skills and review performance

In this section, you will demonstrate the stages involved in achieving a sale in a face-to-face situation with a customer. To help you carry out this practical task, we will look step-by-step at the selling process:

- preparing to make the sale
- contacting and meeting the customer
- finding out the customer's needs
- providing the solution
- dealing with objections
- closing the sale
- after-sales service.

Preparing to make the sale

It is essential to have a very good knowledge of all the products that your company sells, especially the ones you will be involved in selling. Customers will expect you to know the products, how they work, their advantages and benefits, details of any simple maintenance needed to ensure efficient working, the prices, any special offers that may apply, any warranties that are available and details of the after-sales service. Part of your preparation should also include being able to demonstrate the products and making sure they work. There is nothing more embarrassing in a sale situation when the product you go to demonstrate doesn't work or won't even switch on! For example, if your company sold computers, you would need to be able to:

- find out the customer's exact requirements in order to ensure that you could advise on suitable models within the customer's price range
- inform the customer of any special offers or Manager's special deals
- tell the customer about any warranties available
- offer an after-sales service – e.g. what happens if the customer can't get the computer to work when he or she gets it home.

It is also good preparation to know about the products and prices your nearest competitor offers.

Part of your preparation should also be that you ensure you are smart and tidy. First impressions are very important! Some companies provide a uniform – ensure it is clean and uncreased. As well as your clothes, think about your hair and your shoes. If you look the part, are neat and tidy, the customer is more likely to want to buy something from you.

ACTIVITY

Use this activity and the others in this section, to help you prepare to make a sale. Ask someone to help you by taking the part of the customer and someone to be an observer.

For each activity, you might find it helpful to make notes immediately after completing each one to help you review the sales situation.

You work in a music shop selling CDs, videos, DVDs etc. and will role play selling a CD to a customer. Before you start, put together a variety of CDs so that you can use these in the activity. Prepare for this activity by finding out everything about the artistes, the type of music, prices etc.

Contacting and meeting the customer

Greeting the customer is really important for a successful sale. Customers who are met by a cheerful, helpful salesperson who smiles and says 'Hello, may I help you?' are likely to be more willing to buy something than if a sales person is unapproachable. Nothing is more infuriating for a customer than sales staff who are not prepared to offer any type of service. When greeting the customer, be confident – you've prepared well and know your products. The customer will respond to your confidence.

ACTIVITY

Working in groups of four, practise greeting the customer. One of the group should act as the customer, one as the salesperson and two to act as observers. Consider different sales situations by thinking about the range of stores in your local area. How would one store differ from another in the way the customer was greeted? On completion, ask the group for feedback. Then all change round until all members of the group have practised greeting a customer.

You may find it helpful to practise this again, especially if you found it difficult to do. It might also be useful to try this on people you don't know – other tutors, students etc. Your confidence will grow with practice.

On completion, make notes as to what went well and what more you could have done to ensure the customer was greeted in a warm and friendly manner.

Finding out the customer's needs

You will have done your research and should now be confident enough to offer advice or information designed to meet the customer's needs. Use open and closed questions to help you ensure you find out everything about the customer's exact requirements. Use open questions such as who, what, why, where, when, how? Use closed questions (those answered by 'yes' or 'no' to help confirm or clarify what the customer has said. Try to show empathy when questioning the customer. Listen carefully and keep good eye contact.

It may help to summarise the customer's needs at this point, giving the customer the opportunity to change his or her mind or to add something important.

ACTIVITY

Work with a student colleague to sell one of the CDs you chose in the activity on page 292. Use questioning to find out what music the customer likes (hopefully one of those you have!).

Providing the solution

Once you have talked to the customer and found out exactly what he or she wants to buy – and the price he or she is prepared to pay – you can offer a sales solution. This means that you will be able to recommend a particular product that fits the customer's requirements. Hopefully, you will have easy access to the products you feel will suit. Guide the customer to the products you feel are suitable and within the customer's price range. If you're not sure about anything, don't be afraid to say so and offer to find out. A customer will soon be able to see through someone who is obviously not sure about something. Offer as much information as possible, including brochures, leaflets and any special offers which may help you to complete the sale. Enable the customer to try the product if possible or offer a demonstration, depending on what the product.

Give the customer all the facts about the product, the advantages and benefits and, of course, prices. Bear in mind that a customer is more likely to buy from someone whose relaxed style reflects his or her faith in the products made by the company.

Dealing with objections

Throughout the discussion with the customer, watch the customer's body language to help you gauge how the customer is feeling. Look for the obvious signs of posture, arm waving, facial expression, eye contact etc. – look back at page 283 to revise the topic of body language and the signs to watch for.

A customer may tell you that a shop down the road is offering a similar product at a much cheaper price. The customer isn't just telling you what other shops are offering, but is telling you in order to try to encourage you to reduce your price. You may be able to offer a small discount or maybe a special offer if purchase is completed within a time limit.

Sometimes, an objection can result from a misunderstanding between the customer and sales person, or because the customer wants more

ACTIVITY

In this next stage of the role play of selling a music CD, when you have discovered your customer's (colleague's) needs, you will then be able to offer one of the CDs you have to sell. Go through the sales process as outlined above to achieve a sale.

information. The customer may query the reliability of the product, the delivery times or the after-sales service. Tact will be needed to ensure any objections are cleared up quickly, perhaps with gentle questioning.

You will need considerable selling skills to ensure the customer is assured on all the above points. With practice, these skills can be acquired.

Closing the sale

You will probably receive some form of verbal confirmation of a sale, as well as the body language to back it up. You will then be able to move on to closing the sale. You could perhaps say something such as 'Do you have all the information you need – is there anything else I can do for you?' or 'We could deliver next Tuesday – would that be convenient?'

You would then complete the paperwork or take the customer, with the purchase, to a till to arrange payment and to give advice on any after-sales service etc.

After-sales service

After-sales service may be divided into two parts:

- the warranties that may be available with the product
- what the customer should do if dissatisfied for any reason.

It may not be possible to demonstrate an after-sales service to a customer but you should be able to provide evidence in your portfolio that you understand what after sales is about and how it works.

For example, when you are selling your product to a customer, you would include what after-sales service is included depending on the product, such as a warranty. For example, manufacturers of electrical goods offer a 12-month guarantee with a product and this would normally cover parts and labour. Another aspect would be what happens if the customer is dissatisfied with the product. For example, a customer buys a microwave oven but discovers that it doesn't work. The light comes on, but it won't microwave the food. The usual procedure would be for the customer to return the appliance for a replacement or a total refund.

Review the sales performance and propose training or changes to leading to improvement

On completion of the demonstration of sales skills, you will then review your performance during each stage of the sales process and propose training or changes leading to improvement.

During each part of the sales situation, you should have made notes of what went well and what you would do differently next time. These notes should help you to review your performance in the practical task and to enable you to propose further training that might help you in the future. You may also wish to consider any changes you could make that may lead to improvement in your sales techniques.

Portfolio tip

In order to provide the evidence required in your portfolio for this assessment objective, you need to demonstrate good sales skills in dealing effectively with a customer in a sales situation as outlined above and to identify scope for improvement.

You and your assessor should sign and date the completed witness statement.

Video and/or tape recordings should also be submitted as part of your evidence, if appropriate.

SKILLS CHECK

1. Identify and describe the different types of customers that use the business you have selected for your studies (AO1 and AO2 only).

2. Show how good customer service may help the performance of the business you have selected.

3. Describe ways in which customers are protected by consumer law.

4. Describe ways in which customers can obtain advice and support.

5. Deal with customers to meet a range of their requirements:
   - giving advice
   - providing information
   - resolving problems, complaints
   - offering extra services.

6. Review your performance and identify areas for development.

7. Demonstrate sales skills.

8. Review your performance and propose further development.

ACTIVITY

Ask your 'customer' for feedback on the various stages of the sale of the CD. Review your performance in the role-play sales situation and identify scope for improvement e.g. additional training or other changes that may help to improve your sales techniques.

ACTIVITY

You may find it helpful now to use role play to undertake all the steps in a sale – all in one go. Ask your tutor if he or she could arrange for a member of staff or another student whom you do not know to act as your 'customer'. The products you could offer for sale should be real – to ensure the role play is as realistic as possible.

Career planning for business

Getting Started

This unit is all about careers and planning for your future. It looks at the variety of careers available, the help that is available to you, what skills you require and how to go about getting the job you want. You will look at the recruitment process, from the time the vacancy occurs to the interview – all from your point of view, that is you, as a job applicant.

There are so many careers that the choice can be bewildering. You may wish to use the opportunities provided by your studies to explore all aspects of the job you are already doing, including the promotion prospects. However, you may prefer to investigate the possibility of a very different career, perhaps one you would very much like to do in the future. Your studies may result in you deciding that the career you had in mind may not suit you after all and, in that case, you may find yourself looking at a career you hadn't thought of previously.

First of all, you will select a sector of business on which to base your studies. You will then investigate the national trends in two career areas within that sector.

You will assess your own personal skills and achievements – and consider whether these are appropriate for the career areas you have chosen and perhaps what you may need to do to improve your chances of getting a job in one of these career areas.

Finally, you will look in detail at the recruitment process for a specific job that you choose. Your studies will help you to investigate the job market, to see what is on offer, decide whether a particular job might suit you – and whether you suit it – and prepare for the process of finding and getting the job you want.

This unit will cover

- AO1 Identify the main areas of employment within a selected sector of business and describe national trends within the sector.
- AO2 Use sources of information to extract information on two career areas within the selected sector.
- AO3 Review progression opportunities for the two career areas within the selected sector.
- AO4 Assess own personal skills and achievements and analyse implications for progression in the two career areas chosen.

- AO5 Describe the steps in identifying job opportunities and the recruitment process for a specific job role.

- AO6 Complete written application documentation for a specific job role.

- AO7 Plan for an interview for a specific job role.

- AO8 Take part in an interview for a specific job role, presenting personal information effectively and reviewing own performance.

AO1 The main areas of employment and national trends within the sector

To enable you to select the sector on which you would like to base your investigations for this unit, you need to investigate the different sectors of business and then explore:

- the main areas of employment
- growth areas and areas of decline
- the inter-relationship of different industries and different communities
- the impact of new technologies.

As you can see from Figure 12.1, there is a large variety of business sectors. Look at the main areas of employment and you will be able to see the business sector to select. For example, if you were interested in the work of a lorry driver, you would select the Transport, Storage and Distribution sector. For a television presenter, the sector you would choose would be Creative Services and Media and if you were interested in becoming a soldier, you would select the Armed Forces sector.

Main areas of employment

The area of employment you select may be one in which you already work – this will give you the added advantage of knowing about the business, giving you easy access to the different departments or sections, as well as to managers and others who work with you.

Sector of business	Examples of areas of employment
Agriculture and Fishing	Farming, fishing, forestry, agricultural work
Armed Services	Air Force, Army and Navy
Biotechnology, Medical and Chemical	Biochemistry, medical research and chemistry
Business Services	Advertising, PR and marketing, event organiser, cleaning and security services
Communications	Telecommunications including mobile phones and internet providers
Construction and Building Services	Architect, builder, construction worker, maintenance personnel
Creative Services and Media	Television, radio and the performing arts – actor, presenter, behind the scenes
Education	Teacher, trainer, support staff
Energy and Water	Electrical, gas and water board personnel
Financial Services	Banks, building societies, insurance
Forestry	Forester, tree surgeon, lumberjack
Government Services	Police officer, firefighter, paramedic, ambulance technician, coastguard
Health and Social Work	Nurse, doctor, consultant, ancillary worker
Hospitality, Leisure and Sport	Hotels, leisure and sports centres, hospitality industry
Information Technology (IT)	Programmer, computer operator, data processor, call centre worker
Manufacturing and Engineering	Clothing, food and drink, furniture, boat building, paper production, electrical and mechanical engineering, including the motor industry
Mining	Miner – coal, iron, quarry
Personal Services	Hairdresser, beauty therapist, care worker (e.g. in residential care home)
Professional Services	Accountant, legal, personnel, vet, doctor
Publishing, Printing and Packaging	Publishers of books, magazines etc., printers, manufacturers of packaging materials, editors, typesetters
Real Estate	Estate agent, auctioneer, conveyancer, surveyor
Retail and Wholesale	Supermarket, general store, pet shop, pharmacy, wholesale depots
Transport, Storage and Distribution	Lorry driver, coach driver, taxi service, storage and distribution worker
Travel and Tourism	Travel companies, travel reps, tourist information centre staff

Figure 12.1 *Sectors of business and areas of employment*

However, you should bear in mind that, later, you will investigate two career areas within your sector. As a result, you may prefer to select a business in which you are interested in finding work, rather than one in which you are already working. Your studies may help you to decide on the career that you would like to follow or to make a decision that a career you had previously considered may not, after all, be suitable for your talents and skills.

CASE STUDY

Coombe Farm

Peter and Debi Coombe have run their farm in the south of England for over 10 years. The farm has been in Peter's family for several generations. Peter and Debi took over from Peter's father when he retired.

They keep sheep and cattle and grow a variety of crops, including wheat, barley and oil seed rape. The wheat is used mainly for bread products and the barley for brewing, animal feed and pearl barley, with the oil seed rape being harvested for its oil.

The Coombe family has seen many changes and Peter and Debi have had a tough few years, with scares over disease as well as finding it more and more difficult to earn sufficient income to keep going. Only last year they decided to sell off their dairy herd because they had not been able to earn enough money from the milk their cows provided to make it worthwhile continuing.

Peter and Debi have now decided that they must diversify. This means that they must find other ways in which to earn money from their business. The farm is not providing them with sufficient money for them to live. They have a large stone barn that is not used at present and they are considering changing the barn to two self-contained cottages. Debi is keen to offer bed and breakfast accommodation to tourists as the farm is situated in the heart of tourist country, on a major 'A' road near the seaside. She is convinced that holidaymakers will be attracted to the farm as they will experience a taste of country living, while being close to beaches and other attractions offered by the nearby seaside towns.

In which sector of business and in which main area of employment is Peter and Debi's business located?

Growth areas and areas of decline

Coalmining in the UK has suffered a serious decline

Whether or not a business is in decline will be influenced by many factors and you should investigate those within your sector. For example, the mining industry has been in decline since the 1980s. There are many reasons for this but some of the major reasons are that very few people use coal to heat their homes compared with a few years ago. Another reason for the decline may be that power stations changed to using gas or oil, because they were cheaper to buy, rather than burning coal in order to produce electricity. The power stations stopped buying coal and so production had to be reduced, mines were closed and, as a result, miners and others employed in the industry were made redundant. In the 1980s there was also an increase in the amount of coal that was imported into the UK. It was thought to be cheaper to import coal from other countries than it was to use coal mined here. All these factors led to a decline in the mining industry.

One growth area is the motor industry as more new cars are currently being sold than ever before. One of the reasons for this may be that money is much more readily available than previously. People are able to borrow from many sources such as loans, overdrafts and credit cards etc. Although it would appear that the motor trade is a growth area, there is another side to this as the sales of second-hand cars have declined rapidly. People are buying new cars with three-year warranties and as a consequence, they are not buying second-hand cars, as they once did. Therefore, the market for these has declined. The purchase of new cars has also affected the job prospects of many in the motor trade, such as garage proprietors and motor vehicle technicians because of the reduction in the numbers of cars being repaired and maintained. The annual testing of cars (MOTs) has also reduced, as cars do not need to be tested until they are three years old. Consequently, many small garage businesses have closed down and jobs have been lost. The motor industry is, therefore, a sector of business that is in a growth area for some, but in an area of decline for others.

ACTIVITY

1 Refer to the case study on the previous page. Working with a student colleague, investigate the growth areas and areas of decline in the area of employment in which Peter and Debi's business is located.

2 Use as many different resources for your research as possible, including the Internet. Discuss and then word-process or write your findings.

Inter-relationship of different industries and different communities

Different areas of the country will have different industries, different communities and, therefore, different inter-relationships between them. It may be appropriate for you to consider the differences between people who live in rural areas and those who live in cities or towns. For example, many large supermarkets in towns and cities regularly invite schoolchildren to their stores and often provide sponsorship for projects, as well as money for a variety of competitions e.g. paintings the children have done of the store or scenes of the local area. Some have special schemes where customers can give money directly to local charities. One major store, for example, rewards its customers for re-using plastic carrier bags. The customers then directly donate the money to local charities. Most small village shops, however, do not have the resources of the big stores. Some are able to help in a small way by helping to sponsor local organisations or by providing produce at village fetes, carnivals etc.

Some businesses have special relationships with their communities. For example, companies that quarry stone often provide funding for environmental projects, such as wildlife schemes. The companies are able to help the wildlife that may have been disturbed by the quarrying process. When a quarry has given up all its stone and becomes redundant, the companies need to consider what to do with the site. Often, local people work together with the quarry companies to draw up plans to restore the site, or to build houses or to provide a much-needed local amenity such as sports facilities.

Some industries also have inter-relationships with other industries. For example, a company of architects who are designing and overseeing the construction of a building would have close links with the builders, planners and everyone else concerned in the construction of that building.

Many businesses have good, close relationships with their local communities. You will need to investigate those in your chosen sector and in your own locality and to provide examples, giving as much detail as possible.

ACTIVITY

Refer to the case study on page 299. Investigate the inter-relationships that may exist between Peter and Debi's business and other industries and also those between their business and different communities.

Use as many different resources for your research as possible, including the Internet. Discuss your findings with other students in your class and word-process or write the result of your discussions.

Impact of new technologies

New technology, particularly information technology, has made a huge impact on many businesses. For example, before the 1970s people producing newspapers (Publishing, Printing and Packaging business sector), manually put together all the blocks of type needed to make up each page. These people were called compositors and they handled tiny rubber blocks of type and set them in racks so that they made complete sentences. The introduction of information technology meant that the compositors had to learn new skills – they had to learn to type proficiently and quickly. Their old skills were no longer needed. It was quickly discovered that anyone with good keyboard skills could do the work that once only very skilled compositors could do.

The new technology meant that many of the older, experienced compositors either took early retirement or were made redundant.

You should investigate the impact technology has had on your chosen area of employment, but you should not limit your investigation to that of information technology only. For example, if you choose car manufacture as your chosen career area, you would need to consider the effect robots have had on the industry and the results for the workforce.

Mechanisation has had a major impact on car manufacturing

Portfolio tip

In order to provide the evidence required for this assessment objective, you will need to choose a business sector, identify the main areas of employment, give a detailed description of the national trends, showing good knowledge why the trends exist and how they impact on the sector, describe the inter-relationships of different industries and different communities and the impact of new technologies.

AO2 Researching information on two career areas

In this section, you will find out as much as you can about the career areas you choose. You will need to choose two career areas in the business sector you have already selected. You may prefer to investigate career areas in which you currently work or to look at career areas that are of interest to you but you are not sure, at present, whether they are suited to you, and you to them. However, you must make sure that the areas you choose will give you ample opportunity to provide all the evidence you need for your portfolio.

Sources of information

The sources of information you will explore are:

- personal advisers
- Connexion service
- library
- Internet
- employers
- job centre
- job advertisements
- people employed in the workplace.

Personal advisers

Almost all young people in the UK have access to their own personal advisers. These men and women are able to arrange frequent and regular contact meetings to discuss all the issues that you may wish to discuss with them. Advisers are experienced and qualified and come from a wide range of backgrounds. Some have worked solely in careers advice, some have been youth workers, others have worked in education, social or health services and in different occupations. Advisers provide information on a wide range of topics, including learning choices, advice and support on careers.

Connexion service

A Connexions branch

This service, commonly known as Connexions, is aimed at young people aged 13 to 19. The Connexion service employs personal advisers who give advice and guidance on careers, as well as practical help in preparing young people for the world of work. The service is completely free of charge.

> **Portfolio tip**
>
> *You might find it easier to do the research for one of your career areas first, before you investigate the second one. Some of the results from the research you do on the first career area may be useful when you come to research the second one.*

All young people are able to speak to Connexions personal advisers, who are trained to give up-to-date information. They are friendly, will make you feel welcome and will be happy to listen to you. They will ensure that everything you say to them will remain completely confidential.

Connexions is not just about finding jobs. There are experts able to give support and guidance on many subjects, such as your rights, health issues, help with housing and money etc.

Library

As well as your school or college library and the local library, ask your tutor if you have access to a career library. Many schools and colleges now provide these for students and most are open and available at any time. Career libraries are particularly useful, as they stock a large variety of leaflets, reference guides and other materials to help you decide on your career.

Local and college or school libraries have a vast range of information on all kinds of topics. Ask your tutor to organise a visit to your local library, if you haven't already made contact yourself. You may be surprised at the resources that are available. If you want to do research on a particular topic, and you are not sure how, ask the library staff – they will be only too pleased to help you and to guide you to the area in the library where you will find this information. Use of libraries is free of charge and opening hours are generous, but vary from region to region.

Internet

The Internet is a wonderful technological development. It is a worldwide system of networks, which is the reason many people often refer to it as the World Wide Web. The Internet enables people to find just about anything, at any time of the day or night – it never closes! You can easily access a large variety of resources, including photographs, images, text, graphics etc. Ask your tutor what access to the Internet you have in your school or college. To research on the Internet successfully, you should make use of search engines, details of which may be found on page 141.

Employers

Your tutor may have already arranged for local employers to come into your school or college to give a presentation about their business and possible career prospects within it. Many local business people are happy to do this. Your tutor may also be able to arrange for you to visit local offices, factories and other places of employment and these can be very useful and informative. Most employers give ample opportunity for you to ask questions during their presentations and to talk to people who are actually working there.

ACTIVITY

Use the Internet to find out the address and telephone number of:
- your local job centre
- three recruitment agencies in your area
- your local Connexions office.

Job centre

There are job centres in most towns and cities in the UK. Job centres provide a public recruitment service for all types of vacancies that are displayed in self-service vacancy exhibits. If you see a job that appeals to you, then you can make a note of the job reference and ask the job centre staff for more details. They may be able to arrange a job interview with an employer for you while you wait. As well as giving advice on vacancies, staff can offer help and support to people, including those with disabilities, in finding work or appropriate training. They also have good contacts with employers, who they often advise on suitable candidates for vacancies.

Job advertisements

Jobs are advertised in many different ways. They may be displayed on noticeboards, in newspapers, magazines and journals. People also often tell others when a job becomes vacant. Job advertisements give all the information a person looking for a job would need to know – the employer's name, address, telephone number, the job title and, most importantly, how to go about applying for the job.

People employed in the workplace

If you want to know about a job, the very best people to be able to tell you about that job are the people who are actually doing the work. Of course, people who are happy in their work will give you a very different view of the work than those who are dissatisfied. You will need to keep a balanced view of what you are told. Many businesses are happy for their workforce to talk to prospective employees. They often arrange this during visits to their premises. Your tutor may be able to arrange visits for you.

ACTIVITY

Look in a local newspaper, magazine or journal and cut out at least two advertisements related to your chosen career areas. Read them carefully and take note of the information each of them contains. (Keep them safe as you will use these advertisements in an activity later.)

Information on jobs

You will, by now, have selected your two career areas. Now you need to find out specific information on jobs within these career areas as follows:

- the range of job roles within the career areas
- skills needed to work within the areas
- training requirements
- types of employers
- location of employers
- starting packages
- content of job roles
- working conditions (e.g. self-employed, home-working).

Range of job roles within the career areas

Your investigation should explore the range of job roles that are available in your career areas. The range would normally start at the bottom, with the most junior job, and lead up to the most senior position. For example a person starting a career in banking would probably start as a clerk, then progress to junior management, to manager and eventually to senior manager.

Skills needed to work within the area

These are the skills a person would need to be able to work in their chosen career area. These may be skills such as computer and keyboard skills, as well as personal skills such as interpersonal and communication skills. Some of these skills may have been acquired on work placement or during part-time employment and are likely to be specific to a particular career area. For example, a person working in a call centre, selling insurance to members of the public, would need good telephone and communication skills.

Training requirements

Most new employees have training requirements, especially those who are at the beginning of their careers. Many companies provide induction training for new employees, giving them opportunities to learn about the company as well as specific training in using equipment or specialised training in the handling of hazardous materials. To progress in their work, most people need training so that they possess the skills necessary to do their jobs efficiently and to attain qualifications in order to gain promotion in their career. The type of training required will depend very much on the career area, the type of employment and the needs of both employer and employee.

Types of employers

There are many different types of employers and sizes of businesses, which vary from the sole owner to the very large multinational company, with possibly many branches all over the world. Businesses may be very large, employing many thousands of people or may be very small, just employing one or two.

Location of employers

There are businesses in your local area, in cities throughout the United Kingdom (national) and all over the world (international). For example, a florist shop could be a single-owner business in a small village or town or it could be a very large international business, such as Interflora. The location of businesses will often depend on the career areas you choose.

Starting packages

The starting package will vary from employee to employee and from business to business. It is not just about pay, usually it can also consist of bonuses, commission (if appropriate) as well as company car or van (if appropriate). Other benefits such as housing, health and life insurance, pensions etc. may be included in a starting package.

Content of job roles

Every job has its own job description – this will contain a great deal of information about a specific job, including the tasks that each employee is expected to carry out. The job description will also include to whom the employee will directly report, such as a team leader, supervisor or section manager. These tasks will vary from one job to another and from one employee to another, even those doing similar work, within the same business.

Normally, the hours of work and benefits such as sickness benefit, paid holidays and any other benefits will also be included.

Working conditions

Working conditions usually refer to the place where the employees will be based for their normal everyday tasks. These vary tremendously depending on the work. For example, a telephone engineer who is repairing telephone lines (and therefore out and about in different locations each day) will have very different working conditions to a hairdresser who will often work in one salon every day.

You should also consider whether your career areas offer opportunities for people to become self-employed. For example, someone who has worked in public relations may decide to use the experience and knowledge gained by running his or her own public relations business.

Another consideration is home working. Some companies now offer their employees the chance to work at home but this varies considerably from business to business, depending on the type of employment. Some employees are able to work at the company's premises for part of the week and to work at home for the remainder.

CASE STUDY

Simon

Simon is 16 years old and is studying for his Nationals in Business. He intends to leave school as soon as he has finished his studies. He is very keen to get into hotel management – the Hospitality and Leisure business sector.

Simon has good keyboard skills and has a Level 1 IT qualification. He likes talking to people and is friendly and helpful. He has recently been on work placement in a local accountant's office where he had contact with customers, dealt with cash and credit cards and acquired good telephone skills.

Simon is very keen to do well. There are some large hotels in his town and he feels these offer good opportunities for promotion and of getting the qualifications he needs through excellent training schemes provided by the hotels. He is hoping, in a few years, to move on and get his own flat.

He realises that his salary will not be much to start with but he is happy that it will improve as his experience increases and each time he passes an exam, he will get an automatic pay rise.

He wants to work full-time and realises that this will entail shifts, mainly days and evenings to start with, but probably some weekends and bank holidays as well. Eventually, he might have to take his turn in working nights, as many reception desks are staffed all day, every day.

CASE STUDY

Rajinder

Rajinder is very interested in working as a chef in a hotel. She is 16, hasn't any qualifications as yet and will be leaving school soon. She wants to find work as a junior chef and hopes eventually to be a head chef.

Rajinder has a very keen interest in all kinds of food. She is eager to learn and is well organised. She is very patient and handles working under pressure really well. Her uncle owns a restaurant in her town and she has helped out on many occasions.

Rajinder hopes to be able to go to college to study for her exams while she is working. Her uncle has offered her a full-time job in his kitchen but she has decided not to take this. She wants to work in a large hotel as she feels the opportunities for training and promotion are much better. She hopes this will also give her greater experience and the chance to get some qualifications.

There are very few large hotels in her town and Rajinder realises that she might have to move to a city, perhaps 50 miles away, in order to get a job with a large hotel. She is hoping that her employer will be able to offer her accommodation and she is aware that her salary will be reduced as a result.

Rajinder knows that she will probably have to work late into the evening, as well as at weekends and public holidays.

ACTIVITY

Find out all you can about Simon's and Rajinder's job roles. Use as many sources of information as possible to help you with your research. Word-process or write the information, with as much detail as possible.

Portfolio tip

In order to provide the evidence required for this assessment objective, you will need to choose two career areas and accurately use the various sources of information in order to find out all the information specified.

AO3   Review progression opportunities

In this section, you will review the progression opportunities for your two career areas, which means that you will look again at the career areas you have chosen, to investigate the further opportunities for you to progress within those areas. To help you to do this you will look at:

- local, national and international opportunities
- progression opportunities
- transferability to other career areas and to different types of employment e.g. employee to self-employed
- the impact of employment trends within the career area – global.

Local, national and international opportunities

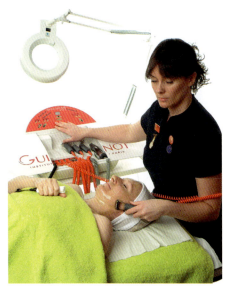

Several career options are open to beauty therapists

You should give a detailed description of the local, national and international opportunities that exist in both of your career areas. Opportunities to work in different regions will depend on the career and the person's own wishes. For example, a beauty therapist may wish to work in a local salon, dealing with local people; another therapist might prefer to work in a large salon in a city such as London or Birmingham, and a third might prefer to work abroad, perhaps in Australia or America, or on a cruise liner, travelling around the world.

Local opportunities

These can be found in job advertisements in local newspapers, in Connexion offices, job centres and the offices of recruitment agencies. You will look at all the information available on the jobs in your career areas in your local area – your village, town, city etc.

National opportunities

For these opportunities you are likely to need to look at the national newspapers such as the *Daily Express*, the *Daily Mail* or *The Times* and *Daily Telegraph*, although some national advertisements do appear in local newspapers from time to time. Websites of companies that specialise in finding jobs for people are also useful sources of information. Use a search engine to locate information on the Internet (see page 141 for more information on search engines).

International opportunities

The chance to work abroad varies very much from one job to another. For example, a salesperson who works for a large multinational company in a city in the UK may be offered the chance to work in New York or Hong Kong.

Progression opportunities

These are the opportunities that enable you to gain promotion – to get ahead in your career. Different jobs will have different progression opportunities. You will investigate those for your career areas and will need to consider many aspects, including the fact that people are different and will have different interests and ideas as to what they want to do with their lives, even those who work in similar jobs. For example, a motor mechanic would probably start his working life as an apprentice, would gain qualifications, knowledge and experience enabling him or her to get a job as a qualified motor vehicle technician. This may then lead to work in sales or management and possibly to self-employment, or to teaching or lecturing.

Transferability to other career areas

Think about other types of jobs and different types of employment people could transfer to and the skills they would acquire in their careers that could be transferred to other careers. You will need to describe the skills in your career areas that may be transferred to other career areas and also those which may be transferred to different types of employment. For example, a word-processor operator who currently works for an estate agent could use these skills in a different career area and different job type – such as a communications officer working for the police service, as a booking clerk or travel rep in the travel industry or as an administrator in the health service, perhaps working for a manager, consultant or registrar in a hospital.

All these jobs are different but all require good keyboard skills – these skills are therefore said to be transferable.

You should also include information on opportunities that may be available for people working in your career areas to become self-employed, such as a word-processor operator who could set up and run his or her own business, offering a word-processing service to businesses to cover employees' sick leave, holidays or to help out at particularly busy times.

Impact on employment trends

Although manufacturing is currently declining, at least in some parts of the UK, other businesses are booming. New technologies have meant that people's jobs have disappeared and they have had to look at other career opportunities. A global factor that can affect employment trends is business costs. For example, some clothes retailers have moved the manufacture of their clothes to other countries in the world, such as China, where rates of pay are lower than those paid to workers in the UK. The retailers suggest that it is cheaper to have the clothes made abroad and to import the finished products to their shops, which has led to factories closing and the loss of many manufacturing jobs in the UK. However, it isn't just employees of the manufacturers involved who are affected. Workers of businesses that supply the manufacturers have also seen their businesses decline, resulting in job losses.

There are likely to be numerous factors that influence the impact on employment trends within your career areas and you should investigate the national, local and international (global) factors.

ACTIVITY

Refer to Simon and Rajinder's case studies on pages 307 and 308. Investigate the progression opportunities for Simon and Rajinder. Ensure you include a detailed description of the local, national and international opportunities; their progression opportunities, transferability to other career areas and to different types of employment and the impact of employment trends within Simon's and Rajinder's career areas, including global factors.

Portfolio tip

In order to provide the evidence required for this assessment objective, you will need to give a detailed description: of the progression opportunities for your two career areas, giving factually correct information; of the local, national and international opportunities within your career areas; of the transferability of your career areas to other career areas and to different types of employment; and of the impact of employment trends within your career areas, including global factors.

AO4 Personal skills and achievements and implications for career progression

In this section, you will have opportunities to assess your own personal skills and achievements – to help you decide whether your own skills and achievements would enable you to progress within the two career areas you have chosen.

Personal skills

There are many personal skills that you may have already or that you may acquire in the future. What skills and interests do you have? Do you enjoy solving problems? Are you practically minded – can you do practical tasks? Do you enjoy handling difficult situations? Would you prefer to use skills you already have or would you like the challenge of learning new ones? If you have decided you want to work with people, have you identified a particular group of people with whom you would like to work? Have you thought whether you would prefer to work in a one-to-one situation or in groups, with young or old people? You may have decided you would like to work with small children. Have you ever spent a whole day with noisy and demanding children?

To help you assess your own personal skills, you will investigate the following:

- interpersonal skills
- communication skills
- eye for detail
- artistic/creative skills
- team skills
- employment skills
- formal achievements (e.g. qualifications, sports achievement, Duke of Edinburgh Award, Young Enterprise)
- informal achievements (e.g. through leisure activities/personal interests).

Interpersonal skills

Interpersonal skills include such things as:

- listening to people
- finding information
- understanding information
- talking to people
- explaining information clearly and concisely
- coping with difficult situations
- getting on well with all kinds of people
- solving problems
- making decisions quickly and decisively
- being creative
- having empathy for people
- working as a team member
- working as an individual
- working on your own initiative
- being practical

Figure 12.2 *Interpersonal skills required in different jobs*

You should consider the interpersonal skills you have and those you will need in your career areas.

CASE STUDY

Joshua

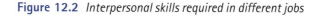

Joshua is 17 years old but celebrates his 18th birthday next month. He is very keen to be a firefighter. He lives with his parents in Bristol opposite the local fire station and has wanted to join the fire brigade since he was very young. He has visited his local station on many occasions and has got to know the Station Officer and others working there and they have been very supportive and have guided him on what he needs to do to be accepted as a firefighter.

Joshua is very fit and has won various athletics awards, mainly for the decathlon and long-distance running. In the winter, he plays football for a local team, as a midfielder. He works out in the gym as often as he can and swims regularly.

He knows that the fire brigade will expect him to be fit and strong and that, as competition for places is very tough, his fitness will work in his favour.

Joshua is hoping to get two GCSEs and will be leaving college soon. He works as a shop assistant in a local supermarket three evenings a week. Mainly as a result of this work experience, he has good communication skills and works well in his team – the dry goods section. Joshua intends to apply to his local fire brigade next year.

Investigate the interpersonal skills Joshua will need as a firefighter. Use as many sources of information as possible, including the Internet, in your investigation.

Communication skills

Everyone has communication skills of one kind or another. Some people may be shy and not so willing to participate; others may be over-willing and too domineering. Communication involves not only talking to customers, colleagues and to seniors such as managers, but also an ability to understand another person's point of view.

However, communication is not just about talking to people. Non-verbal communication (body language) is also important. For example, when someone is talking to you, watch his or her body language. Does what they say match the way they are behaving? Take note of their posture, their willingness to keep eye contact with you and the way in which they use their arms to express themselves. Notice their facial expressions – for example, do they look angry? Sometimes you know that what the person is saying is not what they are feeling – it is not supported by their body language. It is a really good indicator as to how someone is actually feeling and enables you to respond appropriately.

Eye for detail

This relates to people who have a knack for picking up on detail. For example, fashion and furniture designers often have an excellent eye for detail and they need this for tasks such as choosing suitable fabrics, materials and colours for their designs. Architects and surveyors usually have a good eye for detail when designing or constructing buildings. They have the knack of being able to pick out immediately whether something will work, whether something looks right – that is what an eye for detail is. All these people possess an important ability to pick up on small, but vitally important, detail.

Others who have an eye for detail are proofreaders – they need to be able to identify errors in printed work, sometimes very tiny mistakes that are difficult to see.

Artistic/creative skills

People who can come up with new ideas are said to be creative. Those with creative and artistic skills often make excellent designers, actors, ballet dancers, fashion designers etc. These people are able to picture something in their mind and then design it or draw a sketch of how it should look. Some people consider you either have artistic and creative skills or you don't. For example, could an artist who paints portraits in oils produce a picture of beauty in proper proportions with no artistic or creative skills?

Team skills

Many people work well in teams and enjoy the spirit of teamwork. Others prefer to work alone, using their own initiative. Are you a good team player or do you prefer your own company? The ability to be a good team player is important in jobs such as the armed services, firefighting, and the police service, but may also be important in other jobs, such as office work, sales, factory work etc.

ACTIVITY

Refer to the case study on the previous page. What communication skills do you think Joshua will need as a firefighter? Use as many sources of information as possible, including the Internet, in your investigation.

ACTIVITY

Refer to the case study regarding Joshua on the previous page. State whether Joshua is likely to require an eye for detail and artistic/creative skills in his career as a firefighter.

Being part of a team means you have responsibility for members in that team. Even though you may not be the principal person in the team, your role is to support others and to be there for them.

Employment skills

An employer may have a particular type of person in mind when advertising a vacancy. For example, someone with practical skills or a number of years' experience in similar employment, or some work experience in a work placement, may be required. Age may be a factor, especially for an apprenticeship scheme. Before applying for a job, it is important to consider whether you possess the skills an employer is looking for. Your application is unlikely to be considered if you do not possess these skills.

All jobs require employment skills, but these will vary tremendously depending on the work involved.

Formal achievements

As well as employment skills, an employer may require **qualifications** for a specific job. There are many qualifications, some specific to a particular career (e.g. an NVQ in Vehicle Technology) and some that are more general (e.g. GCSEs). Employers will state what qualifications they require people to have for specific vacancies. People may have already achieved these qualifications before applying for a job or may be prepared to study to get them while working.

Sports achievements will show an employer that someone is fit and active – this will be especially important in a job requiring physical strength or agility. Playing a team sport, for example rounders, netball, football or rugby, would indicate that you work well as a team player and have experience of teamwork. Taking part in a solo sport such as tennis or golf may indicate that you prefer to work on your own. Competition can be important in some job roles – the desire to win is strong in many sports and this can be transferred to a desire to win in business. Fair play is also regarded as an important part of sport and in business. Self-esteem and confidence can grow when people take part in sport and this can help to ensure that employees are fit in both mind and body.

The Duke of Edinburgh Award scheme consists of three awards – Gold, Silver and Bronze, each representing different levels and lengths of commitment. Anyone below the age of 23 years of age can take part. To achieve the Silver and Bronze awards, four sections must be successfully completed – Expedition, Service, Skill and Physical. To achieve the Gold award, a fifth section – Residential – must also be attained. The benefits of the Duke of Edinburgh Award are that its achievement is respected worldwide as it enables people to work as a team, it requires a high level of commitment, good time-management skills, is very challenging and can lead to other awards such as life-saving certificates.

Young Enterprise is a UK-registered charity that runs a range of business and enterprise education programmes for young people through the support

ACTIVITY

Refer again to the case study on page 313. What team and employment skills will Joshua need to be a firefighter?

Duke of Edinburgh Award Scheme logo

of various businesses. The Young Enterprise programme offers students the opportunity to run a real company and to learn about aspects of business from the first-hand experience of volunteers. Young Enterprise operates through support from the business community and the government and this support may be financial.

Informal achievements

These are the achievements people gain through **leisure activities** or **personal interests**.

For example, a person may gain a first aid qualification as part of a leisure activity. There are many people, such as factory and office workers, firefighters, police officers and nurses, who have gained first aid qualifications in their leisure time which they use in their jobs.

Other leisure activities or personal interests through which people can gain achievements are by helping local voluntary organisations, such as youth clubs, sports clubs, and charities. There are other national bodies that offer opportunities to attain informal achievements as follows:

- ASDAN
- Fairbridge
- The Guides
- The Prince's Trust Award
- The Scouts
- The Trident Trust
- Weston Spirit
- Youth Achievement Award Bronze/Silver.

ACTIVITY

Read the case Study again concerning Joshua on page 313. Joshua has already gained some sporting achievements – what other formal and informal achievements should Joshua consider to help his application for a job as a firefighter?

Training requirements

Training requirements will vary from one career area to another. You will need to investigate:

- opportunities to develop relevant skills/experience for the selected area
- key decision points (e.g. self-financed or funded)
- timescales (e.g. short, medium, long term).

Opportunities to develop relevant skills/experience

Many employers provide induction training for new employees and this may include training to use new equipment (such as driving a fork lift truck) and providing protective clothing and equipment (such as work involving chemicals or other harmful substances).

Day release courses are often available to employees who wish to gain further qualifications or to learn new skills to enable them to gain promotion at work. Evening classes are another possibility, as these provide opportunities for employees to study in their own time. These are of little help, however, to shift workers who may choose a home study course so that they can study in their own time, at a place convenient to them.

Key decision points

Some employers will pay for the additional training of their staff. Others will pay for the course fees and materials upon successfully passing certain examinations. There are some training courses where a trade union or trade organisation will provide the training or the funds for training.

Schemes, such as The Prince's Trust, can sponsor young people, to help them with course fees and materials they need to do the training and sometimes living expenses may be available.

Those who are not able to obtain funding for their training have to pay for themselves (self-financing). Some people do overtime in their work or extra shifts at weekends etc. to finance their studies. The Open University and Open College offer a wide range of subjects to enable people to study in their own time. Another possibility is home study courses and these are available in many subjects, but can be expensive, although payment can often be made by instalments. To be successful in these training schemes needs a great deal of self-discipline, because people are usually working on their own, without the constant support of a tutor.

Timescales

In order to gain promotion, it will be necessary to consider a long-term training programme. Studying for a qualification with a home study training organisation or with the Open University or College can take several years. This would be long-term training.

Medium-term study refers to shorter courses e.g. a year's evening classes for a GCSE. This is often more popular because people can see results more quickly. Fees are usually lower, so funding is easier and can often be paid for in a one-off payment.

Short-term study includes short courses, seminars, workshops or conferences, which are offered on specific topics and held during working hours or at weekends. Companies often send employees on these short courses and pay for the course fees, materials and accommodation (if residential). For example, hairdressers often update their skills, such as learning new techniques in hair colouring, by attending one-day workshops.

ACTIVITY

Refer to the case study on page 313. What opportunities to develop relevant skills and experience is Joshua likely to have in his career as a firefighter?

ACTIVITY

Refer to the case study on page 313. Use as many sources of information as possible to find out the answers to these questions:

1 Will Joshua's training as a firefighter be self-financed or funded?

2 What are the likely timescales in Joshua's bid to be a successful firefighter?

Portfolio tip

In order to provide the evidence required for this assessment objective, you will need to fully describe your personal skills and achievements and whether these match those required for your career areas, explain whether your personal skills and achievements would allow you to progress within your chosen career areas and describe any extra training that might be required in order for you to progress to a management position (including details on likely timescales and key decision points).

AO5 Identifying job opportunities and the recruitment process

In this section, you will describe the steps involved in finding job vacancies and opportunities and the recruitment process for *a specific job* in one of the career areas you have selected. You will look at the recruitment process from your point of view, as a job applicant.

Job opportunities

The majority of companies advertise their job vacancies in such a way that everyone has access to them. This may involve advertising; many companies also pass the details of vacancies to the local job centre and recruitment agencies. Job opportunities may be found in the following ways:

- advertisements
- recruitment agencies
- writing to potential employers directly.

Advertisements

These are compiled to attract the attention of suitable people to a particular job vacancy. Advertisements may appear on various noticeboards within the company premises (such as staff canteens etc.), in company newsletters, in local and/or national newspapers, trade journals, magazines, and some may appear on websites. Advertisements will usually include all the details that a person wishing to apply for a vacancy would need to know: job title, company name, address and telephone number, name of person to contact, pay and hours of work etc. Another very important aspect of job advertisements is that they contain the exact recruitment process that should be followed in order to apply for the job. For example, applicants may be instructed to write to a person named in the advert for more information or to send a CV with a covering letter, or to telephone or email for information or for an application form.

Whatever process is included in the advert, it is most important that you do exactly as instructed. For example, if two copies of your CV are required with a covering letter, then you must be sure to send two copies with a letter. If the advert asks you to telephone or email for an application form and you send a copy of your CV instead, then your application is unlikely to be considered.

CV is an abbreviation for 'Curriculum Vitae', which is Latin for 'the story of your life'.

DRIVERS

Have you ever had the following excellent benefits?

Excellent rates of pay	8 days' bank holiday
20 days' sick pay	Accident insurance
Pension	Discounts and bonuses

We have won some major business and we are looking for experienced fridge and cage drivers with either C+E or C.

Pay rates start from £7.00 up to £10.50 per hour

Please call Driver Hire on: 01392 114433

Remember Driver Hire = excellent money, contracts, uniform and 24-hour support

**DRIVER HIRE
01392 114433**

ENJOY COMPUTER GAMES?

**PC
X-Box
PlayStation
Nintendo**

We have them all – Games Store is currently recruiting energetic individuals for a new store opening in Exeter soon.

The ideal candidates will be self-starters, with strong interpersonal skills who are self-motivated with the ability to work within a vibrant, fast-paced environment.

Previous retail experience is not necessary but a good working knowledge of computer games is essential.

Interested candidates should apply with a CV and covering letter (quoting reference number W211) to Asma Siraj, Manager, The Games Store, Head Office, Blackpool Lane, Bristol, BS1 2YU.

Games Store is an equal opportunities employer

ACTIVITY

Read through the advertisements displayed above. Word-process or write a separate list of instructions to apply for each of the jobs advertised. Bulleted points are sufficient for this activity.

SECRETARY

Required for our Coventry office

We are looking to recruit a competent secretary with some audio experience for our busy Coventry office. The successful candidate must be able to work under pressure, meet stringent deadlines with minimum supervision and be fully conversant with Microsoft Office. Previous experience in a secretarial role is essential, as is attention to detail.

To obtain an application form, or for more information telephone

Michelle Birch *on*

024 7646 8012

Figure 12.3 *Examples of job advertisements*

Recruitment agencies

These agencies can be very useful to find job vacancies and some companies (especially large, national companies) use them to make the first selection of applicants. Agencies are also very useful if you are interested in obtaining temporary work and this type of work can often lead to permanent posts.

Many people who sign on with recruitment agencies do so because it gives them a great deal more flexibility than permanent jobs – they are often able to choose the days and hours they want to work. Working for a company in a temporary position can also be of help if you are not sure what kind of work you want to do. You can use temporary work to find out whether you enjoy working in a particular type of employment or for a specific company before taking a permanent job.

Many recruitment agencies specialise in a particular sector of employment, such as office work, driving, warehousing/retailing or factory work and are often able to offer vacancies in these areas of employment that are not available elsewhere.

Some considerations to bear in mind when dealing with agencies include:

- you should not have to pay a fee
- do not let anyone talk you into doing a job you are not interested in.

ACTIVITY

Working in groups, visit two or three recruitment agencies (preferably ones that deal with different sectors of employment). Pick up information, such as job details and person specification as well as registration forms and application forms for jobs in different areas of employment. (You will use these later to help you in the practical tasks).

Writing to potential employers directly

You may decide to write to a company because you are particularly interested in working for that firm, or you have heard that there may be a vacancy coming up soon because you know someone who is leaving. In these circumstances, you may wish to write to the company direct. Some companies will respond and give you details of any jobs that are currently vacant. However, don't be disappointed if you don't get a reply, as some companies have a policy of not responding because they rely solely on advertisements or recruitment agencies to fill their vacancies.

If you decide to write to an employer directly, you must ensure that your letter is well constructed, neatly written and contains no errors. The letter should be handwritten – employers prefer to receive handwritten letters in the first instance because they can see your handwriting, and can also assess your grammar, spelling and neatness. You are more likely to get a response if you enclose a stamped, addressed, A4 sized envelope.

22 Maple Avenue
Exeter
EX2 6HQ
[insert date]

Personnel Officer
Chimera Airways
Chimera House
Acorn Business Park
Selly Oak
Birmingham B20 3OL

Dear Sir or Madam

I am writing to enquire if you have any vacancies for cabin crew. I am very keen to work for your airline and would be grateful or any information you can give me.

At present, I work part time in a cafe which has given me opportunities to gain communication skills, as well as taking orders, serving food and other duties.

I enclose a stamped addressed envelope for your use, and look forward to hearing from you.

Yours faithfully

Yuri Petrov

Mr Y Petrov

Enc

Figure 12.4 *An example of a letter of enquiry to an employer*

Recruitment process

The recruitment process you will look at will be from the applicant's point of view – and not from the employer's point of view. (Please note that you will have lots of opportunities to actually produce the documents involved in the next section.)

The recruitment process will include:

- telephoning/writing for application form and/or information
- complete application form/CV/letter of application/registration form for the recruitment agency
- prepare covering letter
- attend interview.

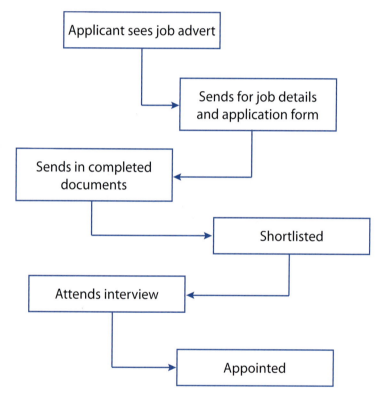

Figure 12.5 *The recruitment process*

Telephoning/writing for application form and/or information

Remember that there is a time limit for the receipt of applications. As soon as you see the advertisement, telephone or write a letter requesting an application form. Don't be tempted to leave it until a week later as you need to allow time for your letter to get there, for the details about the job and the application form to be sent to you and for you to complete the form and return it – all within the time limits given. If a company receives your completed form after the deadline, your application is unlikely to be considered.

An advertisement may give telephone contact details. This means that the company expects you to telephone that person – but beware! The company may also use this as the first stage of the interview process. Be very careful what you say, how you say it and, when asked any questions, be sure to think before you answer. Use a friendly approach but do not be too friendly or chatty. Keep in mind that the person you are speaking to may be making judgements about you concerning your suitability for the vacant post. This also applies if you are telephoning to get more information about a vacancy.

ACTIVITY

Working in groups of three, practise telephoning for information and/or an application form. Take it in turns to be the employer, the applicant and the observer. Before you start, the person taking the part of the applicant should decide what type of job vacancy he or she is applying for and the type of employer and should tell the others in the group.

The person acting as the employer should make a list of the questions he or she should ask to obtain the details that would be needed – e.g. name, address, telephone number etc.

The observer should make notes and make an audio recording of the conversation if possible.

Then change round and when everyone in the group has taken part in the different roles, listen to the audio recordings and to the feedback from the observer and employer and discuss together what went well and perhaps not so well. Decide what you could do differently next time.

Completion of an application form

There are many different application forms. Some are quite short, and others are more detailed, depending on the type of job involved. However, all will require details such as your full name and address, telephone number, date of birth, work experience, education, qualifications etc.

You should consider all the details that will be required. Read the job description and person specification carefully to ensure that you include everything necessary on the application form for that specific job.

Completion of a curriculum vitae (CV)

A CV is very important. It is used by people applying for jobs as a way of promoting themselves. Use your CV to 'sell yourself'. More details and an opportunity to produce a CV can be found in the next section.

Completion of a letter of application

Sometimes an employer will ask for a letter of application. If this is the case, you must ensure you include all the details about yourself in the letter that the prospective employer wants to know. Read the job advert again

Did you know?

Your completed application form is your passport to the job you want. Make sure it impresses everyone who reads it.

and again and check that you have included all the information that is required. Make sure your writing is very clear – take time to produce a well displayed and neat letter, with no mistakes.

Completion of a registration form for the recruitment agency

Most recruitment agencies use a registration form, which is quite similar to an application form but varies in that it is used as a form of application to register with the agency, rather than for a particular job. When you go to see a recruitment agency, take your up-to-date CV with you, as this will be a great help when completing the registration form – it will save you a lot of time and hassle when completing information such as dates etc.

Prepare covering letter

This does not need to be a lengthy letter, but is simply a letter to accompany your application form or CV. However, it is just as important as any other document that you will send. It also gives you the opportunity to show off your handwriting and grammar skills. Covering letters may be word-processed – it depends on the job and the requirements of the employer. If you decide to word-process your letter, make sure it is accurate and well displayed. Take some time over this to make sure it looks professional.

Attend interview

Once all the applications have been received, someone who has been appointed to do this will examine them, such as the Human Resources department or the person who is in charge of the department or section where the vacancy has arisen. A list is compiled of several people who have applied for the job and these will be invited for interview. This list is called a shortlist.

An interview in progress

For some jobs, practical skills tests (such as keyboarding, or arithmetic) may be carried out as part of the interview process.

ACTIVITY

Carefully read the job advertisement below. Describe the steps in the recruitment process for the job advertised.

QUALIFIED MOTOR MECHANIC REQUIRED

Must be qualified mechanic to NVQ Level 3 with a minimum of 2 years' experience. MOT testing certificate would be an advantage. Main duties include service and repair of customers' vehicles including petrol and diesel. Wages: £17,500 per annum. Immediate start. Hours of work: 40 per week, 8.30 am to 5.00 pm Monday to Friday and alternate Saturdays. 20 days per year annual leave.

Please send CV and covering letter to Gordon Jenkins, Jenkins Garage, Fishponds, Bristol, BS16 2RT within 7 days.

For further information regarding this post, please telephone Jacki Simmons on 0117 924 6518.

Portfolio tip

In order to provide the evidence required for this assessment objective, you will need to describe the steps in identifying the job opportunities and the recruitment process for a specific job role in one of your career areas. You should bear in mind that the steps you describe must be from your point of view, as the job applicant.

AO6 Complete written application documentation for a specific job role

In this section, you will be completing the documentation when applying for a specific job role. This will include:

- follow instructions e.g. produce a CV
- select appropriate information – identify relevant information for specific situations
- present additional information relevant to specific job to highlight relevant skills/achievements
- layout
- use of appropriate tone and manner
- accuracy in English.

Follow instructions

It is important to read the advertisement very carefully to ensure that you apply for the job using the process outlined in the advert. Be very careful that you complete the documentation that is asked for in the advert. If it asks for a CV, be sure to prepare a CV – one that is relevant to the job for which you are applying. An employer is unlikely to consider an application from someone who has not provided the exact application documents required.

Letters

Any letters you write should be neatly written – your handwriting will tell the employer a great deal about you. After all, you can ask someone else to word-process a letter for you and no one would be able to tell if you had done it yourself or not but your handwriting is yours – your style, neatness etc. will be individual to you.

You must be prepared to spend time writing a neat letter, stating all the facts clearly and concisely. Be sure that your letter is well displayed and use an appropriate tone. Be careful that you don't make any spelling mistakes. Check all words you are not sure about in a dictionary.

Use good quality paper – buy a stationery pad from a stationery shop such as W H Smith or Menzies. Try to use a good quality pen – a roller ball or felt tip pen is suitable, but try to avoid using a ballpoint pen. Avoid bright colours such as pink – black gives a much better photocopy and all documents in the recruitment process are likely to be photocopied many times to ensure all the people involved have copies of their own to study.

22 Maple Avenue
Exeter
EX2 6HQ
[insert date]

Mr V A Williams
Personnel Officer
Excel Airline
58 Teignmouth Road
Exeter
EX1 7PM

Dear Mr Williams

I am writing in response to your advertisement in last night's Evening Echo for cabin crew.

I am very interested in a position as a member of the cabin crew and would be grateful if you could send me an application form and full details.

Yours sincerely

Yuri Petrov

Mr Y Petrov

Figure 12.6 *An example of a letter requesting an application form*

Application form

It is helpful to take a photocopy of an application form and complete it in draft form first. This will enable you to check details, such as dates, very thoroughly. When you are happy that you have all the information requested, then you can complete the original application form carefully, preferably in black ink. When you have completed the form, check it thoroughly to ensure there are no errors. Then take a photocopy for you to keep before you send off the form.

Some companies will only accept an application form completed by hand as the means to apply for a job.

ACTIVITY

Refer to the activity on page 320 where you visited recruitment agencies and picked up registration and application forms for different areas of employment. Complete a registration and application form for *one* of these, using the job details and person specification to ensure you provide as much information as possible.

CV

Employers often receive hundreds of CVs in reply to advertisements for vacancies. It is important, therefore, that your CV stands out from the others. Take time to prepare a comprehensive CV that is word-processed, accurate, well displayed (using a variety of fonts where appropriate) and produced on good quality paper. Remember, however, that your CV is not used merely to help you get an interview. During the interview, the interviewer may refer to it to help focus on your achievements and it may be used again, once the interview has been completed, to help decide who should be offered the job.

Try to restrict your CV to no more than two pages. Employers will not have time to wade through lots of information. Be sure to include:

- your name, address and contact details
- a short profile of yourself, including your skills, experience and goals
- career history starting with your current job
- education
- references.

It is possible to have a professional CV prepared for you, complete with a photograph. However, this can be expensive, it may not enable you to make amendments very easily and some companies are reluctant to accept professional CVs, preferring to have a well-prepared CV done by the applicant.

Referees are people who would give some detail about you and your suitability for the job for which you are applying. Usually you would supply the contact details of two people who are willing to give references for you, one of whom should be your head teacher or your current employer.

ACTIVITY

Use a word processor to create your CV, using the example given for Fatima Rafir to help you. Check it thoroughly for accuracy, especially dates etc. Make sure you keep it safe.

FATIMA RAFIR

ADDRESS   29 Fore Street, Exeter, EX2 1JL

DATE OF BIRTH   12 January 1988

TELEPHONE NUMBER   01392 161233

PERSONAL PROFILE
Very keen to make a career as a beauty therapist. Possess good verbal and written communication skills and am dealing with people all the time, in my part-time job as well as a member of my school's Student Council.

EDUCATION AND QUALIFICATIONS

1999 to present   OCR Level 1 Certificate for IT Users
North Road Comprehensive School (New CLAIT) – August 2004

WORK EXPERIENCE

2003 to present   Junior, helping out at weekends and during
Lulubelle's Hairdressing Salon holidays – mostly washing clients' hair, making
                                appointments for them, answering the
                                telephone and other general duties

REFEREES

Ms Lulu Whittaker   Mrs Veronica Baker
Lulubelle's Hairdressing Salon Head of Year
22 High Street   North Road Comprehensive School
Exeter   North Road
Devon   Exeter
EX1 6HJ   EX2 4BQ
Telephone: 01392 226699   Telephone: 01392 141516

Figure 12.7 *An example of a CV*

Select appropriate information

In any documentation you prepare, whether it is an application form, a letter of application or a CV, it is important that you make sure that the information you include is relevant to the job for which you are applying. Read the job advert over and over to ensure that you include the information about yourself that you feel will make you the ideal candidate for the job. You must also resist the temptation to include something that isn't required. For example, if you were a switchboard operator, you wouldn't mention that you enjoy reading your favourite magazine during quiet times!

Additional information to highlight relevant skills/achievements

Again, read the advert many times to ensure that you have included in your documentation those specific pieces of information that are required for the application. For example, if you are applying for a job as a courier and are required to have some driving experience, make sure you include details of how long you've been driving and whether you have a full, clean licence.

Layout

Layout of your documentation is very important because the letter of application, covering letter or CV that you send in is going to be read by the person you are trying to impress. The layout of a document is almost as important as its accuracy. A professional, well-displayed document is likely to attract attention rather than one that has a poor layout.

Use of appropriate tone and manner

Don't be tempted to be chatty and over-friendly in your letters. Make sure the tone you use is appropriate. Remember – when writing letters of application, you wouldn't use the same language and tone as you would if you were emailing a friend.

Accuracy in English

Take great care to ensure that your use of English and all spellings are accurate. Ask someone who has a good knowledge of English grammar if they will look over your documents and be prepared to change anything – or to rewrite. Always remember – the person you want to impress will be reading them.

ACTIVITY

Refer to the activity on page 305 where you cut out two job advertisements from a newspaper, magazine or journal. Prepare the written documentation required (for example a CV and a covering letter) to apply for one of the jobs. Ensure you produce well-displayed documents that are accurate and contain all the information required.

Portfolio tip

In order to provide the evidence required for this assessment objective, you should aim to complete the practical tasks to a high level, showing independence, competence and a high degree of accuracy.

AO7 Plan for an interview for a specific job role

In this section, you will prepare for an interview for the specific job role you have already chosen. In your preparations, you should:

- identify potential interview questions and plan responses
- identify questions to ask the interviewer
- research information on the company.

Most people are nervous when attending an interview. One of the best ways to help you feel more relaxed is to be thoroughly prepared. Some of the things you should consider before you attend the interview are listed below.

- Be sure to check what time and date the interview is to be held and the exact location. Check that you know exactly which building you need to go to.

- Check all the details in the interview letter: will there be any tests, such as a keyboarding skills test, or an arithmetic test if figures are involved?

- You might find it helpful to travel the route beforehand. If you are going by bus or train, check what distance the bus stop or railway station is from the building you need to go to. Give yourself plenty of time to get there. Then you will ensure you are not tired out before you start!

- Take the interview letter and instructions on how to get there with you. The letter will include the name of the person you will be meeting plus the address and telephone number. When you get there, you don't want to be flustered because you can't remember the exact details.

- Check what you need to take with you e.g. a copy of your CV and application form, a list of questions you wish to ask (for a quick, last-minute reminder before you go in for the interview – and also to show the interviewer you are well organised), your mobile phone (but switch it off before you enter the building), some mints to refresh your mouth and possibly tissues.

Did you know?

Before you go for an interview, do plenty of research – being thoroughly prepared will help you feel confident.

Identify potential interview questions and plan responses

It is very helpful to make a list of the questions the interviewer is likely to ask you during the interview and to decide what your replies would be. Some questions to consider are given below.

Why do you want to work for us?

What do you look for in a job?

Do you prefer working as a team or on your own?

How will this job help you with your career plan?

What have been the most important achievements in your life so far?

What are your strong points?

What are your weak points?

Why do you want to leave your current job? (if appropriate)

What hours are you expecting to work?

When can you start?

What questions would you like to ask me?

Identify questions to ask the interviewer

As part of your preparation, try to think of questions to ask the interviewer. If you go prepared with your questions, you will feel more confident. The questions you should ask are not those to do with how much you will be earning or how many days' paid holiday you will get. Try to think of something relevant to the company. For example, if you are applying for a job as a shop assistant in a general store and you've heard that another shop selling general goods is due to open in a month's time, you may want to ask questions such as 'Do you think the new shop will take customers away from your store? How do you propose to keep your customers?' Below is a list of other questions you might like to ask your interviewer.

Why is the position vacant?

Why did the person leave?

Will I receive training?

What are the hours I will work?

What exactly does the job entail?

Will my career progress if I work here?

Who would be my immediate boss?

When would you want me to start work?

Research information on the company

Find out what the company's main business is. Useful sources are the local library, Connexions office or job centre. The Internet is also a very great help – the company may have its own website. You should find out:

- the size of the business
- the products or services it makes or provides
- who the company's competitors are.

Try to memorise the name of the company's Chief Executive. Research the organisation of the company; for example, are there are other divisions of the company and, if so, where are these located?

Portfolio tip

In order to provide the evidence required for this assessment objective, you will need to thoroughly prepare for a job interview, for which you have already prepared the application documentation.

ACTIVITY

Work with a group of three student colleagues. Plan for an interview for the job you previously prepared the job application documents for on page 329. Be sure you take into consideration all the above points and all other relevant details.

AO8 Present personal information effectively in an interview and review own performance

This final section is all about taking part in an interview for a specific job role, for which you should include the points listed below:

- use of appropriate tone and manner
- appropriate personal presentation
- present relevant information
- review own performance.

Use of appropriate tone and manner

The way you behave in an interview can mean the difference between getting the job you want and someone else getting it! Some points to consider are shown below:

- Try not to talk too quickly and keep the tone of your voice as even as possible. Take a deep breath just before you speak – it might help to keep you calm.

- If the person interviewing you (the interviewer) offers his/her hand, shake it firmly. (If there is more than one interviewer, shake hands only if they offer theirs.)

- Make constant eye contact, but be careful that you don't appear to stare.

- When you are asked a question, don't rush to answer. Take your time – wait a few seconds at least before answering. This will not only give you time to think of a good answer but will show that you are thinking about the best response to give.

- Be careful of your language – even if the interview seems low key and informal, watch the words you use carefully; try to avoid using slang and too many 'ums'.

- Try to keep a good posture at all times. Sit upright in the chair with your hands in your lap and don't cross your arms.

ACTIVITY

Give a talk of one minute to a group of student colleagues. Before you start, place a chair at the front, facing your colleagues. Walk into the room and sit on the chair. Tell them as much as you can about what you hope to do in your future career within the time allowed. At the end of the minute, ask your colleagues to give you feedback on your:

- style and tone
- manner and the body language you used (including eye contact).

Use this feedback to help you consider what you can do to improve your style and performance.

Appropriate personal presentation

First impressions DO matter! You need to ensure you dress appropriately. Some companies have a more relaxed approach to what their employees wear but it is a good idea to wear the clothes that people working in a similar job are wearing. If you are not sure, wear a suit. However, you need to be comfortable. If you haven't worn a suit for a while, practise wearing it before you go to the interview - practise sitting, standing and walking around.

As well as your clothes, think about your hair – it must be neat and tidy. If your hair is long, consider tying it back.

As a general rule, you should ensure your overall appearance is clean and tidy, including your shoes – avoid wearing trainers if at all possible. Keep jewellery to a minimum and avoid obvious body piercing.

Working in groups, look at these drawings. Think of any advice you can give to these two applicants on their appearance. You should consider hair, clothes, attitude and shoes. They are both candidates at an interview for a job with the Royal Navy.

Working in groups of three, role-play your first interview:

- one person will be interviewed
- one person will be the interviewer
- one person will be an observer.

You have prepared for this interview – so remember all the plans you have already made. Make sure you are suitably dressed for the interview, even though it is a role play.

If possible, ask the observer to use a video recorder to record the interview.

This will help you to review your performance and to correct anything that is necessary.

All the people in the group should take it in turns to be the interviewer, to be interviewed and to be an observer.

Present relevant information

Ensure you give answers to questions that the interviewer actually wants. Concentrate on getting the information across. Don't be tempted to go off the point and ramble on about something which is not at all relevant. How you answer is very important. Remember to speak clearly and to give truthful answers. If you are not sure about something, say so. Don't try to make something up as you may end up looking foolish.

Review own performance

On completion of the role-play activity, ask the others in your group for feedback and watch the video recording (if appropriate). This will help you to review your performance. You will know what went well and not so well. You can then decide on what you could do differently next time. You may be surprised at how well you did. You may be disappointed. The important thing is to learn from what has happened – you can sail through the real thing and get that job!

You may wish to try this activity again. For your second attempt, your tutor may be able to arrange for an employer or a member of staff whom you don't know to act as the interviewer. This will help by making the role play more realistic.

Portfolio tip

In order to provide the evidence required for this assessment objective, you will need to take part in an interview for a specific job, during which your performance should be of a high level, showing independence and competence. On completion of the interview, you should review your performance. Any video or audio taped recordings of the interview and the witness statements from those present at the interview (including your tutor) should be submitted.

SKILLS CHECK

On completion of this unit you should be able to do the following:

1 Identify the main areas of employment within the selected sector of business.

2 Describe in detail the national trends (including the growth areas and areas of decline) within that sector, showing a good knowledge of why the trends exist and how they impact on the sector.

3 Describe the inter-relationships of different industries and communities.

4 Describe the impact of new technologies within the sector.

5 Use sources of information to extract information on two career areas within that selected sector. This information should include the range of job roles, skills needed, training requirements, types and location of employers, starting packages, content of job roles and working conditions.

6 Review progression opportunities for the two career areas thoroughly, giving factually correct information.

7 Describe the local, national and international opportunities within your career areas.

8 Explain the transferability of your career area to other career areas and to different types of employment.

9 Describe the impact of employment trends within your career areas, including global factors.

10 Assess your personal skills and achievements and analyse implications for progression in the two career areas.

11 Analyse whether your skills and achievements would allow you to progress within your areas.

12 Investigate any extra training that might be required in order for you to progress in your career areas and include details of likely timescales and key decision points.

13 Describe the steps in identifying job opportunities and the recruitment process for a specific job role in one of your career areas from the applicant's point of view.

14 Complete written application documents for that job role to a high level, showing independence, competence and a high degree of accuracy.

15 Plan for an interview for the specific job.

16 Take part in an interview for the specific job, ensuring your performance is of a high level, showing independence and competence.

17 Review your performance and state what you would do differently next time.

Glossary

Above the line promotion The use of independent media such as television and press advertising to promote a firm's products or services.

ACAS (Advisory, Conciliation and Arbitration Service) A publicly funded body which works independently with impartiality and maintains confidentiality in all its dealings. It is best known for its role in helping employers and employees resolve disputes; this is known as 'conciliation'.

Advertisement Written communication displaying pictures and text to catch people's attention – e.g. a job advert, selling a product

AIDA Acronym used to describe the stages involved in getting customers to buy products. It stands for awareness, interest, desire and action.

Autocratic management Decisions are made without consultation with the workforce.

Bad debt A persistent debt where customer has received goods or services on credit and has failed to make payment. If the business is unlikely to receive the money in the future the debt is written off.

Balance sheet Financial record that includes fixed assets, current assets, current liabilities and long-term liabilities. It illustrates the value of the business at a set moment in time.

Bank loan Money borrowed over a fixed time scale with an agreed rate of interest. Payments would be made regularly by the customer to the bank.

Below the line promotion Promotional techniques such as money-off coupons, sponsorship of events and special price discounts aimed at increasing sales or boosting the profile of the business or brand.

Benchmarking A comparison between an organisation and a similar concern made to see where the business could improve.

Board of directors The group of senior managers who make all the key decisions in a limited liability company.

Body language Refers to the use of voice, tone, eye contact, facial expression, posture, gestures etc. when speaking to people.

Brand loyalty Ideal situation which exists when customers make regular repeat purchases of a product. It implies that they have confidence in the product and they may even be prepared to pay more for it than competing brands.

Brand name An identity for a particular product

Break even formula $\dfrac{\text{Fixed costs}}{\text{Contribution}}$

Break even point The point where no profit or loss has been made. The business is neither making a profit nor a loss.

Browser Software that enables you to access webpages.

Business mortgage A long-term loan which will be secured against a fixed asset, for example a factory or office building.

Cash book Book of original entry records all the payments made to the business and by the business.

Cash/Cheque Payment for goods received.

Cash flow forecast The cash flow forecast looks at the money coming into and out of the business over a set period of time.

Chain of command The channel by which instructions and orders pass down the organisation through the different levels of hierarchy.

Chairman Sits at the top of the business hierarchy and is elected by other directors.

Circulation The number of people who buy a newspaper or magazine. The larger the circulation, the more that the publication can charge for advertising space.

Closed questions Questions that limit the possible responses.

Coaching Existing member of staff demonstrates the skill necessary to perform a job. The new member of staff then completes the task under the supervision of the coach.

Codes of conduct Guidelines which encourage desirable behaviour in a particular industry.

Codes of practice Exist in a number of industries including the travel industry and the motor trade.

Communication The process by which information is exchanged between two or more people.

Consultative management Consultation with employees before management decisions are made.

Consumer law Legislation that relates to customers.

Contract of employment Document issued to all employees within 16 weeks of starting work. The contract sets out their terms and conditions of employment, for example their working hours, rate of pay etc.

Contribution = Sales price – variable costs.

Co-operatives All shareholders have an equal vote regardless of how many shares they have in the business.

Corporate image (or corporate identity) How a business is viewed by the wider public. Some businesses are regarded as being up-market and selling high-quality, exclusive products e.g. Mercedes Benz. Others may be seen as having a strong commitment to the environment e.g. Body Shop.

Corporation tax A limited company is a separate legal entity. It will therefore be taxed in its own right. The limited company will therefore pay corporation tax on its profits.

COSHH (Control of Substances Hazardous to Health) Legislation that outlines the precautions employers must take to ensure that employees do not harm employees' health.

Conventions Widely accepted ways of doing something, such as using headings 'To', 'From', 'Ref', 'Date' in a memo.

Credit note If goods are returned by a customer a credit note is sent. This states how much they can reduce the original invoice by.

Creditor Money the business owes to other people for the receipt of goods and services not yet paid for.

Culture The way people are treated in a business.

Curriculum Vitae (CV) Document that gives factual information about a person – Greek for 'story of one's life'.

Customer service Providing goods and services that make customers happy.

Debtor A customer who has received goods or services on credit and has not yet paid for them.

Deed of partnership Another name for a partnership agreement which outlines, among other things, how much capital each partner has contributed and how profits and losses are to be shared.

Deindustrialisation Decline in manufacturing.

Delayering Removing layers of management from an organisation to create a flatter structure and reduce wage costs.

Delivery note Goes with the goods to state what is in the package.

Direct marketing Directly contacting potential customers and attempting to persuade them to buy products and services. Popular approaches are mail shots and telephoning people at home.

Directors Senior executives who decide the long-term plans of the business as well as having responsibilities for departments within the business.

Disabled Person Act Legislation that states that a business must make a reasonable effort to accommodate a disabled person if they have the qualification, skills and knowledge necessary to undertake the job.

Discussion People talking together and informing each other of ideas or opinions.

Disposable income The amount of money people have available to spend on goods and services.

Dividend The share of profits that is paid out to shareholders in a limited liability company.

Economies of scale The benefits that firms enjoy as a result of growth. *Internal economies* are the advantages that one firm enjoys as it grows e.g. it is able to employ more special staff and can afford expensive equipment. *External economies* are benefits that all firms in an area enjoy as a result of an industry being concentrated in one area e.g. a pool of specialist labour locally.

Effective listening Careful listening to a level that you can repeat back what has been said.

Email Electronic mail – A message sent electronically through the Internet (electronic communication).

Employee A person who has agreed to offer their services to a business in reward for payment. The exact terms and conditions of the agreement will be laid out in the Contract of Employment which will be signed by both parties.

Employer A person or persons who pay another person in order to perform duties on their behalf. Their terms and conditions will be clearly outlined in the Contract of Employment drawn up and signed by both parties.

Employment Rights Act Legislation that outlines the rights of employers and employees.

Employment tribunals Judicial bodies established to resolve disputes over employment rights.

Encoding The language, style and images used to put across a promotional message. The language and approach of a business selling extreme sports equipment will differ from that used to sell stair lifts.

Enforcing agencies Agencies that enforce legislation e.g. the Health and Safety Executive

Entrepreneur A person who has a business idea, develops it and starts up in business.

Equal Pay Act Legislation making it illegal for men and women to be paid at different rates if they are doing the same job or a job of equal responsibility.

Equipment The items a business needs in order to operate e.g. a photocopier. These items are not available for re-sale.

Ethics A set of values or beliefs about what is right and wrong. Some businesses such as Body Shop or the Co-operative Bank have a strong ethical dimension to their business.

European Court of Justice Legal forum which deals with disputes and is responsible for upholding the laws of the European Union. Its job is to ensure that all laws are interpreted and applied in the same way right across the European Union.

Factories Act Legislation setting down how employers must ensure the health and safety of the workforce. There are two provisions. One focuses on health and the second focuses on general safety provisions.

Filtering Description of the way in which consumers interpret a promotional message. Some people may respond positively to an advertisement for a product purely because they like the music that accompanies it. Others may be put off a product because they dislike the celebrity who is promoting it.

Fixed costs Expenditure that does not change regardless of the levels of production.

Flat organisation chart Visual representation of a business organisation which has few layers which enables employees to speak directly to managers/owner(s) of the business.

Flat structure An organisation that has few layers of hierarchy and large spans of control.

Flotation Selling plc shares on the stock market for the first time.

Formats How a document looks, for example using standard layout for a letter; different font styles, sizes etc.

Franchise A business idea that is owned by the franchisor who then allows another person to trade under the brand name. The **franchisee** will have to purchase this right and also share a proportion of their profits.

Franchisee Person buying into a business brand (franchise).

Goods received note A notice used to check what items have actually been received from the supplier.

Grievance and disciplinary procedures As from 1 October 2004 all businesses must have a written policy which outlines the procedure an employee must use if they have any concerns or complaints about their work, employment terms, working conditions or relationships with colleagues.

Gross profit The amount of profit a company has made by selling their product. It does not take into account the general expenses of the company. It is calculated by taking the cost of sales away from the sales revenue

Health and Safety at Work Act Legislation that outlines the responsibilities of the employer and employee concerning health and safety matters.

Health and Safety at Work Regulations Legislation that sets out the general duties which employers have towards employees and members of the public, and employees have to themselves and to each other.

Herzberg, Frederick Theorist who considered that there were positive and negative aspects to an employee's working life. He divided these up in to positive motivators which include achievement and the negative aspects which are referred to as hygiene factors. These include company policy, working conditions.

Hierarchical organisation chart Graphical representation of a business structure with lots of layers. There are many managers and authority flows from the top down.

Hierarchy Many different layers of management. This provides a promotion ladder for staff and everyone knows their place in the organisation. However, decision-making and communication may be quite slow.

Income Tax A proportion of income taken by the Treasury to fund government and public expenditure. Everybody is required to pay income tax as soon as they earn over the amount set for the personal allowance.

Induction training The initial training a new employee receives when they join a company.

Inflation The percentage that prices increase by over a set period of time. It is measured through the retail price index.

Informational advertising Advertising which gives the customer a considerable amount of information about the product e.g. a catalogue.

Industrial inertia When a business remains in an area even when the original reasons for locating there have gone.

Interest rate The percentage charged when a business borrows money for another person or organisation.

Interest The cost of borrowing. The percentage charged in order to borrow money from external sources, for example a bank. It is also the percentage paid for investment of money into financial institutions, for example banks and building societies.

Internet A computer network that links millions of computers all over the world via telephone.

Internet Service Provider (ISP) Companies that provide connections to the Internet.

Interview A verbal communication between two or more people – questioning.

Invoice A document sent from the supplier to the customer requesting payment be made for the goods or services received. It will normally also state the terms and conditions of payment.

Job description Description of the tasks and responsibilities of the job.

Labour market All the people in the country who are available for work, whether or not they are currently employed.

Lay members Members of a tribunal with no legal background.

Leaflet Short written communication that displays specific information.

Letter Written communication for external use (and occasionally internal use).

Limited liability A legal concept which means that shareholders in a limited liability company (Ltd or plc) only risk the money that they have invested in the business. Their own personal assets are not at risk if the company fails.

Listener profile A description of the 'typical' listener to a particular radio station or programme. This will usually include data about the gender and age of listeners. This information is useful to potential advertisers who wish to target a particular audience.

Loan Money borrowed over a fixed timescale with an agreed rate of interest. Payments would be made regularly by the borrower.

McGregor, Douglas Theorist who developed two theories of motivation. Theory X was based on the idea that employees had to be told what to do and would not take responsibility for their own work. Theory Y was based on the theory that workers were able to manage their own workloads and take responsibility for their own jobs.

Managers People who run departments and carry out the instructions of the directors.

Managing director A senior executive who advises and co-ordinates the work of other directors and managers.

Marketing mix Observation of the price, product, promotion and place of the product.

Market leader The biggest selling company, product or brand in the market. For example, Tesco currently has the largest share of the UK grocery market.

Market research Research investigating people's opinions and buying habits, usually undertaken by business.

Market share This is the proportion of total market sales that are made by one company or product: $\dfrac{\text{Sales of brand X}}{\text{Total market share}} \times 100$

$= \%$ market sales

Marketing objectives Goals that a business is aiming to achieve with its marketing strategy.

Maslow, Abraham Theorist who developed the idea of hierarchy of needs. Employees have to achieve the first level of need before they can move up the hierarchy.

Materials (or Raw materials) The items a business uses in order to manufacture its products. For example in order to manufacture a chair the raw materials required would be wood, screws, glue, varnish etc.

Matrix management Organising staff into multi-skilled teams who work on particular projects rather than organising staff into departments based upon the job they do such as finance or marketing.

Matrix organisation chart A visual representation showing staff taken from different departments to work together as a team.

Memo Written communication for internal use within a company.

Mentoring Pairing up a new or inexperienced employee with an experienced employee. The new employee can seek help and guidance from the mentor. Mentoring does not offer job-specific training.

Mission statement A statement of the key aims, and sometimes values, of the business.

Modem An electronic device that is used to connect computers via a telephone line.

Mortgage A loan that has been borrowed with the specific purpose of buying property. Mortgages are usually obtained from banks and building societies.

Motivation The invisible enthusiasm that drives people to achieve their goals. The willingness to work hard to achieve.

Multi-skilling Training employees so that they are able to perform more than one task within the business.

National insurance Money deducted from your pay to build up your entitlement to a state pension and other social security benfits.

Net profit The final profit of the company after all expenses have been deducted i.e. gross profit minus the expenses of the business, or sales revenue minus total expenses.

Noise at Work Regulations Legislation that requires employees to be protected from loud noise at work.

Notice Written communication announcing some information.

Observation The practice whereby an employee shadows and watches an experienced person perform their job.

Office, Shops and Railway Premises Act Legislation requiring a business to complete the relevant documentation and submit it to their local authority for any employee working in a shop or office premises. The Act defines the requirements for safety, health and welfare of employees.

Off-the-job training Being trained away from your job.

On-the-job training Being trained while at work carrying out your own job.

Open questions Questions with no limit on responses.

Operating profit The final profit of the business calculated by taking expenses away from sales income.

Operatives Workers required to follow tasks as laid out in their job description.

Organisational charts Graphical representations of how a business is organised. It illustrates who is responsible for the decision making. It will show how an employee fits into the organisation.

Overdraft facility An agreement with the bank to continue to draw money on the business's bank account when the drawer's account is in deficit. The business will be charged interest on a daily basis, usually at a higher rate than the bank loan.

Partnership A business of two or more people that is not incorporated and therefore does not have limited liability. Each partner is responsible for the debts of the other partners.

Person specification The educational qualifications, experience and knowledge/skills a potential job applicant is required to have.

Persuasive advertising Advertising that provides little information about the product or service but instead relies on factors such as image and style to persuade customers to buy.

PEST analysis A business technique for assessing some of the external factors that affect a business. PEST stands for Political, Economic, Social and Technological influences.

Point of sale promotions Methods used to promote the product at the point where it is actually being sold. These may include in-store displays or product demonstrations.

Population The total number of people questioned or interviewed for the purpose of a survey.

Primary industry The first stage in the productive process. Primary industries include agriculture, fishing and mining. They obtain resources from the natural world. Industries such as mining, quarrying and drilling for oil are known as *extractive industries*.

Primary market research Research undertaken by a business for its own use.

Prime location Location ideal for the particular business.

Private limited company (Ltd) An incorporated business which can be sued in its own right. The shareholders who are the owners of the business have limited liability and will only lose their initial investment into the business if things go wrong.

Product placement A business pays the producers of a film or television programme to have its products or brand prominently featured in the film or programme. There are fairly strict rules in the UK regarding product placement in television programmes.

Productivity The amount produced by one person over a set time period.

Profit Money made over and above the expenditure needed to create the good or service. Making a profit is the aim of private sector businesses. A firm makes a profit if the revenue from sales exceeds the firm's costs.

Profit and loss account Account that calculates the gross and net profit of a business.

Public Limited Company (plc) An incorporated business that is able to sell its shares on the stock exchange. It will therefore have many owners and there will be a divorce of ownership from control. The shareholders will appoint a board of directors to run the business on their behalf.

Public relations Promotional activities which aim to present the company in a favourable light to the public but are not directly aimed at selling more products e.g. sponsorship of a local primary school football team.

Purchase day book A daily record of purchase invoices.

Purchase order Written confirmation of a wish to purchase goods from a supplier.

Purchases Goods or services bought in by another business or a private individual.

Quality circles Forums where employees are empowered to investigate quality and productivity issues and suggest and make changes as required.

Questionnaire A number of questions asked of people to find out some information.

Race Relations Act Legislation that makes it illegal for anybody to be discriminated against because of their race or ethnic background.

Raw materials (See Materials)

Reader profile Description of the 'typical' reader of a newspaper or magazine. This will usually include data about the gender and age of readers. This information is useful to potential advertisers who wish to target a particular audience.

Receipt Written confirmation that payment has been received.

Rent The payment made in order to use property that belongs to someone else.

Repeat business When a customer returns again to a particular business to purchase goods or services.

Report A written communication containing information, conclusions and recommendations on a specific topic.

Revenue The money coming into the business from the sale of products and services. Total revenue is found by: number of items sold x selling price.

Review A fresh look at a study carried out previously.

RIDDOR (Reporting of Injuries, Diseases and Dangerous Occurrences) Legislation that requires employers to report work-related accidents diseases and dangerous occurrences.

Risk assessment The identification of any possible hazard.

Running costs The payments the business makes in order to run on a daily basis.

Sales day book Daily record of sales invoices.

Sales promotions Techniques which aim to sell more of the company's products such as money-off coupons and free gifts.

Sales returns day book Daily record of goods returned from customers.

Sampling The method used to choose your sample in a survey. This can be either random or specifically targeted.

Search engine Software that enables you to search the Internet for a website containing specific information.

Secondary industries Industry that takes raw materials and produces finished or semi-finished goods. This includes manufacturing industries such as brewing and steel making and the construction industry.

Secondary market research Research undertaken by another independent organisation other than the business the research refers to; for example data prepared by the Office of National Statistics.

Sex Discrimination Act Legislation that makes it illegal for anybody to be discriminated against because of their gender or marital status.

Share issue Limited liability companies can sell shares in order to raise extra funds. Plcs can sell their shares on the stock exchange. Ltds can sell their shares to private individuals, but only with the full agreement of the other shareholders.

Shareholders The legal owners of a limited liability company (Ltd or plc). They all enjoy limited liability and usually have voting rights.

Shortlisting applicants The process of selecting only the most suitable job applicants to call for interview.

Skills audit Identification of the skills needed to carry out a particular job.

Skills shortage Where the skills required for the job are in short supply.

Sole proprietor or sole trader A person who goes into business on their own. They take all the risks and reap all the rewards. The business is not incorporated and therefore does not have limited liability.

Span of control The number of subordinates (workers) over whom a manager has direct control.

Stakeholders Individuals or groups who have an interest in a business or who are affected by its activities. Stakeholders may be *internal* such as employees and managers or *external* such as local residents.

Standard of living Measure of the goods and services people can buy with their income.

Start-up/set-up costs The costs a business incurs when it initially starts up.

Statement of account A document sent to a customer who purchases regularly from a business. It contains all the invoices sent, credit notes issue and cheques received. The final balance is the amount outstanding at the end of the month. This is normally due for payment within 30 days.

Strategic plan The long-term plan of a business.

Supervisors Workers who oversee the work of the operatives and follow instructions from managers.

Surfing A process of looking through various websites in search of information.

Survey To find out some information by asking questions of people.

SWOT analysis A business technique for assessing the performance of a product, brand or company in its market. SWOT stands for strengths, weaknesses, opportunities and threats.

Target market People that your business expects to buy your product.

Taylor, F. W. Theorist who believed that people were solely motivated by money.

Tertiary industry The service sector of the economy. Includes banks, retailers, advertising agencies and transport companies.

Total quality control The philosophy where everybody in the organisation takes responsibility for the quality of the product(s) being produced or service(s) offered.

Total Quality Management (TQM) A management approach which aims to put the customers' requirements at the heart of all of the business's activities. The business will engage in careful market research to identify customers' needs and then develop products and services to meet those needs.

Total revenue The total amount of money coming into the business.

Trade unions Voluntary organisations which represent the interests of employees. Employees are free to join a union if they wish to do so.

Trading standards officers Local government employees who can investigate and prosecute businesses that are acting in breach of consumer protection laws. Consumers are able to obtain advice on their legal rights and bring complaints about local businesses from their local Trading Standards Office.

Two column cash book Record of the incoming and outgoing money of a business.

Unique selling point (USP) A unique or special feature that distinguishes one product or brand from the competition.

Unlimited liability A legal concept which means that the owner of the business is personally liable for the debts of the business. This is a significant drawback of operating as a sole trader or partnership.

Upgrading skills The updating of employees' skills in order to keep up with new developments.

Variable costs Costs that *change* with the level of production. If production increases so do the variable costs.

Verbal communication Two or more people who are talking to each other.

Wage A wage is the rate of pay an employee will receive.

Website A collection of pages – on the Internet.

Website navigation Finding your way around the websites on the Internet, using known website addresses.

World Wide Web (WWW) A collection of millions of websites.

Working capital The immediate money available within the business to meet its short term debts. It is calculated by taking the value of the current assets away from the value of the current liabilities.

Written communications People communicating with each other using a written document.

index